BAY TABLES

SAVOR THE ABUNDANCE

JUNIOR LEAGUE OF MOBILE

SAVOR THE ABUNDANCE

BAY TABLES

A collection of fresh and
fabulous recipes from the
Junior League of Mobile

BAY TABLES
Copyright © 1999 by
Junior League of Mobile, Inc.
57 North Sage Avenue
Mobile, Alabama 36607-2608
334-471-3348

Photographer: Neil Alexander, Southern Lights

Food Stylists: Martha C. Torres and Rosalind Richard

Text: Sallye English Irvine

Other books published by the Junior League of Mobile, Inc.:
Recipe Jubilee
One of a Kind

Library of Congress
Catalog Number: 98-066535

ISBN: 0-9603054-3-2

Edited, Designed, and Manufactured by Favorite Recipes® Press
an imprint of

FRP™

P.O. Box 305142
Nashville, Tennessee 37230
800-358-0560

Designer: Steve Newman

Book Project Manager: Linda A. Jones

Manufactured in the
United States of America

First Printing: 1999   25,000 copies

The Junior League of Mobile is an organization of women committed to promoting voluntarism, developing the potential of women, and improving communities through the effective action and leadership of trained volunteers. Its purpose is exclusively educational and charitable. The Junior League of Mobile reaches out to women of all races, religions, and national origins who demonstrate an interest in and commitment to voluntarism.

WHITNEY

Bank at the Sign of the Clock

A Proud Sponsor
of the
Junior League
of Mobile

Thank You Message from the Committee

*The cookbook, **BAY TABLES**, is the result of a concerted effort by many people. Countless hours have been spent writing, gathering, testing, and evaluating the recipes. The work has been performed joyously and selflessly by the members of the Junior League of Mobile and community supporters. These efforts have taken us from boxes of recipes, splattered with sauces and spilled chocolate, to the glorious book you have before you. The cookbook development team would like to extend a heartfelt thank you to all those who brought **BAY TABLES** to life.*

Cookbook Committee

Chairman: Helene Hassell
Co-Chairman: Text Editor, Sallye Irvine
Marketing Chairman: Liz Blankenship
Marketing Co-Chairman: Catharine Jernigan
Recipe Selection Chairman: Liza Eldred
Testing Chairman: Lynn Guthans
Photography Chairman: Susan Ham
Restaurant Liaison: Katharine Holmes
Recipe Collection Chairman: Mary Anne Killion
Sustaining Advisor: Austill Lott

Introduction

Welcome to our table. We invite you to indulge in an extraordinary celebration of nature's abundance—for Mobile is truly the land of plenty. Mobile is a vibrant, coastal port city nestled between the fresh waters of the Mobile River and the brackish, beautiful Mobile Bay, just off the glittering Gulf of Mexico. The area is interlaced with an astounding array of other wonderful waterways as well—streams, rivers, bayous, and marshes all surrounded by rich, fertile farmland and dense, wooded hunt country—making Mobile an uncommon paradise and offering all the best of nature's lavish bounty.

Mobile is also a marvelous melting pot of culinary styles. It is a city of unquestionable Southern charm, seasoned by a long and colorful history and spiced with a myriad of cultural influences. Creole-inspired dishes came courtesy of the French. The British and Spanish each added their own additions to the pot, as did the African-Americans. Waves of other settlers, including Greek, Italian, Thai, and Vietnamese, have also played an important role in creating the unique blend of cuisine. And while Mobile has long been famous for its delectable gumbo, fried fish and crab claws, recent decades have brought a splendid redefinition of cooking style. This current focus celebrates the glorious profusion of produce and natural resources with fabulous, creative dishes and updated twists on the traditional along with fresher, healthier techniques.

Not everything has changed, however, for some things never go out of style, such as gracious hospitality. Mobilians have a pronounced passion for entertaining and a jubilant zest for life. The city is the American birthplace of Mardi Gras, and thus it comes as no surprise that its people are forever finding ways to turn every day into an occasion. We invite you to come along—to join us at the table and revel in this joyous celebration of food, family, friends. Enjoy!

—Sallye English Irvine

APPETIZERS

*Appetizers or hors d'oeuvres are often what separates entertaining
and occasions from day-to-day dining. They are that special touch
served to tantalize the taste buds before the feasting and festivity to come.
Since they are first among the offerings, appetizers often set the tone
for the party or gathering.*

*Whether it be as casual as crisp chips and a delectable dip
proffered poolside—or as grand as a selection of the best and briniest
caviar ensconced in an elaborate ice vessel—appetizers always make
guests feel welcome, pampered and indulged.*

*Appetizers can be incredibly fun. They present an invaluable
opportunity to offer a marvelous assortment of tidbits, nibbles and tastes
to enchant your guests. Everyone adores them. Appetizers are also an
excellent way to showcase individual style. Consider clustering
savory Blue Poppy Wafers onto an exquisite sterling card tray
or serving Chinese Dumplings along with a sidecar of Ginger Soy
Dipping Sauce from intriguing, eccentric Oriental serving pieces—
let your imagination run wild.*

Photograph sponsored by Betty R. McGowin

The Grand Hotel

What's so grand about the Grand Hotel? Perhaps it is the unmistakable elegance of this quintessential Southern resort. It could be the ancient oaks, gnarled by the balmy breezes off the Bay and dripping with lacy Spanish moss. It might also be that icy mint julep sipped leisurely as the sun goes down. Or perhaps it is simply the resort's long, lively and colorful history.

The Grand Hotel, in all its glory, has been a landmark in Point Clear, Alabama, for over 150 years. It has weathered a multitude of indignities, including fire, war and hurricanes—yet miraculously The Grand lives on, continuing generation after generation to be a favorite retreat for visitors throughout the South and beyond.

Photograph sponsored by The 1998 Sustaining Class of the Junior League of Mobile

Grilling Oysters

Gathering around the grill to eat hot perfectly ruffled oysters fresh from the fire is truly a treat. Start with a sack of the beloved bivalves. Then lay a fire and let it burn for about 45 to 60 minutes or until the coals have sufficiently turned grey. Place whole unshucked oysters on the grill for approximately 15 minutes or until the shells pop open. Using an oven mitt or a heavy glove, pick up each popped oyster and finish prying off the shell with a strong knife (preferably an oyster knife, but a putty knife or the like will do). Place the empty oyster shell halves back on the grill or set aside. Dab hot oysters with the desired sauce (usually some sort of garlic butter creation) and cook just until the edges of the oysters are curled—be careful not to let the oysters cook too long or they will become chewy and tough. It's fun to eat the oysters hot from the grill, straight from their shells with cocktail forks. (If you are serving a sizable crowd, use the empty shells to cook pre-shucked oysters. Simply spoon an oyster, along with some of its liquor, into the empty shells on the fire, douse with sauce, and cook until the edges curl.)

Broiled Oysters on the Half Shell

12 oysters on the half shell
homemade bread crumbs
melted butter
chopped green onions
salt and freshly ground pepper to taste
Worcestershire sauce to taste
fresh lemon juice to taste

Place the oysters on rock salt beds in 9-inch round baking pans. Sprinkle the oysters with bread crumbs. Drizzle with melted butter. Sprinkle with green onions. Season with salt, pepper, Worcestershire sauce and lemon juice. Broil for 2 to 3 minutes or until the edges curl. Serve with lemon wedges and sprigs of fresh parsley.

Note: Instead of using oysters on the half shell, place 3 shucked oysters each in greased ramekins and prepare as above. Broil for 3 to 5 minutes or until the edges begin to curl.

Yield: 4 servings

Shrimp Ono

5 pounds fresh shrimp, boiled, peeled, deveined
1 cup canola oil
1/2 cup vinegar
1 1/4 cups finely chopped celery
2 1/2 tablespoons minced green bell pepper
1/4 cup grated onion
1 clove of garlic, minced
5 tablespoons minced fresh parsley
3/4 cup spicy hot prepared mustard
1/4 cup paprika
1 1/2 teaspoons salt
1/4 teaspoon pepper

Place the cooked shrimp in a large bowl. Combine the oil, vinegar, celery, green pepper, onion, garlic, parsley, mustard, paprika, salt and pepper in a bowl and mix well. Pour over the shrimp. Marinate, covered, in the refrigerator for 24 hours, stirring occasionally.

Yield: 10 servings

Marinated Shrimp and Artichoke Hearts

1 cup olive oil
3/4 cup balsamic vinegar or
    wine vinegar
1 (14-ounce) can artichoke hearts,
    drained, cut into quarters
1/4 cup sugar
2 teaspoons salt

1 teaspoon dry mustard
3 bay leaves
1 clove of garlic, minced
2 pounds cooked, peeled medium shrimp
1 onion, thinly sliced
lemon slices
pitted olives

Combine the olive oil, balsamic vinegar, artichoke hearts, sugar, salt, dry mustard, bay leaves and garlic in a bowl and mix well. Add the shrimp and onion and toss to coat well. Marinate, covered, in the refrigerator for 3 to 10 hours. Drain the shrimp, reserving half the marinade and discarding the bay leaves. Place the shrimp and reserved marinade in a serving bowl. Garnish with lemons and olives. Set in a bowl filled with ice and serve with wooden picks.

Yield: 4 servings

Marinated Mushrooms

1 pound small fresh mushrooms
1 bunch green onions, sliced
1 cup olive oil
1 cup dry white wine
1/2 cup water
1/4 cup lemon juice

1 clove of garlic, minced
1 tablespoon chopped fresh rosemary, or
    1 teaspoon dried rosemary
1/2 teaspoon coriander
1/2 teaspoon instant beef bouillon
1/2 teaspoon salt

Wipe the mushrooms with a cloth. Trim the stems 1/4 inch. Combine the mushrooms and green onions in a bowl and toss to mix well.

Heat the olive oil, wine, water, lemon juice, garlic, rosemary, coriander, instant bouillon and salt in a saucepan until just to the boiling point. Pour over the mushroom mixture. Marinate, covered, in the refrigerator for 1 to 2 days, stirring occasionally.

Yield: 4 to 6 servings

More Luscious Lime Juice

To get more juice from limes, pierce the lime with a sharp object, such as a knife, and then microwave on High for about 45 seconds. This helps to warm the lime, making it easier to break the pulp down and obtain the juice. After removing the lime from the microwave, roll it on the counter, applying pressure with the palm of your hand, then slice and squeeze out the juice.

Red Snapper Ceviche

1 1/4 cups fresh lime juice
2 pounds red snapper fillets, cut into 3/4-inch cubes
3 medium tomatoes, chopped
1 medium red bell pepper, seeded, chopped
1 medium yellow bell pepper, seeded, chopped
6 green onions, minced
1/4 teaspoon red pepper flakes
4 1/4 tablespoons olive oil
2 tablespoons chopped fresh cilantro
salt to taste
fresh sprigs of cilantro or bell pepper strips

Pour the lime juice over the fish in a glass container. Chill, covered, for 2 hours, stirring 1 to 2 times. Combine the tomatoes, bell peppers, green onions, red pepper flakes, olive oil and cilantro in a bowl and mix well. Add to the fish and mix well. Chill, covered, for 1 hour, stirring occasionally. Season with salt. Spoon into a serving bowl. Garnish with cilantro sprigs or bell pepper strips.

Yield: 10 servings

Escargot in Brie Butter

48 canned escargot
2 tablespoons unsalted butter
2 tablespoons finely minced shallots
1/2 cup dry white wine
8 ounces Brie cheese, softened
1 cup unsalted butter, softened
2 tablespoons minced fresh basil
2 tablespoons flour
2 tablespoons dry white wine
salt and freshly ground pepper to taste
chopped fresh parsley

Rinse and drain the escargot. Melt 2 tablespoons butter in a skillet. Add the shallots. Sauté until the shallots are slightly softened. Add the escargot. Sauté until heated through. Add 1/2 cup wine. Simmer until the liquid evaporates.

Remove the rind from the Brie. Cut the Brie into small pieces. Whip 1 cup butter in a bowl until smooth and creamy. Add the Brie and beat until blended. Add the basil, flour, 2 tablespoons wine, salt and pepper and mix well.

Place the escargot in a shallow baking dish or in individual ramekins. Top with the Brie butter. Bake at 350 degrees for 15 minutes. Sprinkle with chopped parsley. Serve with crusty French bread.

Yield: 10 to 12 servings

Lobster Ravioli with Fresh Basil and Creamy Tomato Sauce

5 large tomatoes, peeled, chopped
1 tablespoon chopped fresh basil leaves
salt and pepper to taste
1 tablespoon olive oil
$1/4$ cup heavy cream
1 pound cooked lobster pieces
$1/4$ cup freshly grated Parmesan cheese
Pasta Dough (page 100) or won ton wrappers

Sauté the tomatoes, basil, salt and pepper in the olive oil in a skillet for 10 minutes or until thickened. Add the cream. Cook for 5 minutes, stirring constantly. Purée in a food processor. Reserve $1/3$ cup of the purée. Pour the remaining purée into a saucepan.

Combine the lobster, Parmesan cheese and reserved purée in a small bowl and mix well.

Lay a sheet of Pasta Dough on a nonstick surface. Spoon the lobster filling 3 tablespoonfuls at a time at 5-inch intervals on the dough. Top with another sheet of pasta dough and press down. Cut the dough into two 4-inch squares with the filling in the centers using a pastry crimper. Repeat with the remaining dough and filling. Add the ravioli to salted boiling water in a large stockpot. Cook for 2 to 3 minutes or until the ravioli rises to the top and drain.

Cook the remaining purée until heated through. Spoon onto individual serving plates and top with the ravioli.

Note: If using won ton wrappers, spoon only 2 tablespoons of the filling at a time onto $1/2$ of the wrappers. Moisten the edges with water and place a second wrapper on top of each. Eliminate any air bubbles and press the edges to seal.

Yield: 6 servings

Thai Chicken with Peanut Sauce

$^1/_2$ cup lime juice
$^1/_3$ cup soy sauce
$^1/_4$ cup packed brown sugar
2 tablespoons crushed red pepper
4 cloves of garlic, crushed
2 pounds boneless skinless chicken breasts, cut into strips
Peanut Sauce (below)

Combine the lime juice, soy sauce, brown sugar, red pepper and garlic in a bowl and mix well. Pour over the chicken in a large greased glass baking dish. Marinate, covered, in the refrigerator for 6 to 10 hours and drain, discarding the marinade. Bake the chicken at 375 degrees for 30 minutes or until cooked through. Serve with Peanut Sauce.

Yield: 4 to 6 servings

Peanut Sauce

$^1/_2$ cup chunky peanut butter
$^1/_3$ cup soy sauce
4 cloves of garlic, minced
$^1/_2$ cup lime juice Juice of 1 lime
$^1/_2$ $^1/_4$ cup coconut milk
crushed red pepper to taste
1 teaspoon paprika
1 teaspoon peanut oil

Combine the peanut butter, soy sauce, garlic, lime juice, coconut milk, red pepper and paprika in a small saucepan and mix well. Cook until heated through, stirring constantly. Remove from the heat. Stir in the peanut oil.

Yield: 1$^1/_3$ cups

Chinese Dumplings with Ginger Soy Dipping Sauce

8 ounces ground turkey,
    chicken or veal
6 green onions, chopped
1 medium carrot, grated
1 teaspoon fresh gingerroot, grated
2 teaspoons sherry
1/2 teaspoon salt
1 1/2 teaspoons sugar
1 teaspoon soy sauce
2 teaspoons sesame oil
1 tablespoon vegetable oil
2 cloves of garlic, minced
1 1/2 tablespoons oyster sauce
1 tablespoon chicken broth
1 1/2 tablespoons cornstarch
25 won ton wrappers
Ginger Soy Dipping Sauce
    (at right)

Combine the ground turkey, green onions, carrot, gingerroot, sherry, salt, sugar, soy sauce, sesame oil, vegetable oil, garlic, oyster sauce, chicken broth and cornstarch in a bowl and mix well. Chill, uncovered, for 4 hours or longer.

Place 1 tablespoon of the filling in the center of each won ton wrapper. Moisten the edges with water. Fold over and press the edges to seal. Place the dumplings in a steamer basket sprayed with nonstick cooking spray. Place over boiling water in a large saucepan. Steam, covered, for 7 minutes or until cooked through. Serve with Ginger Soy Dipping Sauce.

Yield: 25 servings

Ginger Soy Dipping Sauce

While Ginger Soy Dipping Sauce is wonderful with Chinese Dumplings (at left), it can also be served with spring rolls and sushi, or added to a stir-fry to enhance and enliven the flavor.

1 teaspoon sugar
2 tablespoons light soy sauce
3 tablespoons chicken broth
1/2 tablespoon sesame oil
1 1/2 tablespoons grated fresh gingerroot
1 green onion, chopped
pinch of red pepper flakes

Combine the sugar, soy sauce, chicken broth, sesame oil, gingerroot, green onion and red pepper flakes in a small bowl and mix well. Let stand at room temperature for 30 minutes for the flavors to blend.

Yield: about 1/2 cup

Founding of Mobile

Mobile's natural resources and subtropical climate combined with abundant fresh water and food sources made the area attractive to Indian settlers long before Spanish explorers first arrived in 1519. The Spanish established a settlement 75 miles north of present-day Mobile in 1540. The personnel stationed there were to patrol the Gulf Coast to protect the Spanish ships laden with silver and gold that traveled between Vera Cruz and Havana. The settlement ultimately failed, but not before the Maubila Indian tribe, for whom the city is named, was annihilated.

Mobile was not successfully settled until the French arrived over a hundred years later. Pierre le Moyne, sieur de Iberville, a French explorer, established a fort in 1702 on the west bank of the Mobile River, now known as 27-Mile Bluff. This flood-prone fort was a primitive village of wooden huts.

Pesto-Stuffed Mushrooms

12 to 15 mushroom caps
2/3 cup Basil Pesto (page 109)
1/4 cup grated Parmesan cheese
3 tablespoons seasoned bread crumbs
3 tablespoons pine nuts
1/4 cup shredded mozzarella cheese
1/4 cup chopped roasted red bell pepper
2 tablespoons shredded mozzarella cheese

Place the mushrooms cap sides down on a baking sheet. Mix the Basil Pesto, Parmesan cheese, bread crumbs, pine nuts, 1/4 cup mozzarella cheese and red pepper in a bowl and mix well. Spoon into the mushroom caps. Sprinkle with 2 tablespoons mozzarella cheese. Bake at 400 degrees for 8 to 10 minutes. Serve immediately.

Yield: 12 to 15 servings

Beef Pâté in French Bread

1 loaf French bread	*1 1/2 teaspoons pepper*
6 tablespoons butter, softened	*1 tablespoon Dijon mustard*
3 cups chopped cooked tenderloin	*1 teaspoon dry mustard*
1/2 medium onion, minced	*1/4 cup Worcestershire sauce*
6 tablespoons half-and-half	*1/4 cup shelled pistachios*
1 1/2 teaspoons salt	*(optional)*

Cut a slit in the bread lengthwise. Remove the center to form a shell. Process the butter, tenderloin, onion, half-and-half, salt, pepper, Dijon mustard, dry mustard and Worcestershire sauce in a blender or food processor until smooth. Stir in the pistachios. Spoon into the bread shell. Chill, covered, in the refrigerator for 3 hours. Cut into slices just before serving.

Yield: 8 to 10 servings

Crawfish Pie

3/4 cup margarine
1/2 cup flour
2 medium onions, finely chopped
1 green bell pepper, finely chopped
2 cloves of garlic, minced
1 pound frozen crawfish tails,
    thawed

dash of cayenne
3 dashes of Tabasco sauce
Tony Chachere's seasoning
    to taste
chopped green onion tops
20 individual pastry shells,
    baked

Melt the margarine in a saucepan. Stir in the flour gradually. Cook until the roux is light brown, stirring constantly. Remove from the heat and set aside.

Sauté the onions, green pepper and garlic in a nonstick saucepan until the onions are transparent. Add the undrained crawfish tails. Simmer for 10 minutes. Add the cooled roux, stirring constantly. Add enough water to make the desired consistency, stirring constantly. Stir in cayenne, Tabasco sauce, Tony Chachere's seasoning and chopped green onion tops. Cook over low heat for 20 minutes. Spoon into the pastry shells. Serve immediately.

Yield: 20 servings

(Founding of Mobile, continued)

In 1711, Iberville's brother Jean Baptiste le Moyne, sieur de Bienville, moved the fort south to the mouth of the river. This site with its earthen fort and thatched roof huts was improved upon until the fort was finally bricked over and renamed Fort Conde in 1720. (Fort Conde still stands in downtown Mobile.) The French are credited with settling the city, even though Mobile never grew much beyond a military garrison and fur-trading post under French rule.

Mobile came under British control at the end of the French and Indian War in 1763. Fort Conde was renamed Fort Charlotte and the Anglican faith was added to an already strong Roman Catholic religion. Following the American Revolution, Mobile was returned to Spanish rule under the terms of the Peace of Paris in 1783. It was not until the War of 1812 that Mobile came to be, once and for all, an American city.

Goat Cheese Tartlets

12 frozen tartlet shells, thawed
16 ounces cream cheese, softened
3/4 cup sour cream
3 eggs
8 ounces goat cheese, such as chèvre or Montrachet cheese, softened
salt and pepper to taste

Bake the tartlet shells at 425 degrees for 15 minutes. Remove from the oven. Decrease the oven temperature to 350 degrees.

Beat the cream cheese, sour cream, eggs, goat cheese and salt and pepper in a bowl until smooth. Spoon into the partially baked shells. Place on a baking sheet.

Bake for 20 to 30 minutes or until golden brown and the filling is set.

Yield: 12 servings

Feta Cheese Tarts

6 to 8 cloves of garlic
1/2 cup medium dry sherry
1/2 cup heavy cream
2 eggs
1 egg yolk
1 cup crumbled feta cheese
freshly ground pepper
8 frozen tartlet shells, thawed

Combine the garlic and sherry in a saucepan. Simmer, covered, over medium heat for 15 to 20 minutes or until the garlic is tender, adding additional sherry if needed. Stir in the cream. Bring to a boil, stirring constantly. Cook until the mixture is reduced by half, stirring constantly. Combine the eggs, egg yolk and cheese in a blender or food processor. Add the cream mixture in a fine stream, processing constantly until smooth. Season with pepper.

Pour the filling into the tartlet shells. Bake at 350 degrees for 30 minutes or until a wooden pick inserted in the center comes out clean.

Note: The filling can be prepared up to 2 days in advance and refrigerated. Assembled tartlets can be frozen for up to 3 months. Bake frozen and add 10 minutes to the baking time.

Yield: 8 servings

Goat Cheese and Tomato Crostini

5 ounces soft goat cheese, such as
    Montrachet or chèvre
1 tablespoon chopped fresh basil
1/4 teaspoon pepper
2 tomatoes, seeded, diced
1/8 teaspoon salt

1 teaspoon olive oil
1 loaf French bread
1 clove of garlic
1 tablespoon olive oil
1 teaspoon chopped fresh
    parsley (optional)

Combine the goat cheese, basil and pepper in a bowl and mix well. Mix the tomatoes, salt and 1 teaspoon olive oil in a bowl.

Cut the bread diagonally into thin slices. Place on a grill rack. Grill over hot coals for 3 to 5 minutes or until golden brown. Rub with the garlic and brush with 1 tablespoon olive oil. Spread with the goat cheese mixture. Spoon the tomato mixture on top. Sprinkle with parsley.

Yield: 10 to 12 servings

Walnut, Arugula and Gorgonzola Crostini

18 (1/4-inch-thick) diagonal baguette bread slices
butter, softened
6 tablespoons chopped toasted walnuts
3 ounces Gorgonzola cheese, crumbled
3 tablespoons finely chopped arugula
pepper to taste
arugula leaves, garnish

Spread 1 side of each baguette slice with butter. Arrange butter side up on a baking sheet. Bake at 400 degrees for 12 minutes or until golden brown. Cool on a wire rack. Reduce the oven temperature to 350 degrees. Mix the walnuts, cheese and chopped arugula in a medium bowl. Spread over the cooled baguette slices. Season with pepper. Bake for 6 minutes or just until the cheese melts. Cool the crostini slightly. Arrange on a serving platter. Garnish with arugula leaves.

Yield: 6 servings

Crostini vs. Bruschetta

Crostini, a classic Italian appetizer, are small toasts cooked over the open fire of the grill or under the broiler. They are brushed with olive oil and then topped with a mixture of savory delectables. Crostini are usually served with drinks before dinner.

Bruschetta is thick crusty country bread that is also grilled over the open fire, then rubbed with garlic and spread with olive oil. This tasty toast can be topped with any number of ingredients but is traditionally topped with fresh tomatoes, basil, and grated Parmesan cheese. Bruschetta, usually larger than crostini, makes a hearty appetizer or can be served as a light meal.

Crawfish Beignets

1 cup flour
1 teaspoon baking powder
1 cup water
1 teaspoon chopped garlic
1 (2-ounce) jar pimento, drained,
  chopped

3 green onions, chopped
4 drops of Tabasco sauce
8 ounces crawfish tail meat,
  cooked, chopped
2^1/$_2$ quarts peanut oil
Horseradish Sauce (below)

Combine the flour, baking powder, water, garlic, pimento, green
onions, Tabasco sauce and crawfish in a bowl and mix well. Chill, covered, in
the refrigerator for 30 minutes.

Heat the peanut oil to 365 degrees in a large heavy saucepan. Drop the
chilled batter by spoonfuls into the hot oil. Deep-fry for 7 to 8 minutes or
until golden brown. Remove to paper towels to drain. Serve with
Horseradish Sauce.

Yield: 4 to 6 servings

Horseradish Sauce

2 teaspoons minced garlic
3 tablespoons horseradish, or to taste
1 cup mayonnaise
1 teaspoon Creole mustard
2 green onions, finely chopped

Blend the garlic, horseradish, mayonnaise and Creole mustard in a
blender or food processor until smooth. Spoon into a small bowl. Stir in the
green onions. Chill, covered, for 1 hour.

Yield: 1^1/$_2$ to 2 cups

Irresistible Sausage Bites

1 package won ton wrappers
1 pound mild or spicy ground sausage
1 medium onion, chopped
1 red bell pepper, diced
2 teaspoons olive oil
8 ounces Monterey Jack cheese, grated
1/2 teaspoon oregano
salt and pepper to taste

Place 1 won ton wrapper in each greased miniature muffin cup. Bake at 350 degrees for 3 to 4 minutes or until just golden. Remove the cups to a baking sheet.

Brown the sausage with onion and red pepper in hot olive oil in a skillet, stirring until the sausage is crumbly. Drain and cool to room temperature. Add the cheese, oregano, salt and pepper and mix well. Spoon into the prepared cups. Bake at 350 degrees for 4 to 5 minutes or until golden brown. Serve hot.

Yield: 3 to 4 dozen

Jalapeño Gator Eggs

1 (12-ounce) jar jalapeños
1 pound Cheddar cheese, grated
1 pound lean ground sausage
1 (10-count) can biscuits

Drain the jalapeños and remove the stems. Cut the jalapeños lengthwise and remove the seeds under running water. Stuff the jalapeños with the cheese. Shape the sausage into patties. Wrap around the stuffed jalapeños. Arrange on a baking sheet. Bake at 400 degrees for 10 minutes. Drain and cool. Sausage jalapeños can be frozen at this point.

Separate each biscuit into 2 layers. Wrap each around the sausage jalapeños and seal the edges. Place on a baking sheet. Bake at 400 degrees for 10 minutes.

Yield: 20 servings

The Delchamps Senior Bowl

The Delchamps Senior Bowl is the nation's most unique football game and football's premier pre-draft event. The nationally televised game is held annually in January at Ladd-Peebles Stadium in Mobile. The Senior Bowl features the country's best collegiate football players and top National Football League (NFL) draft prospects on teams representing the North and the South. The entire coaching staffs of two NFL teams come to Mobile to coach. Senior Bowl practices are attended by over 600 general managers, coaches, scouts, and other front office personnel from all of the NFL teams.

Many of the greatest names in football history have participated in the contest since its inception in 1950. The list reads like a "Who's Who" of NFL greats, including Joe Namath, Walter Payton, Terry Bradshaw, Frank Gifford, Dan Marino, Bo Jackson, and Brett Favre.

The Delchamps Senior Bowl is also a nonprofit event that has donated over $1 million to charity since 1989. The primary beneficiaries of the event are the University of South Alabama Children's and Women's Hospital and the Children's Miracle Network.

Cheese Straws

Cheese straws are an essential staple at almost every social occasion throughout the South. Everyone seems to have his or her own special recipe for the ideal cheese straw. Generations of Mobilians have served and savored this classic rendition from Recipe Jubilee, the first cookbook published by the Junior League of Mobile.

1¼ pounds extra-sharp Cheddar
    cheese, grated, softened
½ cup butter, softened
1¾ cups flour
⅓ teaspoon salt
¼ teaspoon ground red pepper
pinch of cayenne

Beat the cheese and butter in a bowl until creamy. Add the flour, salt, red pepper and cayenne and mix well. Spoon into a cookie press fitted with a star tip. Press into straws onto baking sheets. Bake at 350 degrees for 30 minutes or until brown.

Yield: 3 to 4 dozen

Blue Poppy Wafers

8 ounces crumbled blue cheese, softened
½ cup margarine, softened
1⅓ cups flour
¼ cup poppy seeds
¼ teaspoon cayenne

Beat the blue cheese and margarine in a bowl until smooth and creamy. Add the flour, poppy seeds and cayenne. Beat until a soft dough forms. Shape into a log 2 inches in diameter on a sheet of plastic wrap. Wrap in the plastic wrap. Chill in the refrigerator for 2 hours. Cut the log into slices ⅛ inch thick. Place on ungreased baking sheets. Bake at 325 degrees for 25 minutes or until crisp. Remove to a wire rack to cool.

Yield: 4 dozen

Boursin Cheese Spread

1 clove of garlic
16 ounces cream cheese, softened
½ cup butter, softened
1 teaspoon dried oregano
¼ teaspoon dried basil
¼ teaspoon dried dillweed
¼ teaspoon dried marjoram
¼ teaspoon dried thyme
¼ teaspoon pepper

Process the garlic in a food processor fitted with a knife blade until finely chopped. Scrap down the sides of the container. Add the cream cheese, butter, oregano, basil, dillweed, marjoram, thyme and pepper. Process until smooth. Serve with crackers.

Yield: 2 to 2½ cups

Crabmeat Dip

1 pound fresh lump crabmeat
3 ounces capers
juice of 1 lemon
2 tablespoons mayonnaise

Mix the crabmeat, capers and lemon juice with just enough mayonnaise in a bowl to moisten. Serve with crackers.

Yield: 4 to 6 servings

Unbelievable Crabmeat Spread

1 loaf white bread
1 pound fresh lump crabmeat
1 small white onion, minced
2 cups mayonnaise

Trim the crust from the bread. Cut the bread into bite-size pieces. Combine the bread, crabmeat and onion in a bowl and mix well. Chill, covered, in the refrigerator for 8 to 10 hours. Stir in the mayonnaise just before serving. Serve with assorted crackers.

Yield: 6 to 8 servings

Capers

Capers are the unopened buds of a shrub that grows throughout the Mediterranean region and India. The largest capers grow in Sicily. The green buds are picked before sunrise, while they are still tightly closed, and then pickled. The delightfully briny flavor of capers makes a wonderfully piquant accent to a wide variety of foods, including fish, chicken, beef, steak tartare, sauce verte, vinaigrettes, rémoulade, hollandaise, pasta sauces, pizza, tomatoes, and an assortment of salads and vegetables.

Tortilla Roll-Ups

Tortillas spread with any number of savory fillings make a most marvelous, quick, crowd-pleasing appetizer. Simply cover a flour tortilla with the mixture of your choice. Roll the tortilla jelly roll-style and cut into 1/2-inch pieces to create fun spiral slices. (For easy slicing, refrigerate and use an electric knife.) Here are some suggestions for several tasty tortilla spreads to create your own combination:

• Spinach alouette.

• Picante sauce, chopped green chiles, cream cheese, sour cream, and a healthy dash or two of Tabasco sauce and garlic salt.

• Thinly sliced smoked turkey, flavored cream cheese (such as garden vegetable or chive and onion), sour cream, and picante sauce for dipping.

• Puréed black beans, chopped green chiles, and sautéed red peppers with sour cream and picante sauce for dipping.

• Cream cheese, sour cream, chopped green onions, minced pickled jalapeños, and a dash of both garlic powder and fresh lime juice, served with picante sauce for dipping.

• Cream cheese with chives and picante sauce for dipping.

Crawfish Dip

1 tablespoon melted butter
1/2 tablespoon Worcestershire sauce
2 tablespoons chopped shallots
2 tablespoons chopped parsley
1/2 pound chopped crawfish tails
4 ounces cream cheese
1/4 cup milk

Combine the melted butter, Worcestershire sauce, shallots, parsley and crawfish in a bowl and mix well. Combine the cream cheese and milk in a small saucepan. Bring to a simmer. Simmer until the cream cheese is melted, stirring constantly. Stir in the crawfish mixture. Spoon into a chafing dish and keep warm. Serve with crackers or French bread.

Note: Recipe can be doubled and prepared in a slow cooker. Crawfish tails can be found in the frozen seafood section of your local grocery.

Yield: 30 servings

Shrimp Butter

16 ounces cream cheese, softened
1/2 cup butter, softened
2 tablespoons mayonnaise
1 tablespoon chopped onion
1/2 teaspoon Tabasco sauce
1/2 teaspoon Worcestershire sauce
1 teaspoon chopped garlic
lemon juice to taste
12 ounces peeled boiled shrimp, chopped

Beat the cream cheese, butter and mayonnaise in a bowl until smooth. Add the onion, Tabasco sauce, Worcestershire sauce, garlic and lemon juice and mix well. Stir in the shrimp. Spoon into a mold sprayed with nonstick cooking spray. Chill for 2 hours or until set.

Unmold onto a serving plate. Serve with toasted French bread or bagels.

Yield: 8 servings

Sun-Dried Tomato Dip with Green Peppercorns

16 ounces cream cheese, softened
1/4 cup cream
2 tablespoons lemon juice
2 tablespoons chopped fresh basil
2 small cloves of garlic, minced
4 sun-dried tomatoes packed in oil, drained, cut into pieces
1/4 teaspoon cayenne
1/2 teaspoon salt
1/2 teaspoon lemon pepper
1 teaspoon cracked green peppercorns

Combine the cream cheese, cream, lemon juice, basil, garlic, sun-dried tomatoes, cayenne, salt, lemon pepper and green peppercorns in a blender or food processor. Process until well blended. Serve with assorted crackers.

Yield: 8 to 12 servings

Spinach and Blue Cheese Dip

1 cup mayonnaise
1 1/2 ounces Roquefort cheese, crumbled
1 teaspoon Worcestershire sauce
pinch of cayenne
1 clove of garlic, pressed
1 (10-ounce) package frozen chopped spinach, thawed, squeezed dry
1/2 teaspoon salt
1/2 teaspoon lemon juice
1 green onion, minced

Process the mayonnaise, cheese, Worcestershire sauce, cayenne and garlic in a blender or food processor until nearly smooth. Combine the spinach, cheese mixture, salt, lemon juice and green onion in a bowl and mix well. Serve on toasted French bread rounds, melba toast rounds or toast points.

Yield: 1 1/2 to 2 cups

Roasted Red Bell Pepper Sauce

This versatile sauce is thick and smooth. It is sensational used as a pasta sauce, pizza sauce, or as a vegetable dip.

1 small purple onion
1 head garlic
2 red bell peppers
4 ounces nonfat cream cheese, softened
3/4 cup chopped fresh basil

Place the onion and garlic in a baking pan. Roast at 270 degrees for 1 hour. Place the red peppers in a baking pan. Roast at 270 degrees until blistered. Place the red peppers in a sealable food storage bag and seal. Let stand for 10 minutes or until cool. Remove the red peppers from the bag and remove the skins. Purée the onion, garlic and red peppers in a blender or food processor. Add the cream cheese and basil and process until smooth.

Yield: about 2 cups

Blue Cheeses

Of all cheeses, the blues continue to be universal favorites. Delicate blue-green veins are created after flavor-producing molds are injected during the curing process. Then the cheeses are aged in caves, where the dampness transforms the curds into a soft ivory color with flavors and textures ranging from creamy and mild to intense and fairly firm. Some of the most popular blues are:

Gorgonzola—from Italy is rich and pungent. When it is young, it is sweet, creamy, and smooth; but as it ages, it becomes sharper and firmer.

Roquefort—made from sheep's milk. It must be aged for at least three months in caves in the South of France.

Saga—created by the Danish, is a rich white triple creme. It is more like a fresh cheese, with its creamy, Brie-like texture and its mellow blue flavor.

Stilton—from England is often referred to as the "King of Cheeses." It is best eaten after four to six months of aging.

Maytag Blue—a tangy, smooth-textured, blue-veined white cheese made in Iowa. It is from the Maytag Dairy Farms, a family-run operation that has been making cheeses since the 1940s.

Savory Blue Cheese Cake

1/4 cup fine bread crumbs	4 eggs
1/3 cup finely grated Parmesan cheese	1/2 cup heavy cream
8 ounces bacon	12 ounces Gorgonzola cheese, Stilton cheese or Roquefort cheese, crumbled
1 Vidalia or white onion, minced	salt and white pepper to taste
24 ounces cream cheese, softened	dash of Tabasco sauce

Coat a buttered 10-inch springform pan with bread crumbs and Parmesan cheese. Cook the bacon in a skillet until crisp-fried and crumbly. Drain the bacon, reserving 1 tablespoon bacon drippings. Crumble the bacon and set aside. Sauté the onion in the reserved bacon drippings in the skillet until transparent. Process the cream cheese, eggs and cream in a blender or food processor until well combined. Add the crumbled bacon, onion and Gorgonzola cheese and process well. Add the salt, white pepper and Tabasco sauce. Process until nearly smooth. Pour into the prepared pan.

Bake at 300 degrees for 1 1/2 hours or until the middle springs back when lightly touched. Turn off the oven. Let stand in the oven for 1 hour.

Yield: 12 to 15 servings

Mushroom Pâté

8 ounces button mushrooms, sliced	2 tablespoons crushed fresh rosemary
8 ounces portobello mushrooms, coarsely chopped	1 tablespoon cracked black pepper
2 tablespoons butter	8 ounces cream cheese, softened
1 tablespoon Worcestershire sauce	1 tablespoon brandy
	1 teaspoon garlic salt
	1/4 teaspoon cayenne (optional)

Sauté the mushrooms in melted butter in a skillet. Add the Worcestershire sauce, rosemary and black pepper. Cook until all of the liquid has evaporated. Remove from the heat. Let stand until cool. Spoon into a blender or food processor. Add the cream cheese, brandy, garlic salt and cayenne and process until smooth, stopping to scrap the side of the container occasionally. Spoon into a mold lined with plastic wrap. Cover with the plastic wrap. Chill in the refrigerator for 24 to 48 hours. Invert onto a serving plate lined with fresh lettuce leaves and remove the plastic wrap. Garnish with sliced button mushrooms and a sprig of rosemary. Serve on toasted baguette slices.

Yield: 8 to 12 servings

Bacon-Wrapped Duck Hors d' Oeuvres

4 duck breasts, boned, cut into 2-inch pieces
¹/₂ cup sliced medium to hot jalapeños
1 (8-ounce) can water chestnuts, drained
1 pound bacon, cut into halves
¹/₄ cup Worcestershire sauce

Soak wooden picks in water in a bowl for 30 minutes. Arrange 1 piece of duck, 1 jalapeño slice and 1 water chestnut on each bacon half. Roll up and secure with wooden picks. Baste with Worcestershire sauce. Place on a grill rack. Grill over medium-hot coals for 10 minutes or until the bacon is crisp and the duck is cooked through. Serve immediately.

Yield: approximately 40 pieces

Brandy Chicken Pâté

1 chicken breast
4 cups chicken broth
1 pound chicken livers
1 small onion, finely chopped
¹/₂ cup butter
1¹/₂ tablespoons brandy
1¹/₂ tablespoons sherry
1 teaspoon salt
¹/₄ teaspoon ground nutmeg
¹/₄ teaspoon pepper
pinch of dried thyme
pinch of dried basil
pinch of dried marjoram
2 hard-cooked eggs, finely chopped
*   (optional)*

Boil the chicken in the broth in a saucepan for 10 minutes or until cooked through. Add the livers. Boil until the livers are brown and cooked through. Drain and place in a blender or food processor. Add the onion, butter, brandy, sherry, salt, nutmeg, pepper, thyme, basil, marjoram and eggs and process until smooth. Spoon into a terrine. Chill, covered, in the refrigerator. Serve with toast points, toasted thinly sliced French bread rounds or crackers.

Note: Pâté can be prepared up to 2 days in advance.

Yield: 4 to 6 servings

Caviar

There are two basic facts about caviar: First, the best caviar in the world comes from the Caspian Sea and its tributaries. Second, while there are many types of fish roe on the market, only the eggs from the sturgeon can be labeled simply "caviar"—other fish roe must be labeled with the name of the fish preceding the word "caviar."

Sturgeon eggs come in several varieties: Beluga, the largest of the basic caviars, is pale to dark gray with a buttery flavor. It is also the most expensive and most difficult to come by. Osetra has a rich nutty flavor and can vary in color from golden brown to bottle green or slate gray. (Golden osetra, at one time reserved for the tsars, is the pale roe of the albino sturgeon. It is milder than the dark osetra and very rare.) Sevruga eggs are smaller than either beluga or osetra and have a more intense sea flavor. This roe is dark gray to black in color.

Pressed caviar is a thick caviar paste made from the damaged or overly mature eggs of various sturgeons. Concentrated and salty, it is a staple of the Russian diet.

Of the non-sturgeon caviars, salmon roe caviar is perhaps the most popular. It is bright orange-red, large-grained, and strongly flavored. Lumpfish caviar, one of the more inexpensive varieties, is naturally golden, but it is often dyed black or

Smoked Trout Pâté

1 pound trout fillets
3/4 cup water
2 tablespoons vermouth
16 ounces cream cheese, softened
2 tablespoons fresh lemon juice
2 teaspoons paprika
1/4 teaspoon liquid smoke
1 teaspoon salt
1 clove of garlic, minced
dash of black pepper

Cook the trout in the water and vermouth in a skillet until the trout flakes easily with a fork; drain. Combine the trout, cream cheese, lemon juice, paprika, liquid smoke, salt, garlic and black pepper in a blender or food processor and process until smooth. Chill, covered, for 8 to 10 hours. Serve with crackers.

Note: Pâté can be frozen for later use.

Yield: about 4 cups

Smoked Salmon Mousse

4 ounces smoked salmon
2 dashes of Tabasco sauce
2 dashes of Worcestershire sauce
freshly ground white pepper to taste
1/2 cup whipping cream
fresh fennel or dill, garnish

Process the salmon, Tabasco sauce, Worcestershire sauce and white pepper in a blender or food processor until smooth. Beat the whipping cream in a bowl until stiff peaks form. Fold in the salmon mixture. Spoon into a serving bowl. Chill, covered, in the refrigerator for at least 1 or up to to 24 hours. Serve on any canapé base and garnish with sprigs of fresh fennel or dill.

Yield: 1 1/2 to 2 cups

Tapenade

1 cup rinsed, pitted calamata olives
2 cloves of garlic, minced
1 tablespoon minced yellow onion
1/8 teaspoon dried thyme
1 teaspoon anchovy paste
1 tablespoon capers
1/3 cup olive oil
1 tablespoon fresh lemon juice

Process the olives, garlic, onion, thyme, anchovy paste and capers in a blender or food processor until finely chopped. Add the olive oil in a fine stream, processing constantly. Spoon into a serving bowl. Stir in the lemon juice. Serve with crackers or French bread.

Yield: 8 to 10 servings

Avocado Salsa

1 tablespoon finely chopped fresh basil
1 tablespoon finely chopped fresh cilantro
2 large tomatoes, finely chopped
2 tablespoons olive oil
juice of 1 medium lime
3 tablespoons minced green onions
1 to 3 teaspoons minced jalapeños
1 clove of garlic, minced
salt and pepper to taste
1 large ripe avocado, peeled, chopped

Combine the basil, cilantro, tomatoes, olive oil, lime juice, green onions, jalapeños and garlic in a bowl and mix well. Let stand for 1 hour or longer. Season with salt and pepper. Stir in the avocado. Serve with tortilla chips.

Yield: 4 to 6 servings

(Caviar, continued)

red. The tinted versions should be added to recipes at the last minute, because the dye has a tendency to run. Whitefish caviar comes from the Great Lakes and Canada and has a mild, crisp, clean taste. Carp roe caviar is almost exclusively used to make the delicious Greek caviar spread taramasalata. Mullet roe, golden in hue, is Alabama's answer to caviar. It is very popular in the Asian markets and thus a majority of it is exported to Japan.

The sturgeon caviars should be placed in the tin or in a caviar server on top of a bed of crushed ice and served with a bone or mother-of-pearl spoon. It is delicious alone or heaped on blini or crustless toast points. Accompaniments can include melted butter, minced chives or green onions, crème fraîche or sour cream, or hard-cooked eggs and lemon wedges.

Mardi Gras

Mardi Gras is a gigantic citywide celebration that consumes Mobile for the two weeks preceding Ash Wednesday and the Lenten season. The term Mardi Gras translates literally to "Fat Tuesday" and refers to Shrove Tuesday, the day preceding the start of the solemn Lent. The season is filled with festive public displays of frivolity, including parades, parties, and balls.

The first Mobile Mardi Gras celebration took place in 1711 when a group of soldiers, calling themselves the Boeuf Gras Society, marked the day by parading with a papier mâché bull's head atop an ox-drawn cart.

When the Spanish controlled the city in the late 18th century, torch-lit parades were held to celebrate Twelfth Night (January 6th, traditionally the start of Carnival). Then on the fateful night of December 26, 1831, a cotton broker, by the name of Michael Krafft had dinner on a ship docked at the foot of Government Street. On his way home, the slightly inebriated Krafft fell into a hardware display, knocking down a number of rakes and some cowbells. Krafft discovered that cowbells attached to the teeth of a rake make a great clamor—with his new instrument in hand, he then proceeded noisily up the street, gathering a crowd

Black-Eyed Pea Salsa

2 cups cooked black-eyed peas
2 tomatoes, chopped
1 bunch green onions, sliced
1 tablespoon chopped fresh cilantro
3 tablespoons lime juice

1 tablespoon olive oil
1 to 2 cloves of garlic, minced
$^1/_2$ teaspoon cumin
$^1/_4$ teaspoon salt

Rinse the black-eyed peas with cold water and drain. Combine the tomatoes, green onions, cilantro, lime juice, olive oil, garlic, cumin and salt in a bowl and mix well. Chill, covered, in the refrigerator.

Note: Salsa needs to be prepared ahead of time so the flavors can blend. Black beans can be substituted for black-eyed peas.

Yield: 2 cups

Corn and Black Bean Salsa

1 (15-ounce) can black beans, drained and rinsed
1 cup corn
$^1/_2$ cup chopped red bell pepper
$^1/_2$ cup chopped cilantro, or to taste (optional)
8 green onions, sliced

3 tablespoons lime juice
2 tablespoons balsamic vinegar
$^1/_2$ teaspoon cumin
3 tablespoons olive oil
pinch of salt
minced garlic to taste

Combine the black beans, corn, red pepper, cilantro, green onions, lime juice, vinegar, cumin, olive oil, salt and garlic in a bowl and mix well. Store, covered, in the refrigerator for up to 3 days.

Serve with blue and white corn tortilla chips.

Yield: 4 cups

Bushwhacker

1 1/4 ounces each light and dark rum
3/4 ounce crème de cacao
1 1/4 ounces Kahlúa
1/4 ounce crème de banana
2 scoops vanilla ice cream
1 cup ice

Process the light rum, dark rum, crème de cacao, Kahlúa, crème de banana, ice cream and ice in a blender until smooth. Pour into glasses.

Yield: 2 servings

Bay Cooler

1 (12-ounce) can frozen limeade concentrate
1 (12-ounce) can frozen orange juice concentrate
1 (12-ounce) can frozen pink lemonade concentrate
1 (10-ounce) jar maraschino cherries
1 to 2 (12-ounce) cans rum
3/4 (2-liter) bottle ginger ale

Process the concentrates, undrained cherries, rum and ginger ale in a blender until well blended. Pour into a freezer container. Freeze, covered, until firm. Let stand at room temperature for 1 to 2 hours before serving.

Yield: 8 to 10 servings

Frozen Wine Cooler

1 (46-ounce) can pineapple juice
1 (12-ounce) can frozen lemonade concentrate
1 (12-ounce) can frozen orange juice concentrate
1 (2-liter) bottle ginger ale
1 (750-milliliter) bottle medium dry white wine

Combine the pineapple juice, concentrates, ginger ale and wine in a large freezer container and mix well. Freeze, covered, until firm. Let stand at room temperature for 1 hour before serving.

Yield: 8 to 10 servings

(Mardi Gras, continued)

as he went. Every night for a week, Krafft and his friends paraded with their rakes and cowbells while the local newspaper recorded their raucous exploits. When the group was eventually welcomed into the mayor's home to partake of food and refreshment, the group's future was assured—thus Mobile's first mystic organization, The Cowbellion de Rakin Society was born.

The Cowbellions were joined by the Strikers Independent Society in 1841. The next few years saw the founding of several more mystic societies. But the celebrating came to a halt with the outbreak of the Civil War. Then, following the war, the festivities gradually picked up again and the emphasis began to shift away from New Year's Eve to Carnival season instead. (The Strikers, now the oldest continuing mystic society, still hold their annual event on New Year's Eve.) Today there are more than 20 parades, and even more balls staged during the weeks surrounding Mardi Gras.

Mobile's Most Famous Hostess: Octavia Walton Le Vert

Over 150 years ago, Madame Octavia Walton Le Vert reigned supreme over Mobile's intellectual and social community. It was in her ivory and gold parlor on the corner of Government and St. Emanuel streets that she entertained guests every Monday afternoon and evening. Madame Le Vert's parlor became a forum for the exchange of ideas with famous actors, poets, musicians, writers, artists, and politicians.

Although Octavia was born in Augusta, Georgia, in 1810, she lived in Florida while her father was governor of the state. In 1835, she and her family moved to Mobile where she met and married Dr. Henry Le Vert. Having cultivated her intellectual interests by conversing with her father's political friends, Madame Le Vert longed to be with people of similar passions and pursuits, so she began the ritual of opening her home on Mondays.

It was during these weekly soirees that her legendary fame as a hostess and conversationalist began. It did not take long for her charming reputation to spread throughout the state, the nation, and even Europe.

Lemon Drop

 The Bubble Lounge

2 ounces citron vodka
1 ounce simple syrup
juice of 1 lemon

Pour the vodka, simple syrup and lemon juice over ice in a martini shaker and shake well. Pour into a chilled sugar-rimmed martini glass. Garnish with a lemon twist.

Note: To make 1 quart of simple syrup, dissolve $2^{1}/_{2}$ cups sugar in 1 quart of warm water.

Yield: 1 serving

Loretta's Mint Julep

 Loretta's

4 fresh mint leaves
$1^{1}/_{2}$ ounces quality bourbon
1 ounce simple syrup (above)
ice
dash of ginger ale
sprig of fresh mint, garnish

Crush the mint leaves in the bourbon and simple syrup in a bowl. Let stand for 8 to 10 hours. Strain the liquid into a silver mint julep cup. Add ice and top off with ginger ale. Garnish with a sprig of fresh mint.

Yield: 1 serving

Peach Juleps

1 medium fresh peach, chilled
1 tablespoon sugar
2 ounces bourbon
crushed ice
sprigs of fresh mint, garnish

Peel the peach and cut into slices. Purée the peach slices in a food processor or blender. Add the sugar and process well. Stir in the bourbon. Pour over crushed ice in a silver julep cup. Garnish with sprigs of fresh mint.

Yield: 1 serving

Ultimate Ice Cream Toddy

1 1/2 pints Breyers vanilla bean ice cream
2 ounces Kahlúa
2 ounces Cognac
1/2 cup milk
1/2 cup ice

Process the ice cream, Kahlúa and Cognac in a blender until smooth. Add the milk and ice a small amount at a time, processing well after each addition until the mixture reaches the consistency of a milk shake. Pour into a frosted glass.

Yield: 1 serving

(Mobile's Most Famous Hostess:
Octavia Walton Le Vert, continued)

No one of celebrity standing visited Mobile without a visit to Madame Le Vert's salon. She was well educated, fluent in five languages, and very knowledgeable about current events of the day. Henry Clay, John C. Calhoun, Washington Irving, and Edwin Booth were all close friends and admirers.

Madame Le Vert also traveled extensively in Europe. During one visit Madame Le Vert was presented to Queen Victoria, and on another trip she met Robert Browning, Napoleon III, Empress Eugenie, and Pope Pius IX. In 1857, she published Souvenirs of Travel, recounting the adventures of these European trips.

During the Civil War, Octavia did all she could for the Confederate war effort, but she secretly did not believe that the Union should be divided. After the war she made a costly mistake that ended her reign in Mobile. When Union troops were dispatched to Mobile, she opened her home to them as she would any guest. Mobilians condemned her, and she fell out of favor and moved north. Though she died in Augusta, ignored and heartbroken, Mobilians will always remember their most famous hostess and her grandiose gatherings.

SOUPS
SALADS
SANDWICHES

Soups, salads and sandwiches are the traditional trio of the lunch table—
but they can be splendid served as a lovely, light supper as well.
The true pleasure is in venturing away from the expected—to explore
new and creative combinations. Consider feasting upon crisp-edged,
golden, fried green tomatoes and ham heaped on a crusty roll, or sampling
shrimp bathed in spicy, pink, rémoulade-style sauce tucked into
a pita pocket in lieu of the standard peanut butter, tuna or turkey.
Try dining on such salads as tart baby greens scattered with
ripe strawberries and candied almonds all bathed in a slightly sweet,
Tabasco-spiked vinaigrette, or fresh spinach leaves crowned with a hail of
blue cheese, pecans and blueberries in a gorgeous, purple-hued dressing,
in place of the usual chef, Caesar, or even more simple salad.
And while it's true there has perhaps never been a better time to buy
ready-made soups—nothing satisfies the soul like a bowl of homemade.
Opt for an ultra creamy Brie soup, soothing and sensational—
or for warmer weather, sip a snappy citrus and cilantro-swirled
avocado concoction chilled to cool perfection. With inventive ingredients,
soups, salads and sandwiches can all cause quite a stir,
becoming the stunning highlight of a meal.

Dauphin Island

Situated at the mouth of Mobile Bay is a little piece of land called Dauphin Island. The island, named for the son of Louis XIV, is the largest and the first in a series of barrier islands off the coast of Alabama and Mississippi.

The island was originally home to a small group of Choctaw Indians. They relied on the bountiful surrounding waters for their daily needs, as well as for commerce. The Choctaws harvested oysters, dried them, packed them in earthenware jars and sold them to people on the mainland.

As the years passed, the little island was also home to French, Spanish, English and American soldiers who all maintained forts on the island at different times.

Today many of the people who live on Dauphin Island make their living from the sea, but there are also those who come to Dauphin Island purely for pleasure and relaxation.

It is still a quiet and relatively undiscovered retreat. For many, it is a wonderful place to come and escape the harsh northern winters or to spend a week at the beach. The only crowds you are likely to encounter here are those you create when you host your friends for an afternoon or evening on the beach.

Antipasto

This classic piquant mixture is extraordinarily versatile. Try it as a condiment on sandwiches, especially muffulettas. It is also great with crackers or on bruschetta, as an appetizer, or atop fresh sliced tomatoes as a side-dish salad.

2 (4-ounce) cans chopped
   mushrooms, drained
1 (14-ounce) can artichoke hearts,
   drained, chopped
1 (2-ounce) jar pimento, drained,
   chopped
1/2 cup chopped green bell pepper
1/2 cup chopped celery
1 (16-ounce) jar salad olives,
   chopped
2/3 cup white vinegar
2/3 cup vegetable oil
1/4 cup dried minced onion
2 1/2 teaspoons Italian seasoning
1 teaspoon each salt, garlic powder
   and sugar
1/2 teaspoon pepper

Mix the mushrooms, artichoke hearts, pimento, green pepper, celery and olives in a large bowl. Bring the remaining ingredients to a boil in a medium saucepan. Boil for 1 minute and remove from the heat. Add to the vegetable mixture and mix gently. Pour into an airtight glass container. Store in the refrigerator for up to 1 month.

Yield: 5 to 6 cups

Cream of Asparagus Soup

 Eats of Eden

2 pounds fresh asparagus
3 cups chopped onion
1 1/2 tablespoons butter
2 cups water
1 cup wild rice
1 1/2 teaspoons salt

pepper to taste
2 teaspoons dill
1/2 cup sliced almonds
3 tablespoons flour
3 tablespoons vegetable oil
2 cups (or more) hot milk

Trim the asparagus, discarding the ends. Chop the asparagus. Sauté the asparagus and onion in butter in a stockpot until tender. Add the water, rice, salt, pepper, dill and almonds. Cook for 30 minutes or until the rice is tender. Stir the flour into vegetable oil in a saucepan. Whisk in the milk. Cook until thickened, stirring constantly. Add additional milk if needed, for the desired consistency. Stir into the asparagus mixture. Ladle into soup bowls.

Yield: 4 to 6 servings

Chilled Avocado Soup

6 ripe avocados
5 cups chicken broth
2 cups light cream
1/4 cup fresh lime juice
dash of Tabasco sauce

pinch of cayenne
salt and pepper to taste
thin lime slices, garnish
cilantro sprigs, garnish

Purée the avocados with the chicken broth in a blender or food processor. Combine with the cream, lime juice, Tabasco sauce, cayenne, salt and pepper in a bowl and whisk well. Chill, covered, in the refrigerator. Ladle into chilled soup bowls. Garnish with lime slices and sprigs of cilantro.

Yield: 8 servings

Black Bean Cassolette

1 medium onion, chopped
2 tablespoons olive oil
2 cloves of garlic, minced
1 tablespoon cumin
2 teaspoons dried oregano
1/8 teaspoon cayenne
1/2 teaspoon salt

1/2 teaspoon pepper
2 (16-ounce) cans black beans
1/4 cup dry sherry
1 tablespoon brown sugar
1 tablespoon lemon juice
1 pound smoked sausage, sliced (optional)
3 cups cooked rice

Sauté the onion in the olive oil in a skillet for 6 minutes or until translucent. Add the garlic. Sauté for 1 minute. Add cumin, oregano, cayenne, salt and pepper. Sauté for 1 minute. Combine with the beans in a medium stockpot. Cook over medium heat for 20 to 30 minutes or until of the desired consistency. Add the sherry, brown sugar and lemon juice. Cook for 5 minutes. Sauté the sausage in a nonstick skillet until cooked through. Stir into the bean mixture. Serve over rice.

Note: This is a French bistro dish, not Tex-Mex. However, it can become Tex-Mex by omitting the sherry, brown sugar and lemon juice.

Yield: 4 servings

Brie Soup

1 cup unsalted butter
1 cup coarsely chopped onions
1/2 cup coarsely chopped celery
1/2 cup flour
1/2 teaspoon white pepper

1/2 teaspoon cayenne
4 cups chicken stock
1 pound Brie cheese, cut into pieces
2 cups milk
1/2 cup sherry (optional)

Melt the butter in a large skillet. Add the onions and celery. Sauté for 5 minutes or until the onions are translucent. Whisk in the flour. Cook for 3 minutes, stirring constantly. Add white pepper and cayenne and mix well. Cook for 2 minutes. Remove from the heat. Bring the chicken stock to a boil in a large saucepan. Stir in the sautéed vegetable mixture. Add the cheese. Cook until the cheese begins to melt, stirring constantly. Reduce the heat. Cook for 4 to 5 minutes longer or until the cheese is melted, stirring constantly. Do not scorch. Remove from the heat and strain into a bowl. Return to the saucepan. Add the milk. Cook for about 2 minutes or until heated through. Stir in the sherry. Ladle into soup bowls.

Yield: 8 servings

Roasting Garlic

Garlic turns buttery soft, subtle, and sweet when roasted. It is glorious spread on crisp hot bread and makes a marvelous healthy condiment. Prepare the garlic for roasting by cutting off the top 1/3 of several heads of garlic. Arrange closely in a baking dish. Drizzle generously with extra-virgin olive oil. Sprinkle with kosher salt. Bake, covered with foil, at 350 degrees for 1 hour or until soft. Remove from the oven. Let stand until cool enough to handle. Separate into cloves. Squeeze the cloves to get the warm fragrant roasted garlic out of its papery skin. Use it as a spread or pizza topping, or purée into salad dressings.

Roasted Garlic Soup

4 heads garlic, unpeeled
1/4 cup olive oil
6 tablespoons butter
4 leek bulbs, chopped
1 onion, chopped
6 tablespoons flour

4 cups chicken stock, heated
1/3 cup dry sherry
1 cup heavy cream
lemon juice to taste
salt and pepper to taste

Cut off the top 1/2 inch of each garlic head. Place cut side up in a small shallow baking dish. Drizzle with olive oil. Cover with foil. Bake at 350 degrees for 1 hour or until golden brown. Cool slightly. Squeeze individual garlic cloves to remove from husk.

Melt the butter in a large heavy saucepan. Add the garlic, leeks and onion. Sauté for 6 minutes or until the onion is translucent. Add the flour. Cook for 10 minutes, stirring constantly. Add the hot stock gradually. Add the sherry. Simmer for 20 minutes. Purée in a food processor until smooth. Return to the saucepan. Add the cream. Cook for 10 minutes or until thickened, stirring constantly. Stir in the lemon juice. Season with salt and pepper. Ladle into soup bowls.

Yield: 4 servings

Portobello Mushroom Soup

1/4 cup unsalted butter
5 leek bulbs, chopped
1 medium onion, chopped
10 ounces portobello mushrooms,
    chopped
1/4 cup flour

3 cups chicken stock
5 tablespoons dry sherry
2 cups half-and-half
1/4 teaspoon cayenne
salt and white pepper to taste

Melt the butter in a large Dutch oven over medium heat. Add the leeks and onion. Sauté for 10 minutes or until tender. Add the mushrooms. Sauté for 5 minutes. Reduce the heat to low. Add the flour. Cook for 3 minutes or until thickened, stirring occasionally. Stir in the stock and 3 tablespoons sherry gradually. Bring to a boil, stirring constantly. Reduce the heat. Simmer for 10 minutes or until thickened, stirring constantly. Stir in the half-and-half, cayenne, salt, white pepper and remaining sherry. Simmer for 5 minutes. Ladle into soup bowls.

Yield: 6 servings

Pilgrim Squash Soup

2 pounds butternut squash, unpeeled
1 large onion, unpeeled
1 head garlic, unpeeled
2 tablespoons olive oil
8 sprigs of fresh thyme, or 2 teaspoons dried thyme
$^1/_2$ cup heavy cream
$1^3/_4$ cups (or more) chicken stock
salt and pepper to taste
minced fresh parsley to taste

Cut the squash into 8 pieces and discard the seeds. Cut the onion vertically into halves. Cut $^1/_3$ inch off the top of the head of garlic. Place the garlic, onion and squash cut side up in a large baking dish. Drizzle with olive oil. Sprinkle with thyme. Bake, covered with foil, at 350 degrees for $1^1/_2$ hours. Uncover and cool for 15 minutes.

Scrape the squash into a food processor. Peel the onion and 9 cloves of garlic and add to the squash. Add any juices from the baking dish and heavy cream. Purée until almost smooth. Add more garlic if desired. Pour into a large heavy saucepan. Whisk in $1^3/_4$ cups chicken stock. Cook until heated through, adding more stock if needed for the desired consistency and stirring occasionally. Season with salt and pepper. Sprinkle with parsley. Ladle into soup bowls.

Note: Soup can be made a day in advance. Chill, covered, in the refrigerator and reheat at serving time.

Yield: 4 to 6 servings

Fried Corn Tortillas

8 thin corn tortillas
vegetable oil for deep-frying

Cut the tortillas into strips. Heat the oil in a heavy skillet to 350 degrees. Fry the tortilla strips in batches for 1 minute or until golden brown. Remove to paper towels to drain.

Note: Can be prepared ahead.

Corn Tortilla Chicken Soup

1 tablespoon olive oil
1 small onion, coarsely chopped
2 large cloves of garlic, minced
1 tablespoon chili powder
2 teaspoons cumin
1/2 teaspoon driee oregano
6 cups chicken stock

1 (8-ounce) can tomato sauce
1 1/2 teaspoons salt
1 teaspoon sugar
1/4 teaspoon pepper
2 large chicken breasts
1 1/2 cups corn
Fried Corn Tortillas (at left)

Heat the olive oil in a skillet. Add the onion. Sauté the onion until translucent. Add the garlic, chili powder, cumin and oregano. Sauté for 1 minute. Add the chicken stock, tomato sauce, salt, sugar and pepper. Bring to a boil. Add the chicken. Simmer, covered, about 15 minutes or until the chicken is cooked through. Remove the chicken to a plate and cool slightly. Shred the chicken, discarding the skin and bones. Add the corn to the soup. Simmer until the corn is tender. Add the shredded chicken. Simmer for 1 minute. Ladle into soup bowls. Serve with Fried Corn Tortillas.

Note: Soup can be prepared 1 to 3 days in advance. Chill, covered, in the refrigerator and reheat before serving.

Yield: 6 servings

Sweet Red Pepper and Crab Bisque

2 tablespoons unsalted butter
1 cup chopped onion
1 cup chopped celery
1 cup chopped red bell pepper
1¼ teaspoons Old Bay Seasoning or other seafood spice blend
3 cups fish stock or bottled clam juice
½ cup chopped peeled baking potato
½ cup half-and-half
1 pound fresh lump crabmeat
salt and pepper to taste

Melt the butter in a heavy medium saucepan over low heat. Add the onion, celery, red pepper and Old Bay Seasoning. Cook, covered, for 10 minutes, stirring occasionally. Add the stock and potato. Bring to a boil. Cook, covered, over low heat for 30 minutes or until the potato is very tender. Purée in batches in a blender. Return to the saucepan. Add the half-and-half. Bring to a simmer. Stir in the crabmeat. Season with salt and pepper. Cover and turn off the heat. Let stand for 2 minutes. Ladle into soup bowls.

Yield: 6 servings

Literary Heritage

Simple to make and unbeatable in taste, the original recipe for this oyster soup comes from a 1942 cookbook by Marjorie Kinnan Rawlings, author of The Yearling.

Oyster Soup

3 cloves of garlic, crushed	2 or 3 bay leaves
4 medium onions, finely chopped	1 teaspoon dried thyme
1/2 cup butter	salt and pepper to taste
3 tablespoons flour	Tabasco sauce to taste
1 quart oysters	2 cups half-and-half
6 cups water	

Sauté the garlic and onions in the butter in a large stockpot until the onions are translucent and just beginning to brown. Add the flour. Cook for 3 to 4 minutes over medium heat, stirring constantly. Add the oysters and water. Bring just to a simmer. Cook over low heat for 1 1/2 to 2 1/2 hours. Add the bay leaves, thyme, salt, pepper and Tabasco sauce. Cook for 30 minutes. Add the half-and-half. Cook until heated through. Do not boil. Discard the bay leaves. Serve immediately.

Yield: 6 servings

Scallop and Spinach Soup

2 tablespoons butter	1/4 teaspoon dried crushed
1/2 cup chopped red bell pepper	red pepper
1/2 cup chopped onion	12 ounces sea scallops
1 (10-ounce) package frozen	2 tablespoons chopped fresh
chopped spinach, squeezed dry	basil
2 cups canned chicken broth	salt and black pepper to taste
1/4 to 3/4 cup heavy cream	

Melt the butter in a heavy medium saucepan over medium heat. Add the red bell pepper and onion. Sauté for 4 minutes or until almost tender. Add the spinach, broth, cream and dried red pepper. Simmer, covered, for 5 minutes or until the spinach is tender. Add the scallops. Simmer, uncovered, for 4 minutes or until the scallops are just opaque. Stir in the basil. Season with salt and black pepper. Ladle into soup bowls.

Yield: 4 servings

Shrimp Confetti Soup

1/4 cup vegetable oil

1 cup chopped yellow onion

1/2 cup chopped green bell pepper

1/2 cup chopped red bell pepper

1/4 cup chopped celery

2 tablespoons chopped garlic

1 pound medium shrimp, peeled, deveined

2 cups chicken broth

1 quart heavy cream

2 cups cream-style corn

1 cup whole kernel corn

1/2 cup tomatoes with green chiles, chopped, strained

1 tablespoon chopped fresh thyme

1/2 tablespoon chopped fresh sage

2 tablespoons chopped fresh parsley

1/2 cup diagonally-cut green onions

1 cup shredded mozzarella cheese

6 crab claws, cooked

Heat the vegetable oil in a heavy stockpot. Add the yellow onion, green pepper, red pepper, celery, garlic and shrimp. Sauté over high heat for 5 minutes. Add the chicken broth, heavy cream, cream-style corn, whole kernel corn, tomatoes, thyme, sage and parsley. Reduce the heat to medium. Cook for 25 minutes, stirring occasionally. Ladle into soup bowls. Sprinkle each serving with green onions and mozzarella cheese. Add a crab claw to each bowl.

Yield: 6 servings

Shrimp and Andouille Sausage Gumbo

1/2 cup vegetable oil
1/2 cup flour
4 ribs celery, coarsely chopped
2 medium onions, coarsely chopped
2 medium green bell peppers,
*   coarsely chopped*
1 clove of garlic, minced
2 bay leaves
2 teaspoons salt
1/2 teaspoon black pepper
2 teaspoons dried oregano
1/2 teaspoon cayenne

3 (8-ounce) bottles clam juice, or 3 cups
*   fish stock*
1 (14-ounce) can chicken broth
2 chicken bouillon cubes
1 (28-ounce) can tomatoes
1 pound smoked andouille sausage, cut
*   into halves lengthwise, sliced*
*   1/4 inch thick*
12 ounces sliced okra
2 pounds peeled shrimp
8 cups cooked long grain rice
2 fresh tomatoes, chopped

Heat the vegetable oil in a stockpot. Add the flour, stirring constantly. Cook until the roux is dark brown; do not burn. Add the celery, onions, green peppers and garlic. Cook for 5 to 10 minutes, stirring constantly. Add the bay leaves, salt, black pepper, oregano, cayenne, clam juice, chicken broth, bouillon cubes, canned tomatoes and sausage. Bring to a medium boil. Cook for 15 minutes. Add the okra. Reduce the heat. Simmer for 20 to 25 minutes or until of the desired consistency. Add the shrimp. Simmer for 5 to 7 minutes or until the shrimp turn pink. Discard the bay leaves. Spoon the gumbo over hot rice. Sprinkle with fresh tomatoes.

Yield: 8 servings

Green Salad with Candied Almonds and Strawberries

$^1/_2$ head Boston lettuce, torn into
    bite-size pieces
$^1/_2$ head red leaf lettuce, torn into
    bite-size pieces
$^1/_2$ cup chopped celery
1 pint fresh strawberries, sliced
2 green onions, thinly sliced
1 cup fresh red grapes (optional)

$^1/_2$ cup slivered almonds
2 tablespoons sugar
$^1/_2$ teaspoon salt
$^1/_4$ teaspoon Tabasco sauce
2 tablespoons vinegar
2 tablespoons sugar
$^1/_4$ cup salad oil

Mix the Boston lettuce, red leaf lettuce, celery, strawberries, green onions and grapes in a large salad bowl. Chill, covered, in the refrigerator.

Cook the almonds and 2 tablespoons sugar in a small cast-iron skillet over high heat until the almonds are coated in syrup and light brown, stirring constantly. Pour onto a foil-lined surface. Let stand until cool. Break into pieces.

Combine the salt, Tabasco sauce, vinegar, 2 tablespoons sugar and salad oil in a jar with a lid. Shake, tightly covered, until combined.

Drizzle the dressing over the salad and toss to mix well. Sprinkle with the candied almonds. Serve immediately.

Note: Use mandarin orange slices when strawberries are not in season.

Yield: 6 servings

Spinach Salad Blues

1 shallot, minced
$1^1/_2$ pints fresh blueberries
1 teaspoon salt
3 tablespoons sugar
$^1/_3$ cup raspberry vinegar

1 cup vegetable oil
2 bunches leaf spinach
$^2/_3$ cup crumbled blue cheese
$^1/_2$ cup chopped toasted pecans

Combine the shallot, $^1/_2$ pint of the blueberries, salt, sugar, vinegar and oil in a blender and blend well. Trim the spinach and rinse well. Pat the spinach dry. Combine the spinach, remaining blueberries, blue cheese and pecans in a large salad bowl and toss to mix well. Add the blueberry vinaigrette just before serving and toss until well coated.

Yield: 6 servings

Roasting or Toasting Seeds and Nuts

Toasting nuts brings out a fuller flavor and aroma. Place nuts on a baking sheet and bake at 375 degrees for 5 to 6 minutes or until toasted and golden brown. Small seeds, such as sesame seeds, can be toasted in a heavy skillet. Place the seeds in a cold skillet. Place on a cold stove burner. Turn the heat to medium-high. Cook until the seeds are light brown and toasted.

Oils Other Than Olive

Some common oils used in today's cuisine:

Peanut oil is widely used in Asian cooking and second only to olive oil with French chefs. It is particularly good for frying, since it has very little smell and no flavor. Less refined peanut oil can impart a slight peanut flavor to foods.

Corn oil is one of the most economical oils for shallow and deep frying, since it has one of the highest smoking points. It can be used for salad dressings and mayonnaise, although its critics complain that it is tasteless. Unrefined corn oil, however, has the distinct flavor of corn.

Sesame oil ranges from light to dark. The light sesame oil has only a delicate nutty taste, usually used in cooking and for salads. The darker sesame oils, made from toasted seeds, are used more for flavoring than for cooking.

Sunflower oil is light, mild, and thin. Excellent for cooking, although it has a relatively low smoking point, it is also good for use in combination with more expensive oils when making delicate salad dressings.

Safflower oil, often confused with sunflower oil, is made from the safflower, a pretty thistle-like plant with orange, red, or yellow flowers. Usually a deep golden color, safflower

Avocado and Grapefruit Vinaigrette

 Michael's Midtown Cafe

4 romaine lettuce leaves
1 grapefruit, peeled, sectioned
1 avocado, peeled, sliced
1 cup extra-virgin olive oil
3 tablespoons balsamic vinegar
2 tablespoons Dijon mustard
2 cloves of garlic, crushed
pepper to taste

Arrange the lettuce on 2 chilled salad plates. Arrange the grapefruit sections and avocado slices in a crescent shape on opposite sides of the plates. Whip the olive oil, balsamic vinegar, Dijon mustard, garlic and pepper in a bowl. Sprinkle over the salad just before serving.

Yield: 2 servings

Roasted Pear Salad

1/2 cup olive oil	1/2 teaspoon pepper
1/4 cup red wine vinegar	4 Bosc pears
1/4 to 1/3 cup sugar	1 head romaine lettuce
1/4 cup chopped fresh parsley	2 cups torn radicchio
1 teaspoon Dijon mustard	1 cup toasted walnuts
1/2 teaspoon salt	1/2 cup crumbled blue cheese

Process 1/2 cup olive oil, vinegar, sugar, parsley, Dijon mustard, salt and pepper in a blender until well blended.

Cut the pears into quarters and remove the cores. Place pear quarters on a lightly greased baking sheet. Brush with additional olive oil. Bake at 400 degrees for 20 to 30 minutes or until tender.

Toss the romaine lettuce, radicchio, walnuts and blue cheese in a large salad bowl. Add the vinaigrette and toss well. Divide between 6 to 8 individual salad plates. Arrange 2 pear quarters on top of each serving.

Yield: 8 servings

Roast Beef Salad with Horseradish Vinaigrette

2 cloves of garlic, finely chopped
3/4 cup olive oil
1/4 cup white wine vinegar
1/4 cup fresh lemon juice
3 tablespoons chopped fresh parsley
1 teaspoon sugar
1 1/2 tablespoons drained prepared
    horseradish
2 tablespoons heavy cream
salt and pepper to taste
1 pint cherry tomatoes, cut into
    halves

1 1/2 pounds small red potatoes,
    boiled, cooled, cut into
    quarters
1 1/2 pounds cold cooked roast beef,
    pot roast or steak, trimmed,
    julienned
1 cup thinly sliced green onions
2 tablespoons capers
shredded romaine lettuce
3 hard-cooked eggs, quartered

Combine the garlic, olive oil, vinegar, lemon juice, 2 tablespoons of the parsley, sugar, horseradish, cream and salt and pepper in a blender and blend well.

Combine the tomatoes, potatoes, beef, green onions, capers and the remaining 1 tablespoon parsley in a large bowl and toss to mix well. Add the horseradish vinaigrette and toss to coat well. Season with salt and pepper. Mound on a platter lined with romaine lettuce. Garnish with hard-cooked eggs.

Yield: 8 servings

(Oils Other Than Olive, continued)

oil is found refined in supermarkets and unrefined in health food stores. It is very light and can be used in the same way as sunflower oil.

Canola oil, also known as rapeseed oil, is widely used in Asia and the Mediterranean countries for frying and in salads. It has recently become widely popular in the United States, because it is the oil lowest in saturated fats. Canola oil is often blended with other oils to make margarine.

Grapeseed oil, popular in France and Italy, is a by-product of the wine industry. The seeds yield a golden oil that is light and aromatic. It is used in salads and for gentle sautéing.

Walnut oil is cold-pressed from walnuts and has a strong, deliciously nutty flavor. It is an unusual salad oil, best mixed with a lighter oil or used a little at a time for flavoring. Walnut oil does not keep well, so it should be bought in small quantities and stored in the refrigerator.

Vegetable oils, the most economical oils, are highly refined. They are pale golden oils that are a blend of a variety of vegetable products. Vegetable oils have little taste, but their high smoking point makes them good for frying.

Chicken and Orzo Salad

1 tablespoon Dijon mustard
$^1/_2$ cup red wine vinegar
1 cup olive oil
$^1/_4$ cup sugar
$^1/_2$ teaspoon salt
$^1/_2$ teaspoon pepper
$^1/_2$ cup chopped fresh basil
1 pound orzo
chicken stock

2 pounds chicken, cooked, chopped
2 cups slivered toasted almonds
1 red bell pepper, chopped
1 cup chopped celery
1 green bell pepper, chopped
1 pound cherry tomatoes, cut
    into halves
salt and pepper to taste

Combine the Dijon mustard, red wine vinegar, olive oil, sugar, $^1/_2$ teaspoon salt, $^1/_2$ teaspoon pepper and basil in a bowl and mix well.

Cook the orzo using the package directions until firm and tender, substituting chicken stock for the water. Let stand until cool. Toss with $^1/_3$ of the vinaigrette.

Toss the chicken with $^1/_2$ of the remaining vinaigrette. Add the orzo, almonds, red pepper, celery, green pepper, tomatoes and salt and pepper to taste. Add the remaining vinaigrette and toss to mix well. Chill, covered, in the refrigerator. Serve cold.

Note: Crumbled feta cheese can be added to the chilled salad before serving.

Yield: 4 to 6 servings

Smoked Salmon and Chilled Asparagus Salad with Hazelnut Vinaigrette

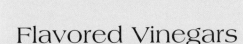

2 bunches fresh asparagus
6 cups mixed greens
Hazelnut Vinaigrette (below)
1/2 cup finely chopped hazelnuts
6 smoked salmon strips

Rinse and trim the asparagus. Blanch the asparagus in boiling water in a saucepan until just tender. Drain and let stand until cool. Chill in the refrigerator.

Tear the mixed greens into bite-size pieces and place in a salad bowl. Add Hazelnut Vinaigrette and toss until the greens are well coated. Place on individual salad plates. Sprinkle with a small amount of the hazelnuts. Arrange the chilled asparagus and salmon beside the mixed greens. Sprinkle with the remaining hazelnuts.

Yield: 6 servings

Hazelnut Vinaigrette

1 1/2 cups olive oil
3 to 4 tablespoons hazelnut oil or salad oil
1/2 cup rice wine vinegar
1 tablespoon chopped shallots
salt and pepper to taste

Combine the olive oil, hazelnut oil, vinegar, shallots, salt and pepper in a bowl and mix well.

Yield: 2 1/4 cups

Flavored Vinegars

Flavored vinegars look fabulous in decorative glass bottles with cork caps. Use your imagination and have fun creating your own variations. Place the desired additions, such as herbs, fruit, or spices, into a container (a wide-mouthed pint-sized jar works well). Pour in vinegar that has been heated to just below the boiling point. Cap the container tightly and let stand for a week or two in a cool dark place, giving the jar an occasional shake. Then strain the vinegar, discard the herbs, etc. and pour into the chosen bottles. (Be sure to sterilize the bottles first to prevent the vinegar from clouding.) Add a fresh sprig of herbs, a few berries, or a twist of citrus peel for garnish. Apple cider vinegar is ideal to use with fruit. Distilled white vinegar works well with herbs. And wine vinegar is best for strong-flavored additions, such as garlic or jalapeños.

Vinegars

Vinegar, a word derived from the French word vinaigre, means sour wine. It is produced by an acid fermentation of fresh wine. By the same process, cider vinegar is made from cider, malt vinegar from malted barley, and Chinese and Japanese vinegars from fermented rice.

Apart from its role in salad dressings, vinegar can be used instead of lemon juice in mayonnaise, hollandaise, and bèarnaise and is essential in horseradish and fresh mint sauces. It is used in countless marinades for meat, poultry, and game—and a little vinegar can also improve the flavor of stews and soups, or do wonders for a dull sauce or gravy.

Among the vinegars available today are:

Wine vinegar—The best wine vinegars are produced by a slow gentle process that allows them to mature naturally. The French wine vinegars are probably the best and the purest.

Cider vinegar—Apple cider vinegar has been touted as a cure for a variety of ills, from indigestion to hair loss. It has a strong distinctive taste of cider and is good for making pickles and fruit chutneys.

Malt vinegar—This vinegar is brewed from malted barley and colored with caramel to varying shades of brown. Malt vinegar is good for

Seafood Bow Tie Pasta Salad

1 medium red bell pepper, chopped
1 medium green bell pepper, chopped
1 cup chopped celery
2 teaspoons minced garlic
2 tablespoons olive oil
1 pound bow tie pasta, cooked
$1/2$ to $3/4$ cup milk or cream
1 pound peeled cooked shrimp
1 pound fresh lump crabmeat
1 cup Homemade Mayonnaise (below)
1 teaspoon salt, or to taste
1 teaspoon pepper, or to taste

Sauté the red pepper, green pepper, celery and garlic in the olive oil in a skillet until tender-crisp. Add the pasta, milk, sautéed vegetables, shrimp and crabmeat in a large bowl and toss to mix well. Add 1 cup Homemade Mayonnaise and mix well. Season with salt and pepper.

Note: Mushrooms and onions can be sautéed with the vegetables. Salad can be sprinkled with shredded Parmesan cheese and baked until slightly melted.

Yield: 6 servings

Homemade Mayonnaise

1 tablespoon lemon juice
2 egg yolks, or $1/4$ cup egg substitute
$1/2$ teaspoon Dijon mustard
$1/2$ teaspoon Kosher salt
pepper to taste
2 teaspoons vinegar
$1 1/2$ cups vegetable oil

Process the lemon juice, egg yolks, Dijon mustard, Kosher salt, pepper and vinegar in a food processor until well blended. Add the vegetable oil in a fine stream, processing constantly. Process until the mixture is very thick.

Yields: 2 cups

Beet, Arugula, Mint and Goat Cheese Salad

10 small beets, trimmed
1/4 cup olive oil
3 tablespoons fresh lemon juice
1 large clove of garlic, minced
salt and pepper to taste
1 tablespoon chopped fresh mint
10 cups arugula leaves
4 dozen mint leaves
2/3 cup crumbled goat cheese

Wrap the beets in foil. Bake at 350 degrees for 1 hour or until tender. Let stand until cool. Peel the beets and cut into thin slices.

Whisk the olive oil, lemon juice and garlic in a small bowl. Season with salt and pepper.

Combine the beets, 1 tablespoon chopped mint and 2 tablespoons of the dressing in a bowl and toss until the beets are well coated. Combine the arugula and mint leaves in a large bowl. Add the remaining dressing and toss until well coated. Arrange on a serving platter. Top with the beet mixture. Sprinkle with goat cheese. Serve immediately.

Yield: 4 servings

Crawfish Salad Bienville

1 pound crawfish tails	3 tablespoons capers
1 tablespoon plus 1 teaspoon fresh lemon juice	salt to taste
1 1/2 tablespoons mayonnaise	1/2 teaspoon pepper
1 teaspoon Creole mustard	Bibb lettuce leaves
1 green onion, chopped	1 tablespoon chopped parsley
	lemon slices, garnish

Rinse the crawfish tails. Place in a bowl and toss with 1 tablespoon of the lemon juice. Combine the mayonnaise, Creole mustard, green onion, capers and remaining teaspoon lemon juice in a small bowl and mix well. Add to the crawfish tails and mix well. Season with salt and pepper. Spoon onto Bibb lettuce leaves on individual serving plates. Sprinkle with parsley. Garnish with lemon slices.

Yield: 4 servings

(Vinegars, continued)

pickling and is an indispensable addition to the English specialty of fish and chips.

Distilled vinegar—Being colorless, this is often simply labeled white vinegar. It is used for pickling onions and for any pickling where color is important.

Sherry vinegar—Sherry vinegar is a delightful vinegar made from sweet sherry. Mixed with an equal amount of lemon juice, it gives a delicious nutty taste in a vinaigrette. The best sherry vinegars come from Spain.

Balsamic vinegar—This farm-made vinegar comes from the region surrounding the town of Modena in Italy. It is made from the unfermented juice of pressed grapes, which is boiled until it is thick and then matured in barrels. Each year for five years, as it reduces by evaporation, it is moved to a smaller barrel made from a different wood: oak, chestnut, mulberry, ash, and cherry are favorites. It may be left to age further, sometimes for as long as 50 years. Balsamic vinegar is sweet, dark, pungent, highly concentrated, and mellow.

Rice vinegar—White rice vinegar has a sweet and delicate flavor and is a staple of Asian cuisine. In China, rice vinegar may be black with a rich smokey flavor, or a clear pale red, which is slightly tart. There is also a sweet rice vinegar, which is dark, thick, and aromatic.

Olive Oil

Olive oil, much like wine, can be rich and complex or simple and almost flavorless. Prices vary greatly—like wine, you get what you pay for, with the more expensive oils offering more intensity, elegance, and taste. Buying olive oil can be a confusing experience. Choices range in color from deep green to light amber and in flavor from strong to mild. Olive oils also vary according to the region where the olives are grown. The Spanish, Greek, and Southern Italian olives produce a heavier flavored oil than the olives of Tuscany and Provence.

Olive oil is graded according to the process used to extract the oil. The best oil, the extra-virgin, is made from hand-picked olives that are cold-pressed in large circular stone presses. The lesser quality oils, labeled virgin,

Tomato Bread Salad

1 clove of garlic, minced
pinch of salt
1 tablespoon red wine vinegar
freshly ground pepper
1/4 cup extra-virgin olive oil
2 cups (3/4-inch) cubes crusty French bread
8 ounces tomatoes, cut into 3/4-inch wedges
1/4 cup niçoise or calamata olives, pitted
1/4 cup finely chopped fresh basil leaves
1 tablespoon finely chopped fresh marjoram leaves, or
    1 teaspoon dried marjoram
salt to taste

Mash the garlic with a pinch of salt in a bowl until a paste forms. Add the vinegar and pepper and whisk well. Whisk in the olive oil until emulsified. Add the bread cubes, tomatoes, olives, basil, marjoram and salt to taste and toss to coat well. Let stand at room temperature for 15 minutes before serving.

Yield: 2 servings

Tomato, Bacon and Basil Salad

5 cups cherry tomato halves

6 slices bacon, cooked, crumbled

1/3 cup chopped fresh basil

2 tablespoons red wine vinegar

2 teaspoons sugar

1/2 teaspoon dry mustard

1 small clove of garlic, minced

salt and pepper to taste

1/4 cup extra-virgin olive oil

fresh lemon juice to taste

balsamic vinegar to taste

sprigs of fresh basil, garnish

Combine the tomatoes, bacon and chopped basil in a bowl and toss to mix well. Combine the vinegar, sugar, dry mustard, garlic, salt and pepper in a small bowl and mix well. Add the olive oil in a fine stream, whisking constantly. Add to the tomato mixture and toss lightly until well coated. Sprinkle with lemon juice and balsamic vinegar. Garnish with sprigs of basil.

Yield: 6 servings

Tossed Tomato, Cucumber and Artichoke Salad

4 tomatoes, cut into quarters

1 red onion, thinly sliced

2 cucumbers, peeled, sliced

1 (14-ounce) can artichokes, drained, cut into halves

6 tablespoons olive oil

1/4 cup red wine vinegar

1 teaspoon salt

1/2 teaspoon sugar

1 clove of garlic, pressed

1 teaspoon crushed dried basil

salt and pepper to taste

Combine the tomatoes, onion, cucumbers and artichokes in a bowl and toss to mix well. Mix the olive oil, wine vinegar, 1 teaspoon salt, sugar, garlic and basil in a small bowl. Pour over the vegetable mixture and season with salt and pepper to taste. Marinate, covered, in the refrigerator for a few hours or up to 2 days.

Yield: 6 servings

(Olive Oil, continued)

pure, or simply olive oil, are extracted from the subsequent pressings of the olive residue.

Extra-virgin olive oil is unrefined oil extracted from the first pressing of the highest quality olives. It is intensely flavored and aromatic.

Virgin olive oil, extracted from the second pressing of the olives, is flavorful, lightly fruity or nutty, yet not as intense as the extra-virgin.

Pure olive oil, often referred to simply as "olive oil," is generally a mixture of refined olive oil and extra-virgin or virgin oils and can be used as an all-purpose cooking oil.

Light olive oil is refined olive oil with a small amount of extra-virgin oil for flavor. It has "light" flavor and color—it is not, however, lighter in caloric or fat content.

Tomato, Basil and Couscous Salad

2¹/₄ cups chicken broth
1 (10-ounce) package couscous
1 cup chopped tomatoes
¹/₃ cup julienned basil
¹/₂ cup olive oil
¹/₄ cup balsamic vinegar
¹/₄ teaspoon crushed dried red pepper

Bring the broth to a boil in a medium saucepan. Add the couscous and remove from the heat. Let stand, covered, for 5 minutes. Spoon into a large bowl and fluff with a fork. Let stand until cool. Add the tomatoes, basil, olive oil, vinegar and red pepper and mix well. Chill, covered, in the refrigerator until serving time.

Note: Salad can be prepared 1 day in advance. Best if served at room temperature.

Yield: 6 servings

Orzo with Dilled Lemon Sauce

3 tablespoons fresh lemon juice
1 tablespoon Dijon mustard
5 green onions, chopped
3 tablespoons chopped fresh dill
salt and freshly ground pepper to
  taste
1 cup chicken broth, heated
¹/₄ cup olive oil
1 pound orzo, cooked, drained

1 cup calamata olives, pitted, cut
  into halves
2 (14-ounce) cans artichoke
  hearts, drained, rinsed, cut
  into quarters
4 ounces feta cheese, crumbled
6 to 8 Bibb or Boston lettuce
  leaves

Combine the lemon juice, Dijon mustard, green onions, dill, salt and pepper in a blender or food processor. Add the hot chicken broth and olive oil 1 at a time in a fine stream, processing constantly until well blended.

Add the sauce to the orzo in a large bowl and toss to mix well. Pat the olives dry. Add the olives, artichokes and feta cheese to the orzo mixture and toss to mix well. Serve at room temperature on lettuce leaves on individual salad plates. Garnish with additional fresh dill.

Yield: 6 to 8 servings

Roast Beef, Tomato and Red Onion Sandwich with Peppery Balsamic Vinaigrette Sauce

Peppery Balsamic Vinaigrette Sauce (below)
8 slices crusty French bread
8 ounces roast beef, sliced
1 to 2 tomatoes, sliced
1 medium red onion, thinly sliced
1/2 bunch arugula, rinsed, drained

Spread Peppery Balsamic Vinaigrette Sauce on each slice of bread. Layer the roast beef, tomatoes, onion and arugula on 1/2 of the bread slices. Top with the remaining bread slices. Cut into halves.

Yield: 4 servings

Peppery Balsamic Vinaigrette Sauce

2 tablespoons olive oil
2 tablespoons mayonnaise
1 tablespoon balsamic vinegar
1 teaspoon freshly ground black pepper

Combine the olive oil, mayonnaise, vinegar and pepper in a small bowl and mix well.

Yield: 1/4 cup

Homemade Mustard

This marvelously pungent mustard is a snappy addition to a variety of sandwiches as well as to baked ham. It also makes a thoughtful holiday or hostess gift.

2 (2-ounce) cans dry mustard
1 cup apple cider vinegar
3 eggs
1 cup sugar

Soak the mustard in the vinegar in a bowl for 6 hours or longer. Mix the eggs and sugar in a double boiler. Add the mustard mixture and mix well. Cook over boiling water until the mixture is of a spreadable consistency. Pour into hot sterilized small jars. Store, covered, in the refrigerator.

Yield: 6 small jars

Herbed Mayonnaise

This homemade herbed mayonnaise is marvelous on fresh tomatoes, as a salad dressing, or on turkey sandwiches. It keeps for one week in the refrigerator. . . if it lasts " that long!

1 egg, or $^1/_4$ cup egg substitute

1 teaspoon dry mustard

1 tablespoon wine vinegar

$^1/_2$ teaspoon salt

$^1/_4$ teaspoon lemon pepper

1 cup olive oil

$^1/_2$ cup chopped parsley or basil, or $^1/_2$ cup combination

Process the egg or egg substitute, dry mustard, vinegar, salt and lemon pepper in a food processor fitted with a metal blade for 10 seconds. Add the olive oil in a fine stream, processing constantly until thick. Add the herbs. Process for 30 seconds.

Yield: 1 cup

Fried Green Tomato and Ham Sandwich

3 green tomatoes, cut into $^1/_4$-inch-thick slices

1 cup cornmeal

$^1/_4$ teaspoon salt

$^1/_4$ teaspoon black pepper

$^1/_8$ teaspoon red pepper

vegetable oil for frying

8 slices French or sourdough bread, toasted

mayonnaise to taste

8 ounces ham, thinly sliced

salt and black pepper to taste

Coat the tomato slices with a mixture of cornmeal, salt, $^1/_4$ teaspoon black pepper and red pepper. Heat 1 inch of vegetable oil in a large heavy skillet. Add the tomato slices in a single layer to the skillet. Fry until golden brown, turning once. Remove to paper towels to drain.

Spread each toasted bread slice with mayonnaise. Layer ham and hot fried green tomatoes on $^1/_2$ of the bread slices. Sprinkle with salt and black pepper to taste. Top with the remaining bread slices. Cut into halves. Serve immediately.

Yield: 4 servings

Chicken, Roasted Red Pepper and Watercress Sandwich

8 slices bread, lightly toasted

mayonnaise to taste

Dijon mustard to taste

2 chicken breasts, cooked, sliced

$^1/_2$ to 1 cup roasted red pepper strips

4 slices fontina cheese

4 to 8 lettuce leaves

salt and freshly ground black pepper to taste

Spread 4 slices of the bread with mayonnaise. Spread the remaining bread slices with Dijon mustard. Layer chicken, roasted pepper strips, cheese and lettuce on the bread slices. Sprinkle with salt and pepper. Top with the bread slices. Cut into halves.

Yield: 4 servings

Caesar Chicken Sandwich

6 tablespoons olive oil
3 tablespoons red wine vinegar
2 tablespoons water
1/4 teaspoon dry mustard
1/4 teaspoon fresh ground
    black pepper
1/2 teaspoon anchovy paste

1 clove of garlic, crushed
dash of Worcestershire sauce
1/2 cup grated Parmesan cheese
2 chicken breasts, cooked, sliced
romaine lettuce leaves
4 pita bread rounds, cut into halves

Process the olive oil, vinegar, water, dry mustard, pepper, anchovy paste, garlic, Worcestershire sauce and Parmesan cheese in a blender until smooth. Place the chicken and lettuce in each pita. Spoon the dressing over the lettuce.

Note: Can omit anchovy paste and add salt to taste.

Yield: 4 servings

Open-Faced Crabmeat Sandwiches

1/2 pound fresh lump crabmeat
8 ounces cream cheese, softened
1 teaspoon lemon juice
1 teaspoon salt
1 teaspoon Worcestershire sauce
1 teaspoon grated onion
4 large tomato slices
4 Holland rusks
1/2 cup grated baby Swiss cheese

Combine the crabmeat, cream cheese, lemon juice, salt, Worcestershire sauce and onion in a bowl and mix well. Place a tomato slice on top of each Holland rusk. Top with the crabmeat mixture. Sprinkle with cheese. Place on a baking sheet. Bake at 400 degrees until the cheese melts.

Yield: 4 servings

Lime Basil Mayonnaise

This lively homemade mayonnaise is perfect spread on sandwiches starring chicken, smoked turkey, or fresh tomatoes.

1 egg, or $^1/_4$ cup egg substitute
$^1/_2$ teaspoon salt
2 tablespoons lime juice
1 cup vegetable oil
6 to 10 basil leaves

Process the egg or egg substitute, salt, lime juice, $^1/_4$ cup of the vegetable oil and basil leaves in a blender or food processor until the basil is well chopped. Add the remaining $^3/_4$ cup cold vegetable oil gradually, processing constantly.

Note: Can substitute $^1/_2$ cup of the vegetable oil with olive oil.

Yield: about 1$^1/_4$ cups

Summer Vegetables in a Pita

$^1/_4$ cup Lime Basil Mayonnaise (at left)
4 pita bread rounds, cut into halves
2 tomatoes, sliced
1 Vidalia onion, thinly sliced
1 medium avocado, peeled, seeded, sliced
4 fresh lettuce leaves
1 small cucumber, grated
alfalfa sprouts
salt and freshly ground black pepper to taste

Spread Lime Basil Mayonnaise on the inside of each pita pocket on 1 side. Layer the tomatoes, onion, avocado and lettuce leaves in each pocket. Spoon 2 tablespoons cucumber into each pocket. Top with alfalfa sprouts. Sprinkle with salt and pepper.

Yield: 4 servings

Portobello, Tomato, Basil and Mozzarella Sandwich

8 ($^1/_2$-inch-thick) portobello mushroom slices
$^1/_4$ cup olive oil
8 slices crusty Italian bread
1 clove of garlic, cut into halves
8 ounces fresh mozzarella cheese, cut into $^1/_4$-inch-thick slices
16 to 20 fresh basil leaves
2 tomatoes, cut into $^1/_4$-inch-thick slices
salt and pepper to taste

Brush both sides of the mushrooms with olive oil. Place on a grill rack or rack in a broiler pan. Grill or broil over hot coals or over high heat for 3 minutes on each side.

Rub each slice of bread with garlic and brush with remaining olive oil. Place on a rack in a broiler pan. Broil for 1 minute or until golden brown. Watch carefully so as not to burn. Layer 2 mushrooms, cheese, basil and tomatoes on each of 4 bread slices. Sprinkle with salt and pepper. Top with the remaining bread slices. Cut into halves.

Yield: 4 servings

Shrimp Sandwich with Pink Sauce

4 to 8 romaine lettuce leaves
2 to 4 pita bread rounds, cut into halves
1 pound shrimp, boiled, peeled
1/2 cup Pink Sauce (below)

Lay a couple of lettuce leaves in each pita half. Spoon the shrimp into each pita. Drizzle with Pink Sauce.

Yield: 4 to 6 servings

Pink Sauce

1 large onion, quartered
2 to 3 cloves of garlic, crushed
1 cup mayonnaise
1/2 cup vegetable oil
1/2 cup chili sauce
1/2 cup catsup
2 tablespoons Worcestershire sauce

1 tablespoon water
2 teaspoons prepared horseradish
juice of 1 lemon
1 teaspoon pepper
1 teaspoon paprika
1 teaspoon prepared mustard

Combine the onion, garlic, mayonnaise, vegetable oil, chili sauce, catsup, Worcestershire sauce, water, horseradish, lemon juice, pepper, paprika and mustard in blender or food processor. Process until puréed.

Note: Can also use as a salad dressing.

Yield: about 3 cups

BREAKFAST
BRUNCH
BREAD

Balmy, sun-washed mornings are ideal for entertaining alfresco.
Brunch or breakfast is extra special served in the backyard abloom with a
profusion of flowers and greenery—or on the porch or patio amid plush,
pillow-stacked wicker and unstructured arrangements of azaleas,
hydrangeas, gardenias and the like, all spilling decadently from creamy
china pieces or crystal bowls. It's a magnificent time for luxuriating in
the gentle breeze and delighting in good food and good company.
Velvet-textured egg casserole along with heirloom, linen-lined baskets
heaped with homemade muffins, biscuits and sweet breads accompanied
by shining silver pitchers filled with tart, pulpy orange juice or
classic cocktails, such as Bellinis, Bloody Marys or brandy-laced
milk punch—all add to the elegance of a morning event.
Freshly baked breads make such occasions all the more memorable.
The aroma is entrancing—warm and wonderful as it wafts lazily
through the house. Biscuits are especially beloved among Southerners
for breakfast, brunch, lunch or dinner. Steaming, tender biscuits
slathered with melting butter and sweet, dense berry preserves—
the perfect way to start, or end, the day.

Photograph sponsored by The Friends of the Junior League of Mobile

Photograph sponsored by The Past Presidents of the Junior League of Mobile

Point Clear

Point Clear became a thriving resort area in the 1800s, when South Alabama's elite discovered the Point as a place to escape the stifling heat of Mobile in the summer. All along the Eastern Shore of Mobile Bay, prominent Mobile families built charming summer homes. The Grand Hotel, at the cusp of the Point, drew visitors from other parts of the United States as well, who came to enjoy the pleasant summer climate found "over the Bay."

Travel to Point Clear in the early days was by steamboat. A boardwalk ran in front of the homes in Point Clear, starting at the Grand Hotel and stretching two miles south. The picturesque boardwalk still remains today.

Marshall Turner built what has come to be known as the Slaton House on the boardwalk in 1923. The Slaton family purchased the house in 1946. The glorious 90-foot porch of this house is one of the few remaining open porches left along the Bay in Point Clear.

Spinach and Ham Strata, page 71
Mixed Berry French Toast, page 72
Baked Crabmeat Benedict, page 74
Angel Biscuits, page 86
Deluxe Corn Bread, page 87

Joe Cain

After the Civil War, Mobile's economy, based on agriculture upstream, was in a shambles and the residents' spirits were sagging. Joe Cain, a well-known roustabout, had a remedy—the revitalization of Mardi Gras in Mobile. Cain decided that Mobile could use a little dose of festivity. So, for Mardi Gras 1866, Cain costumed himself as Chickasaw Indian Chief Slacabamorinico. Legend held that the Chickasaw under this chief never suffered defeat in battle. By choosing such a hero, Cain veiled his merriment with a message of hope for the defeated city.

Cain, as old Chief Slac, rode in a charcoal wagon. Six associates, dressed in comic outfits, marched behind playing discordant musical instruments. The procession cheered the citizenry. When the group paraded the

Midnight Supper Eggs

6 large or 8 small hard-cooked eggs
1 tablespoon butter
1 tablespoon flour
1 pint heavy cream
salt and pepper to taste
1 cup buttered bread crumbs

Cut the hard-cooked eggs into halves. Separate the egg yolks from the egg whites. Grate the egg whites and egg yolks separately. Melt the butter in a saucepan over low heat. Stir in the flour. Add the cream gradually, stirring constantly. Cook until thickened, stirring constantly. Season with salt and pepper. Stir in the grated egg whites. Pour into a buttered 1 1/2-quart casserole. Cover with 1/2 of the buttered crumbs. Sprinkle with the grated egg yolks. Sprinkle with the remaining crumbs. Bake at 350 degrees for 30 to 45 minutes or until bubbly.

Yield: 6 servings

Savory Egg Casserole

2 cups seasoned croutons
2 cups shredded Cheddar cheese
4 to 6 eggs, beaten
2 cups milk
1/2 teaspoon prepared mustard
salt and pepper to taste
Tabasco sauce to taste
6 to 8 slices bacon, cooked, crumbled

Sprinkle the croutons and cheese in a greased 9x9-inch baking dish. Mix the eggs, milk, mustard, salt, pepper and Tabasco sauce in a bowl. Pour in the prepared dish. Bake at 325 degrees for 45 to 60 minutes or until set. Sprinkle with crumbled bacon.

Note: Can add Creole seasonings, sautéed onions and bell peppers or tomatoes and green chiles for a spicier casserole. This casserole can be assembled the night before and refrigerated.

Yield: 6 servings

Spinach and Ham Strata

2 (10-ounce) packages frozen
    chopped spinach
1 teaspoon butter
2 tablespoons chopped onion
1/2 teaspoon pepper

18 slices dry bread, crusts trimmed
12 slices sharp American cheese
2 cups cubed honey-baked ham
6 eggs, lightly beaten
3 cups milk

Steam the spinach in a saucepan and drain well. Add the butter, onion and pepper and mix well. Cut 6 of the bread slices into triangles. Layer the remaining 12 bread slices, cheese, spinach mixture and ham 1/2 at a time in a greased 9x13-inch baking dish.

Arrange the bread triangles in 2 long rows on top, keeping right angles facing the same direction and letting triangles in each row slightly overlap. Pour a mixture of the eggs and milk over the layers. Chill, covered, in the refrigerator for 8 to 10 hours. Bake at 325 degrees for 1 hour. Let stand for about 10 minutes before serving.

Yield: 12 servings

Sausage Egg Bake

8 ounces bulk sausage
1 cup cooked grits
4 eggs
salt and pepper to taste
1/2 cup shredded Cheddar cheese

Brown the sausage in a skillet, stirring until crumbly and drain well. Place the sausage in a lightly greased 1-quart casserole. Spoon the grits over the sausage. Press 4 indentations in the grits with the back of a tablespoon. Break 1 egg into each indentation. Sprinkle with salt and pepper. Sprinkle with cheese. Bake at 350 degrees for 20 to 25 minutes or until set.

Yield: 2 servings

(Joe Cain, continued)

next Mardi Gras, they had named themselves the Lost Cause Minstrels. That same year, in 1867, Cain also helped establish Mobile's oldest parading organization, the Order of Myths. Cain is credited with rejuvenating Mardi Gras after the war and thus is responsible for Mobile's largest public party.

Many years after Joe Cain's death, a group of ladies calling themselves the Merry Widows of Cain began holding an elaborate celebration in the cemetery where he is buried on the Sunday prior to Mardi Gras day. The Widows' party eventually outgrew the cemetery walls to become the "Joe Cain Day" celebration that now covers most of Mobile's downtown area.

Mixed Berry French Toast

4 cups mixed berries, such as blueberries, raspberries and blackberries
1 cup plus 1 tablespoon sugar
1 teaspoon cinnamon
6 eggs, lightly beaten
1¹/₂ cups milk
2¹/₂ teaspoons vanilla extract
10 (¹/₂-inch-thick) diagonal slices French bread
1 cup sour cream
sugar to taste

Place the berries in a shallow 2-quart baking dish. Sprinkle with 1 cup sugar and cinnamon. Combine the eggs, milk and vanilla in a bowl and beat well. Add the bread. Let stand until the bread is saturated with the egg mixture. Place the bread in a single layer over the berries. Pour any remaining egg mixture over the bread. Sprinkle with 1 tablespoon sugar. Bake at 400 degrees for 20 to 25 minutes or until golden brown. Mix the sour cream with sugar to taste in a small bowl. Serve the French toast topped with the berry sauce and the sweetened sour cream.

Yield: 6 servings

Grillades

1 cup chopped onions
3/4 cup chopped celery
1 1/2 cups chopped green bell pepper
2 cloves of garlic, minced
2 tablespoons butter
8 veal cutlets
1/2 cup bacon drippings
1/2 cup flour
1 cup water
1 cup red wine (optional)

2 cups chopped tomatoes, or
   1 (16-ounce) can chopped
   tomatoes
2/3 teaspoon dried thyme
1 teaspoon salt
1/2 teaspoon pepper
1/2 teaspoon Tabasco sauce
2 tablespoons Worcestershire sauce
1 tablespoon chopped parsley
2 medium bay leaves

Sauté the onions, celery, green pepper and garlic in the butter in a skillet until light brown.

Brown the cutlets in 1/4 cup of the bacon drippings in a skillet. Remove the cutlets to a warm plate and keep warm.

Add the remaining 1/4 cup bacon drippings to the skillet. Stir in the flour. Add the sautéed vegetables, water, wine, tomatoes, thyme, salt, pepper, Tabasco sauce, Worcestershire sauce, parsley and bay leaves and mix well. Return the cutlets to the skillet. Cook over low heat for 1 hour or until the veal is cooked through. Discard the bay leaves. Serve with Garlic Cheese Grits Soufflé on page 120.

Yield: 8 servings

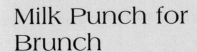

Milk Punch for Brunch

Milk punch is the epitome of the "eye-opener"—an ideal libation for sipping during the morning and early afternoon hours, splendid served with breakfast or brunch.

For the uninitiated, milk punch is a decadent, delightfully spiked, slightly sweet concoction laden with milk and laced with either bourbon or brandy, all divinely dusted with nutmeg.

There is always much ado amongst cocktail connoisseurs as to which is best for creating the quintessential milk punch—bourbon or brandy. Milk punches made with bourbon tend to taste more potent and, not surprisingly, more like bourbon. Brandy milk punches are slightly sweeter and a bit more subtle in flavor. You'll just have to experiment and decide for yourself.

1 cup ice cubes
1 1/2 ounces brandy or bourbon
2 tablespoons simple syrup (page 36)
1/2 cup half-and-half
3/4 teaspoon vanilla extract
pinch of nutmeg

Combine the ice cubes, brandy, simple syrup, half-and-half and vanilla in a cocktail shaker and shake vigorously. Pour into a chilled old-fashioned glass. Sprinkle with nutmeg and enjoy.

Yield: 1 serving

Hollandaise Sauce

3 egg yolks
1/4 teaspoon salt
dash of cayenne
1/2 cup melted butter, hot
2 tablespoons lemon juice

Process the egg yolks at high speed in a blender or food processor until thick and pale yellow. Add salt and cayenne. Add 3 tablespoons of the hot butter a small amount at a time, blending constantly. Add the remaining butter and lemon juice gradually.

Note: Can be made the day before serving and chilled in the refrigerator. Reheat in a double boiler over lukewarm water until softened.

Yield: 1 cup

Baked Crabmeat Benedict

1/4 cup butter
1 cup fresh lump crabmeat
1 hard-cooked egg, grated
2 tablespoons sherry
1/2 tablespoon lemon juice
dash of Tabasco sauce
4 English muffin halves, toasted
1 1/2 cups Hollandaise Sauce (at left)

Melt the butter in a skillet. Add the crabmeat, grated egg, sherry, lemon juice and Tabasco sauce. Cook until heated through. Place the English muffin halves in a baking dish. Spread each with the crabmeat mixture. Top with Hollandaise Sauce. Place under a broiler. Broil until brown. Serve immediately.

Yield: 4 servings

Alsatian Meat Pie

1 medium zucchini or summer
    squash
$1/4$ cup chopped onion
1 tablespoon butter
$1^{1}/_{2}$ pounds ground pork
$1/4$ cup chopped green onions
salt and pepper to taste
$1/8$ teaspoon nutmeg

2 teaspoons curry powder
1 egg
1 egg yolk
1 cup heavy cream
$1/2$ cup milk
1 (9- or 10-inch) pie shell, partially
    baked

Cut the unpeeled zucchini into $1/2$-inch pieces. Sauté the onion in the butter in a skillet until wilted. Add the pork, green onions and zucchini. Cook until the liquid has evaporated. Add salt, pepper, nutmeg and curry powder. Beat the egg, egg yolk, cream and milk in a bowl. Add to the pork mixture and mix well. Pour into the pie shell. Place on a baking sheet. Bake at 375 degrees for 30 to 35 minutes or until set and the top is golden brown. Cool for 10 minutes before serving. Serve warm or at room temperature with chutney.

Note: To partially bake a pie shell, line the pie shell with parchment paper or waxed paper and fill with pie weights or dried beans. Place the shell on a baking sheet and bake at 400 degrees for 10 minutes. Remove the weights and parchment and bake for 2 minutes longer. Freezes well.

Yield: 6 to 8 servings

Plantation Iced Tea

This iced tea recipe, with its lively citrus flavor and hint of mint, is a refreshing favorite.

1 quart boiling water
7 tea bags
12 mint stems
1 cup sugar
1 (6-ounce) can frozen lemonade
    concentrate
1 (12-ounce) can pineapple juice

Pour boiling water over the tea bags, mint and sugar in a pitcher. Steep for 30 minutes. Remove the tea bags, squeezing out the excess liquid. Remove the mint. Prepare the lemonade concentrate using the package directions. Add with the pineapple juice to the tea and stir to mix well. Let stand until cool before adding ice.

Yield: 3 quarts

Individual Ham and Cheese Tarts

2 eggs
3/4 cup half-and-half
1 tablespoon Dijon mustard
1 tablespoon minced green onioins or grated onion
1 cup grated sharp Cheddar cheese
1/2 cup ground or minced ham
freshly ground pepper to taste
8 frozen (3-inch) pastry shells, baked

Whisk the eggs, half-and-half, Dijon mustard and green onions in a bowl. Stir in the cheese, ham and pepper. Pour into the baked pastry shells. Bake at 350 degrees for 30 minutes or until set. Let stand for 10 minutes before serving.

Yield: 8 servings

Smoked Salmon Tart

1 (9-inch) pie shell
1 egg white, lightly beaten
8 ounces smoked salmon, chopped
1 cup grated Gruyère cheese
4 eggs
1 1/4 cups half-and-half
1 tablespoon finely chopped fresh dill, or
    1 teaspoon dried dill
1/2 teaspoon salt
1/4 teaspoon freshly ground pepper
salmon roe caviar (optional)

Brush the pie shell lightly with egg white. Bake at 400 degrees for 5 minutes. Cool slightly. Increase the oven temperature to 450 degrees. Layer the salmon and cheese in the prebaked pie shell. Beat the eggs, half-and-half, dill, salt and pepper in a bowl. Pour over the cheese. Bake for 15 minutes. Reduce the oven temperature to 350 degrees. Bake for 15 minutes longer or until the top is golden brown. Garnish with salmon roe caviar.

Yield: 4 servings

Seafood Quiche

2 (9-inch) deep-dish pie shells
1/4 yellow onion, chopped
1/4 cup vegetable oil
1/2 cup flour
1/2 cup crabmeat
4 ounces shrimp
1/4 cup sherry

3 eggs
2 cups heavy cream
1 teaspoon salt
1 teaspoon white pepper
1 cup grated Swiss cheese
1/4 cup grated Parmesan cheese
1 teaspoon chopped fresh parsley

Bake the pie shells at 350 degrees for 5 minutes. Let stand until cool.
Increase the oven temperature to 375 degrees.

Sauté the onion in the vegetable oil in a skillet until crisp. Add the
flour. Cook for 3 minutes, stirring constantly. Add the crabmeat and
shrimp. Sauté until the shrimp turn pink but not until cooked through. Add
the sherry gradually, stirring constantly. Cook for 5 minutes. Spread in the
partially baked pie shells.

Beat the eggs in a mixer bowl. Add the cream, salt and white pepper
and mix well. Pour into the prepared pie shells. Sprinkle with Swiss cheese,
Parmesan cheese and parsley. Place on baking sheets. Bake for 35 minutes or
until set. Let stand for 1 hour.

Note: Can store in an airtight container in the refrigerator for up to
2 days.

Yield: 12 servings

Bloody Mary

Bloody Marys are often an integral part of entertaining—and nothing says Sunday brunch better than this classic cocktail.

1 (10-ounce) can beef broth
10 ounces vodka
2¹/2 cups vegetable juice cocktail
¹/4 teaspoon Tabasco sauce
1 tablespoon Worcestershire sauce
2 tablespoons lemon juice
    concentrate
juice of 1 lemon

Combine the beef broth, vodka, vegetable juice cocktail, Tabasco sauce, Worcestershire sauce and lemon juice concentrate in a pitcher and mix well. Add the juice of 1 lemon and mix well.

Yield: 4 to 6 servings

Basil and Cheese Tart

1 prepared pie pastry
8 ounces cream cheese, softened
¹/3 cup ricotta cheese
¹/4 cup butter or margarine,
    softened

2 eggs
2 tablespoons flour
¹/8 teaspoon salt
¹/4 teaspoon pepper
2 tablespoons chopped fresh basil

Unfold 1 pie pastry on a lightly floured surface and press out the fold lines. Roll ¹/8-inch thick. Cut into a 10¹/2-inch circle. Fit into an 8-inch springform pan and prick with a fork. Freeze for 10 minutes. Bake at 450 degrees for 8 minutes. Combine the cream cheese, ricotta cheese and butter in a bowl. Beat at medium speed for 1 to 2 minutes or until light and fluffy. Beat in the eggs 1 at a time. Add the flour, salt, pepper and basil and beat until blended. Pour the filling into the pastry. Bake at 350 degrees for 35 to 40 minutes or until set. Garnish with tomato slices and sprigs of fresh basil.

Yield: 6 to 8 servings

Blue Cheese Soufflés

¹/2 cup grated Parmesan cheese
2 tablespoons unsalted butter
3 tablespoons flour
²/3 cup milk
¹/2 teaspoon ground pepper

8 ounces blue cheese, crumbled
4 eggs, separated
¹/2 tablespoon chopped fresh thyme, or
    ¹/2 teaspoon dried thyme
salt to taste

Grease 6 ramekins and sprinkle with ¹/4 cup of the Parmesan cheese. Melt the butter in a saucepan over low heat. Add the flour. Cook for 2 minutes, stirring constantly. Add the milk gradually, whisking constantly until smooth. Add the pepper. Remove from the heat. Add the blue cheese and the remaining ¹/4 cup Parmesan cheese and mix well. Cool for 10 minutes. Whisk 4 egg yolks in a large bowl. Add several tablespoons of the warm cheese mixture and whisk until blended. Fold in the remaining cheese mixture. Stir in the thyme. Beat the egg whites with salt in a bowl until stiff peaks form. Stir in ¹/3 of the beaten egg whites into the cheese mixture. Fold in the remaining beaten egg whites. Fill each prepared ramekin ³/4 full and place in a larger pan. Pour boiling water into the larger pan, filling halfway up the sides of the ramekins. Bake at 350 degrees for 20 to 25 minutes or until the soufflés rise and are light brown. Serve immediately.

Yield: 6 servings

Portobello Leek Frittata

2 leeks, sliced
1/4 cup butter
1 cup chopped portobello mushrooms
1 cup French bread cubes
6 eggs
1 cup shredded Gruyère cheese
salt and pepper to taste
1/2 cup grated Parmesan cheese
1/4 cup sliced green onions

Sauté the leeks in 1 tablespoon of the butter in a skillet until soft. Add the mushrooms. Sauté for 3 minutes or until tender. Remove from the heat and let stand until cool. Sauté the bread cubes in 1 tablespoon of the butter in a 10-inch skillet until toasted. Mix the eggs, Gruyère cheese and salt and pepper in a bowl. Add the cooled leek mixture and mix well. Heat the remaining 2 tablespoons butter in an ovenproof 10-inch skillet until the foam subsides. Add the egg mixture and reduce the heat to low. Sprinkle with bread cubes, Parmesan cheese and green onions. Cook for 15 to 20 minutes or until set. Place under a broiler. Broil until the top is set and brown. Serve immediately.

Yield: 4 to 6 servings

Bloody Mary Madness

The original Bloody Mary was developed by the English as a variation of the martini. It consisted of equal parts gin and tomato juice, with a dash of Worcestershire sauce and a squeeze of lemon juice. Since its inception, the ratio of tomato juice to alcohol has gradually been altered, and vodka is now the more commonly used liquor for the classic cocktail. Some popular variations include:

Classic Mary—vodka, tomato juice, Worcestershire sauce and lemon juice with a celery stick

Proud Mary—vodka, tomato juice, Worcestershire sauce, lemon juice and horseradish

London Mary—gin, tomato juice, Worcestershire sauce and lemon juice

Cajun Mary—vodka, tomato juice, Worcestershire sauce, lemon juice and Tabasco sauce with a pickled okra

Bloody Maria—tequila, tomato juice, lime juice and a jalapeño

Caribbean Mary—light rum, tomato juice, lime juice with a green onion

Other intriguing additions to the Bloody Mary include celery salt, celery seeds, Beau Monde seasoning, Greek seasoning, lemon pepper, crushed red pepper flakes, vegetable juice cocktail, clam juice, beef broth, soy sauce, pickled green beans, peperoncini, green olives, pickled onions, and a vast variety of hot sauces.

Red Bell Pepper and Cheese Frittata

1 red bell pepper, chopped
¹/4 cup flour
¹/2 teaspoon baking powder
¹/4 teaspoon salt
pepper to taste
3 eggs
3 ounces cream cheese, softened

12 ounces small curd cottage
*   cheese*
¹/4 cup butter, softened
¹/2 cup milk
1 cup grated Cheddar cheese
2 to 3 tablespoons minced
*   green onions*

Sauté the red pepper in a nonstick skillet until tender-crisp. Mix the flour, baking powder, salt and pepper in a bowl. Beat the eggs in a large bowl until frothy. Add the cream cheese, cottage cheese and butter and beat until almost smooth. Add the flour mixture and mix until blended. Add the milk and beat well. Pour into a greased 9-inch pie plate. Sprinkle with Cheddar cheese, sautéed red peppers and green onions. Bake at 350 degrees for 30 to 40 minutes or until set.

Yield: 4 to 6 servings

Spinach and Ricotta Pie

2 pounds fresh spinach, finely
    chopped
3 tablespoons olive oil
4 ounces prosciutto, chopped
1 clove of garlic, minced
3 eggs, separated

3/4 cup grated Parmesan cheese
salt to taste
1 pound ricotta cheese
2 prepared pie pastries
1 egg, lightly beaten

Cook the spinach in a small amount of water in a saucepan until tender. Drain and squeeze dry. Heat the olive oil in a small skillet. Add the prosciutto. Cook for 3 minutes. Stir in the garlic and remove from the heat. Beat 3 egg yolks, Parmesan cheese and salt in a large bowl. Add the ricotta cheese, spinach and prosciutto and mix well. Beat 3 egg whites in a bowl until stiff peaks form. Fold into the spinach mixture.

Line springform pan with 1 of the pie pastries. Fill with the spinach mixture. Cover with the remaining pie pastry. Pinch the edges together and trim excess dough. Prick the top in several places with a fork. Brush the top with a beaten egg. Bake at 375 degrees for 50 minutes or until golden brown. Let stand until cool. Remove the side of the pan. Cut into serving pieces.

Note: Can use one 10-ounce package frozen spinach for the fresh spinach.

Yield: 8 servings

Prosciutto and Pancetta

Prosciutto and Pancetta are both Italian cured meats readily available in supermarkets, and often found in today's recipes. Prosciutto, the Italian word for ham, describes a ham that has been seasoned, salt-cured, and air-dried, not smoked. Both domestic and imported prosciutto are available. Those hams imported from Italy will be labeled according to their region of origin. For example, Prosciutto di Parma, believed by many to be the first and the finest, hails from Parma, Italy. Prosciutto is eaten in sandwiches, as an appetizer, or used as a flavoring in other dishes, such as Risotto with Lemon and Prosciutto (page 115), and Spinach and Ricotta Pie (at left). It is also glorious wrapped around fresh cantaloupe wedges or figs and spritzed with fresh lemon juice.

Pancetta is an Italian bacon that is also spiced, cured, and air-dried. This flavorful meat is made in a salami-like roll. Pancetta is served in sandwiches and on pizzas. It can be substituted for ordinary bacon in some recipes, including Garden Green Beans with Hot Bacon Dressing (page 133).

Iced Tea

Serving up a fine pitcher of tasty refreshing iced tea is an essential, expected, and firmly ingrained part of southern hospitality. It's a surefire crowd-pleaser that can be both delicious and invigorating. Hence it has long been a staple at almost every imaginable sort of social gathering.

It can be as friendly and casual as a shared glass of iced tea between neighbors on the front porch swing, or a batch of the icy brew quaffed at a picnic or tailgating party. Tea can be ultra elegant and refined, served at the most stylish of luncheons, parties, and weddings. And because iced tea has intergenerational appeal, it is especially fabulous for family functions, including christenings, reunions, and so forth— perhaps the biggest plus being that iced tea makes a delightfully inexpensive thirst quencher for serving a crowd.

Often it seems as if every host and hostess has his or her own special secret for brewing up just the perfect batch of iced tea. Some rely on mint, others claim citrus fruits are the trick, and still others add exotic extracts, such as almond, vanilla, or peppermint.

Almond Tart

3/4 cup melted butter
1 1/2 cups sugar
2 eggs
1 1/2 cups flour
pinch of salt
1 teaspoon almond extract
1/2 cup sliced almonds
sugar to taste

Beat the melted butter and 1 1/2 cups sugar in a bowl until well mixed. Beat in the eggs 1 at a time. Add the flour, salt and almond extract and beat well. Pour into a foil-lined 10- or 12-inch cast-iron skillet. Sprinkle with almonds and sugar to taste. Bake at 350 degrees for 40 minutes or until light golden brown.

Yield: 8 to 10 servings

Bishop's Bread

2 1/2 cups flour	1 cup chopped dates
2 cups packed brown sugar	1/2 cup chopped nuts
2 teaspoons baking powder	1 cup buttermilk
1/2 teaspoon baking soda	1 egg, beaten
1/2 teaspoon salt	1/2 cup vegetable oil
1 teaspoon cinnamon	cinnamon sugar to taste

Mix the flour, brown sugar, baking powder, baking soda, salt and 1 teaspoon cinnamon in a bowl. Add the dates and nuts and toss to mix well. Add the buttermilk, egg and vegetable oil and mix well. Pour into a greased 9x13-inch glass baking dish. Sprinkle with cinnamon sugar to taste. Bake at 375 degrees for 35 to 40 minutes or until the bread tests done. Serve hot.

Yield: 12 to 16 servings

Blueberry Breakfast Cake

3 1/2 cups flour
1 1/2 cups packed brown sugar
1 teaspoon cinnamon
1/4 teaspoon nutmeg
1/4 teaspoon salt
1/2 cup butter
1 1/2 teaspoons baking powder

1/2 teaspoon baking soda
1 1/2 cups buttermilk
2 eggs
1/4 cup apple butter
1 teaspoon vanilla extract
3 cups blueberries
2 tablespoons butter

Mix the flour, brown sugar, cinnamon, nutmeg and salt in a bowl. Cut in 1/2 cup butter until coarse crumbs form. Reserve 1 cup of the flour mixture. Add baking powder and baking soda to the remaining flour mixture and mix well. Beat in the buttermilk, eggs, apple butter and vanilla. Pour into a 9x13-inch baking dish sprayed with nonstick cooking spray. Top with the blueberries. Cut 2 tablespoons butter into the reserved flour mixture. Sprinkle over the blueberries. Bake at 350 degrees for 50 minutes. Cool before serving.

Yield: 10 to 12 servings

Cinnamon and Brown Sugar Coffee Cake

2 cups flour
1 teaspoon baking powder
1 teaspoon baking soda
1/2 teaspoon salt
1 cup sugar
1/2 cup packed brown sugar
1 to 2 teaspoons cinnamon

1 cup buttermilk
2/3 cup melted butter or margarine
2 eggs
1/2 cup packed brown sugar
1 to 2 teaspoons cinnamon
3/4 cup chopped pecans

Mix the flour, baking powder, baking soda, salt, sugar, 1/2 cup brown sugar and 1 to 2 teaspoons cinnamon in a large bowl. Add the buttermilk, butter and eggs. Beat at low speed just until moistened. Beat at medium speed for 3 minutes. Spoon into a greased and floured 9x13-inch baking pan. Mix 1/2 cup brown sugar, 1 to 2 teaspoons cinnamon and pecans in a bowl. Sprinkle over the batter. Chill, covered, for 8 to 10 hours. Bake, uncovered, at 350 degrees for 30 minutes or until a wooden pick inserted in the center comes out clean.

Yield: 12 servings

An elegant or artistic ice ring can make all the difference between a ho-hum bowl of rather ordinary-appearing punch and a spectacular, showy centerpiece of a punch bowl. Try combining a creative mixture of colorful fruits, fresh herbs, and/or edible flowers (see page 232) to achieve stunning results. Here's how:

Arrange cut fruits, herbs, flowers, or other desired items in the bottom of a ring mold. Add just enough water to cover but not float the decorations. Freeze until firm. Then fill the remainder of the mold with water and freeze. To release, run warm water over the back of the mold until the ice ring slips out. Float in punch in a punch bowl.

Cranberry Pecan Bread

2 cups flour	$^1/_4$ cup shortening
1 cup sugar	$^3/_4$ cup orange juice
1$^1/_2$ teaspoons baking powder	1 egg, beaten
$^1/_2$ teaspoon baking soda	$^1/_2$ cup chopped toasted pecans
1 teaspoon salt	1 cup chopped cranberries

Sift the flour, sugar, baking powder, baking soda and salt into a large bowl. Cut in the shortening until coarse crumbs form. Mix the orange juice and egg in a bowl. Add to the flour mixture and mix just until moistened. Fold in the pecans and cranberries. Spoon into a greased and floured 5x9-inch loaf pan. Bake at 350 degrees for 1 hour.

Yield: 12 servings

Loxley Strawberry Bread

3 cups flour	3 eggs, beaten
1 teaspoon baking soda	1 cup vegetable oil
$^1/_2$ teaspoon salt	1 cup chopped pecans
1 teaspoon cinnamon	2 pints fresh strawberries, sliced
2 cups sugar	

Mix the flour, baking soda, salt, cinnamon and sugar in a bowl. Make a well in the center. Add the eggs, vegetable oil, pecans and strawberries to the well in the flour mixture and mix until thoroughly combined. Pour into 2 greased 5x9-inch loaf pans. Bake at 350 degrees for 40 to 60 minutes or until the loaves test done.

Yield: 24 servings

Petite Orange Muffins

1 cup butter, softened
1 cup sugar
2 eggs
1 teaspoon baking soda
3/4 cup buttermilk

3 cups flour
grated peel of 1/2 orange
1/4 cup orange juice
1 teaspoon lemon extract
Orange Sauce (below)

Cream the butter and sugar in a bowl until light and fluffy. Add the eggs 1 at a time, beating well after each addition. Dissolve the baking soda in the buttermilk. Add to the creamed mixture and mix well. Add the flour, orange peel, orange juice and lemon extract and mix well. Fill nonstick miniature muffin cups 3/4 full. Bake at 400 degrees for 10 to 12 minutes or until light brown. Remove from the muffin cups. Dip the tops and sides of the warm muffins into Orange Sauce. Drain on wire racks or waxed paper.

Yield: 4 dozen

Orange Sauce

3/4 cup orange juice
1 1/2 cups sugar
grated peel of 1/2 orange

Combine the orange juice, sugar and orange peel in a small saucepan. Bring to a boil, stirring constantly. Boil until the sugar is dissolved, stirring constantly. Chill in the refrigerator.

Yield: 2 cups

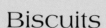

Biscuits

Good biscuit making is an art and a sure sign of a true southern cook. Here are a couple of tried-and-true tips to help make biscuit baking better and easier.

• To ensure lighter, fluffier biscuits, the first step should be sifting the dry ingredients together.

• Stir biscuit dough only long enough to incorporate and moisten the dry ingredients—and don't worry about lumps. It is often over-mixing that leads to tough, leaden biscuits.

• Shortening works better than butter in most biscuit recipes.

• Overworking the dough can also cause heavy biscuits. Knead the biscuit dough only three or four times on a lightly floured surface until the dough is soft but not sticky.

• The most efficient method of biscuit cutting is to cut biscuits into squares instead of the usual circles—thus eliminating scraps and the need to roll the dough out repeatedly. (They might look a little different, but they sure taste good!)

Angel Biscuits

1 envelope dry yeast
1/4 cup warm water
2 1/2 cups flour
1 teaspoon baking powder
1/2 teaspoon baking soda
1 teaspoon salt
2 tablespoons sugar
1/2 cup shortening
1 cup buttermilk

Dissolve the yeast in warm water. Mix the flour, baking powder, baking soda, salt and sugar in a large bowl. Cut in the shortening until crumbly. Add the buttermilk and yeast mixture, stirring until a soft dough forms. Knead on a lightly floured surface 3 or 4 times or until the dough is no longer sticky. Roll 1/2 inch thick. Cut with a biscuit cutter. Place on a greased baking sheet. Let rise for 15 to 30 minutes or until doubled in bulk. Bake at 400 degrees for 12 to 15 minutes or until golden brown.

Yield: 1 dozen

Buttery Biscuits

3/4 cup melted butter
2 cups self-rising flour
1 cup sour cream

Combine the butter, flour and sour cream in a bowl and mix well. Spoon into ungreased muffin cups. Bake at 350 degrees for 10 to 15 minutes or until golden brown.

Yield: 1 dozen

Deluxe Corn Bread

1 cup cornmeal
1/2 teaspoon salt
1 tablespoon baking powder
2 eggs
1/2 cup vegetable oil
1 cup sour cream
1 cup creamed corn

Mix the cornmeal, salt and baking powder in a small bowl. Beat the eggs in a bowl until light and pale yellow. Add the vegetable oil, sour cream and corn and mix well. Stir in the cornmeal mixture. Spoon into greased muffin cups. Bake at 400 degrees for 35 minutes or until brown.

Yield: 1 dozen

Lacy Corn Bread Wafers

1 egg, beaten
1 1/3 cups cornmeal
1 3/4 cups water
1/2 tablespoon salt
dash of pepper
1 small onion, finely chopped
vegetable oil for frying

Combine the egg, cornmeal, water, salt and pepper in a bowl and mix well. Stir in the onion. Heat 1/2 inch vegetable oil in a heavy skillet. Drop the batter by spoonfuls into the hot oil. Fry until golden brown, turning once. Drain on paper towels. Serve immediately.

Yield: 2 to 2 1/2 dozen

Rosemary Flatbread

3 cups semolina flour
3 cups unbleached flour
2 teaspoons sea salt
3 tablespoons chopped fresh rosemary
1²/₃ cups water
¹/₂ cup olive oil
kosher salt to taste

Mix the semolina flour, unbleached flour, sea salt and rosemary in a bowl. Make a well in the center. Add the water and olive oil to the well in the center and stir with a fork until a soft dough forms. Knead on a lightly floured surface for 2 to 3 minutes. Do not overwork the dough. Chill for 1 hour. Divide the dough into 12 to 15 portions. Roll each portion ¹/₈ inch thick. Place on a baking stone or baking sheet. Bake at 450 degrees for 8 to 10 minutes or until golden brown. Brush with additional olive oil. Sprinkle with kosher salt. Let stand until cool. Store in an airtight container.

Yield: 12 to 15 servings

Pepperoni Bread

cornmeal
2 (16-ounce) loaves frozen bread dough, thawed
2 large cloves of garlic, minced
1 package pepperoni slices
3 tablespoons grated fresh Parmesan cheese
2 tablespoons fresh basil
1 egg, beaten

Sprinkle 2 baking sheets with cornmeal. Roll each portion of dough into a 7x12-inch rectangle. Sprinkle each with garlic. Arrange the pepperoni over the garlic, leaving a $^{1}/_{2}$-inch border. Sprinkle with the Parmesan cheese and basil. Roll up from the long end to enclose the filling, pinching the seam to seal. Fold each end under and pinch to seal. Place each loaf seam side down on the prepared baking sheets. Brush with the beaten egg. Cut several shallow slits in the top of the loaves. Bake at 400 degrees for 25 to 30 minutes or until golden brown and the loaves test done. Cool on a wire rack.

Note: Loaves can be tightly wrapped and frozen for up to 1 month.

Yield: 24 servings

Scottish Whole Grain Bread

$2^1/2$ cups flour
$1^1/4$ cups ground rolled oats
$1/4$ cup unprocessed bran or wheat germ
2 tablespoons baking powder
1 teaspoon salt
1 cup margarine
1 cup raisins or currants
2 eggs, beaten
$3/4$ cup orange marmalade
$1^1/2$ cups milk

Mix the flour, rolled oats, bran, baking powder and salt in a large bowl. Cut in the margarine until crumbly. Add the raisins. Combine the eggs, orange marmalade and milk in a bowl and mix well. Add to the dry ingredients and mix well. Pour into a well greased 5x9-inch loaf pan. Bake at 325 degrees for 1 hour or until a wooden pick inserted in the center comes out clean. Let stand for 10 minutes. Invert onto a wire rack. Serve with butter or additional orange marmalade.

Yield: 12 servings

Braided Bread

1 cup milk
1/2 cup butter
1/2 teaspoon salt
1/2 cup sugar
1 envelope dry yeast
1/4 cup warm water
1 egg
4 cups flour

Scald the milk in a saucepan and remove from the heat. Add the butter, salt and sugar and stir until dissolved. Let stand until lukewarm. Dissolve the yeast in 1/4 cup warm water. Add to the cooled milk mixture. Stir in the egg. Add the flour and mix well. Cover with a towel and let rise in a warm place until doubled in bulk.

Knead the dough on a lightly floured surface until smooth and elastic. Divide into 2 equal portions. Divide each portion into 3 equal portions. Roll each portion into a long strip. Braid 3 of the strips together. Place on a buttered baking sheet. Repeat with the remaining 3 strips. Cover and let rise until doubled in bulk. Bake at 350 degrees for 15 minutes or until golden brown and the loaves test done. Remove from the baking sheets immediately.

Note: Can cover dough and let rise in the refrigerator for 8 to 10 hours.

Yield: 24 servings

America's Junior Miss

The America's Junior Miss Program has been an annual event in Mobile since 1958. This program honors the 50 state winners, college-bound senior girls who represent some of the United States' most outstanding youth. The nationwide scholarship program recognizes, rewards, and encourages excellence while promoting self-esteem. These young women serve as positive role models, and the scholarships they win help them pursue their college and career goals. Scholarships awarded at the local, state, and national levels total approximately $5 million.

Rosemary and Calamata Olive Focaccia

2 cups (or more) bread flour
1 envelope fast-rising dry yeast
1 teaspoon salt
1 1/2 teaspoons sugar
3/4 cup hot (125 to 130 degrees) water
1 tablespoon plus 2 teaspoons olive oil
cornmeal
2 tablespoons minced fresh rosemary
20 calamata olives, pitted, halved
salt to taste

Process 2 cups bread flour, yeast, 1 teaspoon salt and sugar in a food processor until blended. Mix the hot water and 1 tablespoon of the olive oil in a glass measure. Add to the flour mixture gradually, processing constantly. Process for 40 seconds or until a moist dough forms. Add additional flour 1 tablespoon at a time if the dough is too sticky. Add additional water 1 tablespoon at a time if the dough is too dry. Shape the dough into a ball. Place in a greased bowl, turning to coat the surface. Cover with a damp towel and let rise for 30 minutes.

Punch the dough down. Knead on a lightly floured surface until smooth and elastic. Cover and let rest for 10 minutes. Grease a 12- to 14-inch pizza pan or baking sheet. Sprinkle with cornmeal. Roll dough 1/2 to 3/4 inch thick in the prepared pan. Press the surface with fingertips to form indentions. Brush remaining 2 teaspoons olive oil over the surface. Sprinkle with rosemary, olives and salt. Press into the dough. Let rise, covered, for 30 minutes. Bake at 400 degrees for 20 minutes or until golden brown. Cut hot bread into wedges to serve.

Yield: 16 servings

French Bread

6 to 7 cups flour
2 envelopes dry yeast
2¹/₂ cups hot water
2 teaspoons salt
2 teaspoons water
1 tablespoon (about) cornmeal

Mix 3 cups of the flour and yeast in a large mixer bowl. Add 2¹/₂ cups hot water and mix well. Beat at low speed for 9 to 9¹/₂ minutes. Add a mixture of salt and 2 teaspoons water. Beat for 30 to 60 seconds longer. Add enough of the remaining flour ¹/₂ cup at a time, mixing until a soft dough forms.

Knead on a lightly floured surface for 10 minutes or until smooth and elastic. Place in a greased large bowl, turning to coat the surface. Cover lightly with plastic wrap. Let rise in a warm place for 2 hours or until doubled in bulk. Punch the dough down. Knead on a lightly floured surface for 3 to 5 minutes and return to the bowl. Cover loosely with a cloth. Let rise in a warm place for 1¹/₂ hours or until doubled in bulk.

Divide the dough into 2 equal portions. Let rest for 2 to 3 minutes. Line a large baking sheet with foil and sprinkle with cornmeal. Shape each portion into long thin loaves for baguettes or round loaves for boules. Place on the prepared baking sheet. Let rise in a warm place for 1 hour. Make diagonal cuts with a sharp knife into the baguette loaves or make a tic-tac-toe design in the boule loaves.

Place a baking pan on the bottom oven rack. Preheat the oven to 450 degrees. Pour 2 cups water into the baking pan and close the oven door. Let steam for 5 minutes. The steam will make the loaves crusty. Place the baking sheet with the loaves on the middle oven rack. Bake for 25 to 30 minutes or until the loaves are golden brown and sound hollow when tapped. Remove to a wire rack to cool.

Yield: 2 loaves

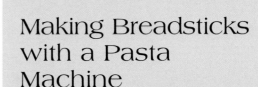

Making Breadsticks with a Pasta Machine

Take half of the dough used for French Bread (at left) and let it rise once. Punch the dough down. Divide into 3 equal portions on a well-floured surface. Press each into a 4x5-inch rectangle ¹/₈ inch thick. Make sure each rectangle is well coated with flour. Roll each of the rectangles through a manual pasta machine fitted with the widest pasta attachment. Separate the strips of dough and place on an ungreased baking sheet. Bake at 350 degrees for 18 minutes or until crisp and golden brown. Cool on a wire rack. Store in an airtight container for up to 1 month. This method makes gorgeous long breadsticks. They look fabulous either tied together with a ribbon as a gift or displayed in a tall vase to serve with cocktails or a buffet supper.

PASTA PIZZA RICE GRAINS

Pasta, rice, grains, and even pizza dough all provide a neutral,
yet nutritious, blank canvas from which to compose the most individual
and innovative of culinary creations. Pungent, blue-laced Gorgonzola
paired with plump, tender dumplings of potato gnocchi.
Delicate pink slivers of smoked salmon and fresh asparagus tops
entwined in creamy dense risotto. A piping-hot homemade pizza
punctuated with goat cheese, leeks, and the ripest of tomatoes.
The possible combinations are limitless.
Long viewed as low-brow, simple foods like pasta, pizzas, rice and
grains (including our beloved grits) have all gone gourmet. There was a
time not so long ago when pasta (known then as noodles) meant
pretty much spaghetti or maybe macaroni, when rice was mainly white
or brown, when pizzas were either delivered to the door,
eaten in casual chain restaurants, or came frozen from the grocery.
All that has certainly changed. Now, as more and more cultures influence
the way we cook and increasingly diverse items become available,
culinary horizons have expanded extraordinarily.

Photograph sponsored by Dusty Wharton Walton and Nancy Tanner Walton

Bellingrath Gardens

In 1917, Walter Bellingrath, Mobile's Coca-Cola bottler, was advised by his physician to stop working so hard and get more rest and relaxation. Bellingrath heeded the sage advice and purchased an extensive piece of property on Fowl River, just south of Mobile.

What began as an overgrown fishing camp soon flourished with azalea and camellia shrubs that Bellingrath and his wife Bessie brought from their home in Mobile. In 1927, the couple further enhanced the surroundings of their retreat by having lavish gardens designed by architect George B. Rogers. Depression-weary Mobilians were invited down on a Sunday afternoon five years later to view the results.

The traffic jams and overwhelming interest of that afternoon in 1932 led to the Gardens being opened to the public. The Bellingraths, delighted with the public's response and the beauty of the area, built their permanent home in the Gardens' center in 1935. The elegant 15-room home was also opened to the public in 1956, following the couple's deaths.

The beautiful Bellingrath Gardens and Home is now one of Alabama's top tourist attractions, receiving thousands of visitors each year to marvel at the spectacular gardens that showcase seasonal blooms year-round and culminating with millions of lights each December.

Photograph sponsored by The Betty Bienvilles

Pasta

Pasta comes in an astonishing array of sizes and shapes. The flat ribbon-shaped pastas are (from thinnest to widest):

Linguini
Fettuccini
Tagliatelle
Pappandelle
Lasagna

For the thin ribbon-shaped pastas, the best sauces are oil and butter, light vegetable, and light cream. The heavier ribbons go better with meat and game sauces, heavy vegetable, and thicker cream sauces.

The strands of pasta are (from thinnest to thickest):

Capellini d'angelo (or angel hair)
Capellini
Vermicelli
Spaghettini
Spaghetti

For the thin strands, use light vegetable or oil and butter sauces, or use them in soups. The thicker strands can take heavy vegetable sauces, light meat sauces, tomato, seafood, and creamy sauces.

The tube-shaped pastas are (from smallest to largest):

Macaroni
Penne
Bucatini
Ziti
Rigatoni
Manicotti
Cannelloni

Creamy Fusilli with Panéed Chicken and Shrimp

2 cups fresh bread crumbs
1/3 cup chopped parsley
salt and pepper to taste
3/4 to 1 pound boneless skinless chicken breasts
2 eggs, lightly beaten
6 tablespoons (or more) olive oil

1/2 to 3/4 pound large shrimp, peeled, deveined
2/3 cup dry white wine
1 cup heavy cream
1/4 teaspoon cayenne
1/2 cup grated Parmesan cheese
1 pound fusilli, cooked, drained

Mix the bread crumbs, parsley and salt and pepper in a shallow dish. Dip the chicken in the beaten eggs. Place in the bread crumb mixture, turning to coat. Heat about 3 tablespoons of the olive oil in a skillet over medium heat. Add the chicken. Cook until the chicken is cooked through. Remove to a warm platter and wipe the skillet clean.

Add about 3 tablespoons of the remaining olive oil to the skillet. Add the shrimp. Cook for 3 minutes or until the shrimp turn pink. Remove the shrimp to the platter.

Add the wine to the skillet. Bring to a boil. Cook for a few minutes or until the liquid is reduced to 1/2 cup. Add the cream. Boil until slightly thickened, stirring constantly. Stir in cayenne and Parmesan cheese.

Cut the chicken into strips. Return with the shrimp to the sauce in the skillet. Cook until heated through, stirring constantly. Add the hot pasta to the skillet and toss until well coated. Season with salt and pepper to taste. Garnish with additional parsley.

Yield: 4 servings

Crabmeat Cannelloni

2 tablespoons unsalted butter
1/2 cup finely chopped onion
1/2 cup finely chopped celery
1 pound fresh lump crabmeat
2 teaspoons Dijon mustard
1/4 cup heavy cream
2 eggs, lightly beaten
juice from 2 medium lemons
2 tablespoons minced flat-leaf
    Italian parsley

1/2 cup fresh bread crumbs
salt and pepper to taste
12 cannelloni shells, cooked, drained
1/2 cup unsalted butter
1/2 cup heavy cream
1 teaspoon grated lemon zest
pinch of salt
1/4 cup freshly grated Parmesan
    cheese

Melt 2 tablespoons butter in a small skillet over medium-low heat. Add the onion and celery. Sauté until tender. Combine the crabmeat, mustard, 1/4 cup cream, eggs, 1/2 of the lemon juice, parsley, bread crumbs and salt and pepper to taste in a medium bowl. Add the sautéed vegetables and toss lightly to mix well. Spoon 3 to 4 tablespoons of the stuffing mixture into each cooked pasta shell. Place in a single layer in a shallow baking dish.

Melt 1/2 cup butter in a small saucepan and remove from the heat. Add 1/2 cup cream, remaining lemon juice, lemon zest and a pinch of salt and mix well.

Pour the sauce over the stuffed pasta. Bake at 350 degrees for 30 minutes. Sprinkle with Parmesan cheese just before serving.

Yield: 6 servings

(Pasta, continued)

The best sauces for small tubes are creamy cheese and light meat. They are also used in salads and soups. The large tubes can take robust vegetable, chunky meat and game, and heavier cream and cheese sauces.

Among the special shapes of pastas are:
    Agnolotti—stuffed half-moon shaped
    Cappelletti—"little hats," which are stuffed
    Cavatelli—small and lip-shaped with curly edges
    Conchiglie—"conch shells"
    Farfalle—"butterflies" or bow ties
    Fusilli—twisted or spiral-shaped strands
    Gnocchi—little dumplings, usually made of potato
    Orecchiette—"little ears"
    Orzo—a rice-shaped pasta
    Radiatore—"little radiators"
    Ravioli—1- or 2-inch squares or circles, stuffed with meat, vegetables, or cheese
    Rotelle—"little wheels"
    Rotini—"little corkscrews"
    Tortellini—little twists stuffed with meat, cheese, or vegetables
    Tortelloni—larger tortellini
    For the small special shapes, the sauces should be light vegetable, light cream, vinaigrettes, or butter and cheese. They can also be used in salads and soups. The larger of the special shapes can take heavier vegetable sauces as well as robust sauces with beef or pork.

Pasta Dough

Pasta dough made in the food processor is much easier and less tricky than making it by hand in a bowl or on a countertop. The end result is much more reliable, takes only a few minutes and tastes the same as handmade dough.

> 2 cups flour
> 3 eggs
> 1/4 cup cold water

Place the flour in a food processor. Add the eggs 1 at a time, processing constantly. Process for 15 seconds longer. Add the cold water a small amount at a time, processing constantly until the mixture forms a ball. Knead on a lightly floured surface until smooth. Let rest, covered, for 30 minutes. Divide the dough into 4 equal portions. Roll 1 portion slightly with a rolling pin, keeping the remaining portions covered. Roll the dough through the widest section of

Italian Sausage and Roasted Red Pepper Fettuccini

> 1 tablespoon olive oil
> 4 sweet Italian sausages, sliced
> 1 (14-ounce) can Italian tomatoes
> 1/4 teaspoon pepper
> pinch of sage
> 1 (10-ounce) package frozen chopped spinach, thawed, drained
> 7 ounces roasted red bell peppers, chopped
> 1 pound fettuccini, cooked, drained
> 1/4 cup freshly grated Parmesan cheese

Heat the olive oil in a large saucepan. Add the sausages. Cook for 10 minutes and drain. Add the tomatoes, pepper and sage. Cook for 10 minutes, stirring frequently. Add the spinach and roasted red peppers. Cook until heated through. Spoon the sauce over the hot pasta. Sprinkle with Parmesan cheese.

Yield: 4 to 6 servings

Prosciutto, Sun-Dried Tomato and Pesto Fettuccini

> 6 to 8 oil-packed sun-dried tomatoes, chopped
> 3 to 4 cloves of garlic, minced
> 1 small white onion, chopped
> 4 ounces prosciutto, chopped
> 2 tablespoons olive oil
> 1/4 cup pesto
> 1 pound fettuccini, cooked, drained
> 1/4 cup freshly grated Parmesan cheese

Sauté the tomatoes, garlic, onion and prosciutto in the olive oil in a skillet until the onion is transparent. Add the pesto. Simmer for 15 minutes. Place the hot pasta in a large serving bowl. Spoon the sauce over the hot pasta. Sprinkle with Parmesan cheese.

Note: May add sautéed shrimp.

Yield: 6 servings

Chicken and Spinach Fettuccini

1 cup chopped onion
1/4 cup olive oil
1/4 cup butter
8 boneless skinless chicken breasts,
    cut into bite-size pieces
1/4 teaspoon garlic powder
1 small zucchini, chopped
2 teaspoons salt

pepper to taste
1 teaspoon dried basil
1 teaspoon dried oregano
4 cups cherry tomato halves
2 cups grated Swiss cheese
1 pound spinach fettuccini, cooked,
    drained

Sauté the onion in the olive oil and butter in a skillet until tender. Add the chicken and garlic powder. Cook until the chicken is just cooked through. Add the zucchini, salt, pepper, basil and oregano. Cook over low heat until the zucchini is tender. Add the tomatoes. Cook until the tomatoes are heated through. Add the chicken mixture and Swiss cheese to the hot pasta and toss to mix well.

Yield: 4 to 6 servings

(Pasta Dough, continued)

a pasta machine. Fold into thirds and roll through pasta machine again. Repeat the rolling process 4 times, folding dough each time. Continue rolling pasta through the pasta machine, reducing the opening each time until the thinnest setting is reached. Repeat the process with the remaining 3 portions of dough. Dough can be cut into various widths or left wide for ravioli. Cook the pasta in boiling water in a saucepan for 2 minutes or until al dente.

Note: Herb leaves can be pressed into the pasta dough about halfway through the rolling process.

Yield: 4 to 6 servings

Creamy Crawfish Bow Tie Pasta

3 quarts water
salt to taste
12 ounces bow tie pasta
1/4 cup butter
1 1/2 teaspoons minced garlic
1 cup thinly sliced red bell pepper
1 pound fresh crawfish tail meat
1 cup heavy cream
1 (14-ounce) can peeled whole
   tomatoes, drained

2 teaspoons paprika
2 teaspoons dried basil
1/4 teaspoon pepper
1 teaspoon chopped dried chives
1 teaspoon Tabasco sauce (optional)
1 cup grated Monterey Jack
   cheese
1 cup grated Parmesan cheese

Bring the water to a boil in a large saucepan. Add salt. Add the pasta. Cook for 10 minutes and remove from the heat. Melt the butter in a large saucepan. Add the garlic and red pepper. Sauté for 2 to 3 minutes or until tender. Add the crawfish. Sauté for 3 minutes. Add the cream, tomatoes, paprika, basil, pepper, chives and Tabasco sauce and whisk well. Stir in the Monterey Jack cheese and Parmesan cheese. Cook until melted. Drain the pasta and place in a large serving bowl. Spoon the sauce over the hot pasta.

Yield: 4 to 6 servings

Crawfish Linguini with Sun-Dried Tomatoes

1 pound crawfish tails
2 tablespoons butter
1 teaspoon salt
$1/2$ teaspoon white pepper
$1/4$ teaspoon cayenne
$1/2$ teaspoon dried basil
$1/2$ teaspoon dried thyme
$1/4$ teaspoon dried oregano

$1/2$ cup chopped green onions
$1/4$ cup melted butter
1 cup cream or 2 percent milk
1 pound linguini, cooked
1 cup chopped, drained oil-packed
   sun-dried tomatoes
$1/2$ cup grated Parmesan cheese

Sauté the crawfish in 2 tablespoons butter in a skillet over high heat for 3 minutes. Add the salt, white pepper, cayenne, basil, thyme, oregano and green onions. Reduce the heat to medium. Sauté for 2 minutes. Stir in $1/4$ cup butter and cream. Add to hot linguini in a large bowl and toss to mix well. Add the tomatoes and toss to mix well. Sprinkle with Parmesan cheese and toss to mix well.

Yield: 4 servings

Oven-Made Sun-Dried Tomatoes

To create the marvelous, dense, concentrated flavor of sun-dried tomatoes at home, fire up your oven. Slice the ripest tomatoes $1/4$ inch thick and arrange the slices in a single layer on a flat baking sheet. Set the oven temperature to the lowest setting and bake the slices for 8 to 12 hours. Monitor them carefully since oven temperatures may vary.

Fettuccini with Caramelized Scallops and Rosemary Beurre Blanc

$^1/_2$ cup dry white wine

3 tablespoons wine vinegar

$^1/_2$ cup chopped shallot

1 tablespoon chopped garlic

2 teaspoons chopped fresh rosemary

$^1/_2$ cup heavy cream

$^1/_2$ cup cold unsalted butter, cut into pieces

1 tablespoon fresh lemon juice or to taste

salt and pepper to taste

2 pounds sea scallops

2 tablespoons vegetable oil

12 ounces fettuccini

Combine the wine, vinegar, shallot, garlic and rosemary in a small heavy saucepan. Simmer until reduced to about 2 tablespoons. Add the cream. Simmer until reduced by $^1/_2$. Add the butter. Cook over medium-low heat just until the sauce is creamy and the butter is incorporated, swirling the pan constantly. Remove from the heat. Stir in the lemon juice, salt and pepper.

Pat the scallops dry. Season with salt and pepper. Heat 1 tablespoon of the vegetable oil in a 12-inch heavy skillet over medium-high heat until hot but not smoking. Add $^1/_2$ of the scallops. Cook for 1 to 2 minutes or until tender and the bottoms are golden brown. Remove to a bowl and keep warm. Repeat with the remaining scallops and 1 tablespoon vegetable oil.

Cook the pasta in boiling water in a large saucepan until al dente and drain. Place in a heated bowl.

Pour the butter sauce through a fine sieve over the pasta. Drain the scallops, reserving the liquid. Add the reserved liquid to the pasta and toss to mix well. Divide the pasta among 6 heated serving plates. Arrange the scallops on the pasta. Garnish with chopped fresh rosemary and parsley leaves.

Yield: 6 servings

Angel Hair Flan

1 cup heavy cream
3 eggs
1 teaspoon chopped fresh thyme
salt and pepper to taste
1 cup freshly grated Parmesan cheese
3 ounces angel hair pasta, cooked, drained

Butter eight $^{1}/_{2}$-cup soufflé dishes or ramekins. Whisk the cream, eggs and thyme in a medium bowl until blended. Season with salt and pepper. Stir in $^{2}/_{3}$ cup of the Parmesan cheese. Divide the pasta evenly among the prepared dishes. Pour the egg mixture over the pasta. Sprinkle with the remaining Parmesan cheese. Bake at 350 degrees for 20 minutes or until set and golden brown. Run a sharp knife around the edge of each soufflé to loosen. Unmold onto serving plates.

Yield: 8 servings

Orzo with Parmesan Cheese and Basil

3 tablespoons unsalted butter
1$^{1}/_{2}$ cups orzo
3 cups chicken stock
6 tablespoons chopped fresh basil
$^{1}/_{2}$ cup grated Parmesan cheese
salt and pepper to taste

Melt the butter in a skillet. Add the orzo and stir to coat with the butter. Add the chicken stock. Bring to a boil and reduce the heat. Simmer, covered, for 20 minutes or until the orzo is tender and the chicken stock is absorbed. Stir in the basil and Parmesan cheese. Season with salt and pepper.

Yield: 6 servings

Olive Oil Tips

• *You can't always judge an olive oil by its color. It is not always true that the darker the oil, the better—usually, but not always.*

• *Olive oil should be stored in a cool, dark place, such as the cupboard or pantry.*

• *When olive oil is refrigerated, it tends to turn cloudy and solidify. When the olive oil returns to room temperature, it becomes clear and liquid once again. The flavor and quality should not be affected.*

• *When stored properly in an airtight container, olive oil will keep optimum flavor for up to two years.*

• *Cook with regular olive oil; reserve the pricier extra-virgin varieties for drizzling over already cooked foods, breads, etc.*

• *Olive oil makes moist, even-textured baked goods, and because it contains antioxidants, baked products stay fresh longer. When baking with olive oil, substitute 3/4 teaspoon for every teaspoon of butter or margarine; 3 tablespoons olive oil for every 1/4 cup of butter or margarine; 3/4 cup olive oil for every cup of butter or margarine.*

• *It is best to use "light" or "mild" olive oil in baked goods so the olive oil will not impart much flavor.*

Fresh Tomato and Basil Pasta

1 pound Brie cheese
4 large tomatoes, cut into pieces
1 cup torn fresh basil leaves
1 clove of garlic, minced
1/4 cup chopped green onions
1/2 to 3/4 cups olive oil

salt and pepper to taste
1 to 1 1/2 pounds penne or
    linguini
1/4 cup freshly grated Parmesan
    cheese
chopped fresh parsley, garnish

Remove the rind from the Brie cheese. Cut the Brie cheese into pieces. Combine the Brie cheese, tomatoes, basil, garlic, green onions and olive oil in a large bowl. Sprinkle with salt and pepper. Let stand at room temperature for 2 hours. Cook the pasta using the package directions and drain. Add to the tomato mixture and toss to mix well. Add the Parmesan cheese and toss to mix well. Garnish with chopped fresh parsley.

Yield: 4 to 6 servings

Four-Season Linguini

1/2 cup sliced onion
1 cup thinly sliced mushrooms
1/4 cup white wine or water
1 (14-ounce) can chopped
    tomatoes
1 (14-ounce) can artichoke hearts,
    drained, cut into quarters

10 pitted medium black olives,
    thinly sliced
2 tablespoons liquid from olives
2 teaspoons provençal herbs or Italian
    herbs
1 clove of garlic, minced
1 1/2 pounds linguini, cooked

Spray a large skillet with nonstick cooking spray. Spread the onion in a shallow layer in the skillet. Cook until the onion is brown. Stir in the mushrooms and white wine. Cook over medium heat until most of the liquid evaporates. Stir in the tomatoes, artichoke hearts, black olives, olive liquid, herbs and garlic. Simmer, covered, for 20 minutes. Pour over the hot pasta and toss to mix well.

Yield: 8 servings

Pasta with Pears and Gorgonzola Cheese

¹/4 cup butter
4 pears, peeled, cored, cut into thick strips
1 tablespoon chopped fresh rosemary
1 cup low-sodium chicken broth
4 ounces Gorgonzola cheese, crumbled
¹/2 cup freshly grated Parmesan cheese
¹/2 cup heavy cream
salt and white pepper to taste
1 pound fettuccini or linguini, cooked, drained
¹/2 cup lightly toasted chopped walnuts

Melt the butter in a large skillet over medium heat. Add the pears. Sauté for 5 to 8 minutes or until tender and beginning to turn brown but not soft. Remove the pears to a large serving bowl using a slotted spoon. Add the rosemary to the skillet. Sauté for 1 minute. Add the broth, Gorgonzola cheese, ¹/2 cup Parmesan cheese and cream. Simmer for 5 minutes or until thickened and smooth, whisking constantly. Return the undrained pears to the skillet. Season with salt and white pepper. (May prepare in advance to this point.) Place the pasta in the serving bowl. Add the pear sauce and toss well until the pasta is coated. Sprinkle with walnuts. Serve with additional grated Parmesan cheese.

Yield: 4 to 6 servings

Penne with Tomatoes, Olives and Cheese

6¹/2 tablespoons olive oil
1¹/2 cups chopped onion
1 teaspoon minced garlic
3 (28-ounce) cans Italian plum
   tomatoes, drained
2 teaspoons dried basil
1¹/2 teaspoons crushed dried
   red pepper
2 cups canned low-sodium chicken
   broth

salt and pepper to taste
1 pound penne
2¹/2 cups packed grated
   Havarti cheese
¹/3 cup sliced pitted calamata
   olives
¹/3 cup grated Parmesan cheese
¹/4 cup finely chopped
   fresh basil

Heat 3¹/2 tablespoons of the olive oil in a large heavy Dutch oven over medium-high heat. Add the onion and garlic. Sauté for 5 minutes or until the onion is translucent. Stir in the tomatoes, dried basil and red pepper. Bring to a boil, stirring to break up the tomatoes with the back of a spoon. Add the broth. Return to a boil and reduce the heat to medium. Simmer for 1 hour and 10 minutes or until thickened and reduced to 6 cups, stirring occasionally. Season with salt and pepper.

Cook the pasta in a large stockpot of boiling salted water until al dente. Drain the pasta and return to the stockpot. Add the remaining 3 tablespoons olive oil and toss to coat well. Add the sauce and toss to mix well. Add the Havarti cheese and mix well. Spoon into a greased 9x13-inch glass baking dish. Sprinkle with olives and Parmesan cheese. Bake at 375 degrees for 30 minutes or until the pasta is heated through. Sprinkle with chopped fresh basil.

Yield: 4 to 6 servings

Basil Pesto with Vermicelli

2 cups chopped fresh basil
1/2 to 1 cup toasted pine nuts
1 teaspoon minced garlic
1/2 cup grated Parmesan cheese
1 (10-ounce) package frozen spinach, thawed, drained (optional)
1/2 to 1 cup olive oil
1 pound vermicelli
salt to taste

Purée the basil, pine nuts, garlic, Parmesan cheese and spinach in a food processor. Add the olive oil in a fine stream, processing constantly. Cook the pasta in boiling salted water in a large saucepan until tender. Drain, reserving 1/2 cup of the liquid. Add the reserved liquid to the pesto and mix well. Pour over the pasta and toss to coat well.

Yield: 4 to 6 servings

Ziti Napolitana

 The Pillars

12 ounces ziti
salt to taste
1/4 cup olive oil
3 cups chopped, seeded, peeled fresh tomatoes
1 teaspoon chopped garlic
1/2 cup chopped fresh basil
pepper to taste
6 ounces freshly grated Parmesan cheese

Cook the pasta in boiling salted water in a large saucepan until al dente. Heat the olive oil in a skillet over medium heat until the olive oil begins to smoke lightly. Add the tomatoes and garlic. Simmer for 5 to 10 minutes. Add the basil and salt and pepper. Drain the pasta. Add the sauce and toss until well coated. Sprinkle with the cheese.

Yield: 4 servings

Pesto

Pesto comes from the Italian word pestare, *meaning to pound. Traditionally, a handful of fresh herbs, a few nuts, a clove of garlic, and a little salt would be ground to a paste with a mortar and pestle. Grated Parmesan cheese or romano cheese would be added and then the olive oil. Today, pesto can be made quickly and easily in a blender or food processor.*

The classic recipe for pesto calls for basil; however, marvelous pesto-style creations can be made from spinach or other flavorful ingredients, such as cilantro, sage, parsley, and arugula. Festive additions to pesto recipes include anchovies, olives, capers, paprika, jalapeños, roasted garlic, sun-dried tomatoes, and grated lemon peel.

Gorgonzola Sauce

1 cup heavy cream
2 cloves of garlic, minced
4 ounces Gorgonzola cheese,
    crumbled

Bring the cream to a simmer in a saucepan. Add the garlic and cheese and whisk until blended and smooth.

Yield: about 2 cups

Gnocchi with Gorgonzola Sauce

 Guido's

4 medium boiling potatoes (about 1½ pounds), or
    8 to 10 new potatoes
1 egg, beaten (optional)
1 cup flour
¼ cup grated Parmesan cheese
salt to taste
Gorgonzola Sauce (at left)

Boil the potatoes in water to cover in a saucepan until tender and drain. Let the potatoes stand until cool. Peel the potatoes and place in a large bowl. Mash with a potato masher or fork. Add the egg and mix well. Add enough flour to make a smooth and slightly sticky dough. Knead in the Parmesan cheese on a lightly floured surface. Divide the dough into golf-ball-size portions. Roll each portion with your hands into a rope ½ inch thick. Cut each rope into marble-size pieces and create indentations with the tines of a fork.

Cook 1 to 2 dozen gnocchi at a time in boiling salted water in a saucepan for 1½ minutes or until the gnocchi float to the surface. Remove each batch to a warm serving platter and pour a small amount of Gorgonzola Sauce over the top to keep warm. Pour the remaining Gorgonzola Sauce over all the gnocchi after the final batch is cooked. Serve hot.

Yield: 4 to 6 servings

French Country Pizza

1 white onion, cut into slices
1 tablespoon butter
4 chicken breast fillets, cooked, cut lengthwise into strips
6 individual baked pizza crusts
fresh spinach leaves
1 (28-ounce) can chopped tomatoes
3 tablespoons chopped fresh oregano
3 tablespoons chopped fresh basil
1 tablespoon salt
1^1/$_2$ teaspoons pepper
3 cups grated mozzarella cheese
1 (2-ounce) can sliced black olives, drained

Separate the onion slices into rings. Sauté in the butter in a skillet until caramelized. Arrange the chicken on the pizza crusts, beginning at the center and moving outward to form a star. Layer the spinach, tomatoes and caramelized onions over the pizza. Sprinkle with a mixture of oregano, basil, salt and pepper. Sprinkle the cheese and olives over the top. Place on baking sheets. Bake at 400 degrees for 10 minutes.

Yield: 6 servings

Pizza Toppings

No one knows the origin of pizza, but it must have evolved over thousands of years. From as far back as Neolithic man, every culture has had a flat, round loaf of bread, often spread with herbs and oil. Pizza, as we know it, comes from early Neapolitans who first spread tomatoes on these rounds of dough. The first pizzeria in the United States was opened in New York City in 1905.

Continuing the tradition requires only a supply of pizza dough and imagination. In addition to the classics of tomato sauce, mozzarella cheese, pepperoni, Italian sausage and dried herbs, possible combinations are:

• chopped tomatoes, red onions, and boursin cheese
• fresh basil and pine nuts, and goat cheese
• sun-dried tomatoes, fresh herbs, and fresh mozzarella cheese
• shrimp, pesto, and fresh tomatoes
• roasted garlic, caramelized onions, and fontina cheese
• smoked salmon, salmon roe caviar, and goat cheese
• prosciutto and Gorgonzola
• cilantro, salsa, and Monterey Jack cheese

Also consider fresh garlic, anchovies, Greek or Italian olives, fennel, provolone cheese, artichoke hearts, salami, spresta, capers, pancetta, tapenade, roasted peppers, feta cheese, and Parmesan cheese.

Pizza with Leeks, Tomato and Goat Cheese

1 1/2 tablespoons butter
2 medium leek bulbs, thinly sliced
salt and pepper to taste
1 tablespoon minced fresh parsley
3/4 cup chopped, seeded peeled tomato
3 ounces soft fresh goat cheese, crumbled
1 tablespoon olive oil
1 (12-inch) pizza dough

Melt the butter in a large skillet over low heat. Add the leeks. Sauté for 10 minutes or until tender. Season with salt and pepper. Stir in parsley. (This can be done a day in advance.) Spread the leek mixture evenly over the pizza dough. Sprinkle with tomato and goat cheese. Drizzle with olive oil. Place on a baking stone or baking sheet. Bake at 500 degrees until the crust is crisp. Cut into wedges.

Yield: 6 to 8 servings

Roasted Vegetable Pizza

1 yellow, red or green bell pepper,
*   sliced*
1 Vidalia, sweet yellow or purple
*   onion, sliced*
2 tomatoes, chopped
4 portobello mushrooms, sliced
asparagus, eggplant or squash, cut
*   into small pieces (optional)*

1/2 cup balsamic vinegar
1/4 cup olive oil
salt and pepper to taste
1 Boboli thin crust
1/2 cup pesto
feta, goat, mozzarella and Parmesan
*   cheese, or a combination of each,*
*   to taste*

Place the vegetables in a bowl. Add a mixture of the vinegar and olive oil. Marinate for 30 minutes or longer and drain. Sprinkle with salt and pepper. Place the vegetables on a rack in a broiler pan or in a grill basket. Broil or grill until the vegetables are light brown. Pat the vegetables dry. Spread the Boboli crust with pesto. Layer the vegetables and cheese over the crust. Place on a baking stone or baking sheet. Bake at 400 degrees or until heated through.

Note: Roasted garlic can be substituted for the pesto.

Yield: 6 to 8 servings

Spinach and Gorgonzola Pizza

1 (10-ounce) package frozen spinach, thawed
1 onion, thinly sliced
1 tablespoon olive oil
2 cloves of garlic, minced
1 (12-inch) pizza crust
4 ounces Gorgonzola cheese
4 ounces mozzarella cheese
1/4 cup toasted pine nuts
pepper to taste

Drain the spinach and squeeze dry. Sauté the onion in the olive oil in a skillet until golden brown. Add the garlic. Sauté for 2 minutes. Add the spinach. Cook for 3 minutes or until all the moisture has evaporated. Spread over the pizza dough. Sprinkle with Gorgonzola cheese, mozzarella cheese and pine nuts. Season with pepper. Place on a baking stone or baking pan. Bake at 450 degrees for 15 minutes or until the crust is golden brown and the cheeses have melted. Cool for 5 minutes. Cut into wedges.

Yield: 6 to 8 servings

Five-Cheese Pizza

1 (12-inch) pizza crust, partially baked
2 tablespoons olive oil
2 tablespoons shredded smoked Gouda cheese
3/4 cup shredded mozzarella cheese
1/2 cup shredded fontina cheese
1 to 2 plum tomatoes
1/2 cup fresh basil leaves, julienned
3 ounces water-packed fresh mozzarella cheese, sliced
1/2 cup shredded Romano cheese

Brush the pizza dough with olive oil. Layer the Gouda cheese, shredded mozzarella cheese, fontina cheese, tomatoes, basil and fresh mozzarella cheese over the pizza. Sprinkle with Romano cheese. Place on a baking stone or baking sheet. Bake at 400 degrees until the crust is brown and the cheeses are bubbly.

Yield: 6 to 8 servings

Pizza Crust

Homemade pizza crust is much easier to make than most folks would imagine. This simple dough can be baked in the oven or over a hot fire on the grill and topped with any number of delectable ingredients.

2 cups flour
1/2 teaspoon salt
1/2 teaspoon sugar
1 envelope fast-rising yeast
3/4 cup warm water
1 tablespoon olive oil
cornmeal

Combine the flour, salt, sugar and yeast in a food processor. Add the water and olive oil in a fine stream, processing constantly until the mixture forms a ball. Process for 1 minute. Knead on a lightly floured surface 9 to 10 times. Place in a bowl sprayed with nonstick cooking spray and turn to coat the surface. Let rise, covered, in a warm draft-free place for 45 minutes or until doubled in bulk. Divide into 2 equal portions. Let rest, covered, for 10 minutes. Roll each portion into a 10-inch circle on a lightly floured surface. Place on baking sheets sprinkled with cornmeal. Place the pizza dough on a grill rack sprayed with nonstick cooking spray. Grill for 3 minutes and turn over. Top with the desired toppings. Grill for 4 minutes or until the crust is brown.

Yield: 6 servings

Great Grains

Grains used to be pretty much limited to grits and rice. But fusion cooking and increased availability have vastly expanded the grain horizons to include a wide variety of grains from a wide variety of cultures. What all grains generally have in common is that they are cooked in steam or boiling water until they are swollen and tender—and most grains can be prepared and served the same as rice.

Among the grains widely available today are:

Barley—Whole grain barley is mainly used in making beer and whiskey but is also eaten hulled as a cooked grain.

Buckwheat—Kasha is toasted buckwheat that has a nutty flavor.

Corn—Cornmeal is ground from white, yellow, or blue corn. Polenta is a cornmeal mush eaten soft and creamy like grits or baked or fried, making it dense and firm. Hominy is white or yellow corn that has been hulled and dried. It can be found either dried or precooked in cans. Hominy is ground to create grits.

Oats—Whole oat groats are hulled whole oat grains. Steel-cut oats are groats that have been cut into smaller pieces. Rolled oats have been steamed and flattened.

Quinoa—Pronounced keen wa, is a tiny nutritious grain. It is

Shrimp, Sausage and Chicken Jambalaya

1 pound smoked sausage, thinly sliced
3 tablespoons olive oil
2/3 cup chopped green bell peppers
2 cloves of garlic, minced
3/4 cup chopped parsley
1 cup chopped celery
2 (16-ounce) cans tomatoes, chopped
2 cups chicken stock
1 cup chopped green onions
1 1/2 teaspoons dried thyme
2 bay leaves
2 teaspoons dried oregano
1 tablespoon Creole seasoning
1/4 teaspoon cayenne
1/4 teaspoon black pepper
1 (3-pound) chicken, boiled, drained
2 cups long grain rice, washed, rinsed 3 times
3 pounds medium shrimp, peeled, deveined

Cook the sausage in a large skillet until firm. Remove to a warm bowl using a slotted spoon. Add the olive oil to the skillet. Add the green peppers, garlic, parsley and celery. Sauté for 5 minutes. Add the undrained tomatoes, chicken stock and green onions. Stir in the thyme, bay leaves, oregano, Creole seasoning, cayenne and black pepper. Chop the chicken, discarding the skin and bones. Add the chicken, rice and sausage to the vegetable mixture. Cook, covered, over low heat for 30 minutes or until most of the liquid has been absorbed, stirring occasionally. Add the shrimp. Cook until the shrimp turn pink. Discard the bay leaves. Spoon the jambalaya into a casserole. Bake at 350 degrees for 25 minutes.

Yield: 10 servings

Risotto with Lemon and Prosciutto

3 1/2 cups chicken stock
2 tablespoons julienned lemon peel
1/4 cup butter
3/4 cup chopped onion
1 clove of garlic, minced

2 ounces prosciutto, thinly sliced
1 cup plus 2 tablespoons arborio rice
1/2 cup white wine
1/2 cup freshly grated Parmesan cheese

Simmer the stock in a saucepan. Blanch the lemon peel in a small saucepan of hot water for 30 seconds and drain. Repeat the process 2 more times, using fresh water each time. Melt the butter in a large saucepan. Add the onion and garlic. Sauté until the onion is translucent. Add the prosciutto. Sauté for 1 minute. Add the rice. Sauté for 1 minute. Add the wine. Boil until almost all of the liquid is absorbed. Add 1/2 cup of the hot chicken stock, stirring constantly. Cook until the liquid is absorbed, stirring constantly. Repeat with the remaining stock until all of the stock has been absorbed. Stir in the Parmesan cheese and lemon peel. Serve immediately.

Note: The total cooking time for the rice is about 20 minutes.

Yield: 4 servings

Salmon and Asparagus Risotto

2 tablespoons olive oil
1 yellow onion, coarsely chopped
4 cloves of garlic, minced
1 cup arborio rice
3 1/2 to 4 cups chicken broth
1/2 cup dry white wine

1 bunch asparagus, cut into bite-size
    pieces
1 to 2 ounces smoked salmon, cut into
    small pieces
salt and pepper to taste
3/4 cup freshly grated Parmesan cheese

Heat the olive oil in a heavy saucepan. Add the onion and garlic. Sauté over low heat for 5 minutes or until soft. Add the rice. Cook for 3 minutes, stirring constantly. Bring the broth to a boil in a saucepan. Reduce the heat and simmer the broth. Add 3/4 to 2 cups of the hot broth 1/2 cup at a time to the rice, stirring constantly after each addition and cooking until the broth is absorbed. Add the wine. Cook until absorbed, stirring constantly. Stir in the asparagus. Add the remaining broth 1/2 cup at a time, stirring constantly after each addition and cooking until the broth is absorbed. Stir in the salmon. Cook for 5 minutes or until the rice is tender, stirring constantly. Add salt and pepper. Stir in the Parmesan cheese.

Note: The total cooking time for the rice is 25 to 35 minutes.

Yield: 4 servings

(Great Grains, continued)

higher in unsaturated fats and lower in cholesterol than most other grains.

    Rice—There are many varieties of rice available today. Among them are brown rice, which is hulled but has not lost its bran; white rice, which is polished rice; Basmati rice, a flavorful long-grain rice; jasmine rice, an aromatic long-grain rice; risotto, a medium short grain rice; and wild rice, which is not actually rice at all but instead the seed of an aquatic grass.

    Rye—Rye berries are hulled whole rye kernels.

    Wheat—A number of products come from the wheat grain. Wheat berries are whole wheat grains. Cracked wheat consists of whole wheat berries that have been cracked. Bulgar is wheat that has been parboiled or steamed, then dried, with some of the bran removed before cracking. Bran is the outer covering of the wheat grain and is an excellent source of fiber. Wheat germ is the heart of the wheat grain. Semolina is the floury part of the wheat grain and is used to make most pasta. Couscous is the flour-coated semolina grain.

Risotto with Mushrooms

3 cups chicken broth
¹/2 cup chopped onion
2 to 3 tablespoons butter
1 cup arborio rice
¹/2 cup white wine
8 ounces mushrooms, sliced
¹/4 cup olive oil
¹/2 cup freshly grated Parmesan cheese
salt and pepper to taste

Simmer the broth in a saucepan. Sauté the onion in the butter in a skillet over medium heat until translucent. Stir in the rice. Add the wine. Cook until the wine is absorbed, stirring constantly. Add ¹/2 cup of the hot broth, stirring constantly. Cook until absorbed, stirring constantly. Repeat until all of the remaining broth has been absorbed and the rice is creamy with a slight crunch at the center. Sauté the mushrooms in the olive oil in a skillet over high heat until all the liquid has evaporated. Fold into the rice. Stir in the Parmesan cheese. Sprinkle with salt and pepper. Serve immediately.

Note: The total cooking time for the broth to be absorbed is about 20 minutes. Can shape any leftover risotto into patties and sauté on both sides in butter or olive oil until golden brown and crunchy.

Yield: 4 servings

Green Peppercorn and Pecan Risotto

3¹/2 cups chicken broth
2 tablespoons olive oil
1 shallot, minced
1 small onion, finely chopped
1 cup arborio rice
¹/2 cup sherry

2 tablespoons green peppercorns packed
    in brine
salt and pepper to taste
¹/2 cup chopped toasted pecans
1 tablespoon unsalted butter
¹/2 cup grated Parmesan cheese

Simmer the broth in a saucepan. Heat the olive oil in a heavy saucepan over medium heat. Add the shallot and onion. Sauté until wilted. Stir in the rice. Cook for 3 to 5 minutes, stirring constantly. Add the sherry and peppercorns. Cook until the sherry is absorbed, stirring constantly. Add ¹/2 cup of the hot broth. Cook until the broth is absorbed, stirring frequently. Repeat with the remaining broth until all of the broth has been absorbed. Add the salt, pepper, pecans, butter and Parmesan cheese and mix well.

Note: Total cooking time for the rice should be about 30 minutes.

Yield: 4 to 6 servings

Golden Squash Risotto

5¹/2 to 6 cups chicken stock
4 tablespoons butter
1 large onion, chopped
1¹/2 cups chopped peeled butternut or acorn squash
1¹/2 cups arborio rice
¹/2 cup dry white wine
1 cup freshly grated Parmesan cheese
salt and freshly ground pepper to taste

Simmer the stock in a saucepan. Melt 3 tablespoons of the butter in a large saucepan. Add the onion. Sauté until light brown. Add the squash and ¹/2 cup of the stock. Cook, covered, for 15 minutes or until the squash is tender. Stir in the rice and wine. Cook until absorbed, stirring occasionally. Add 4 cups of the remaining stock. Simmer for 30 minutes or until absorbed, stirring occasionally. Add 1 cup of the remaining stock. Cook until creamy and the rice is tender, adding the remaining stock if needed. Stir in the remaining butter and Parmesan cheese. Season with salt and pepper.

Yield: 4 to 6 servings

Coconut Ginger Rice

3 cups water
2 cups jasmine rice
1 cup coconut milk
2 tablespoons cinnamon sugar
2 teaspoons grated peeled gingerroot

Combine the water, rice, coconut milk, cinnamon sugar and gingerroot in a medium saucepan. Bring to a boil over high heat. Reduce the heat to low. Simmer, covered, for 25 minutes or until the liquid is absorbed.

Yield: 6 cups

Thai Shrimp with Coconut Ginger Rice

1 cup ground peanuts
1/4 cup soy sauce
3 tablespoons dark molasses
2 cloves of garlic, minced
1/2 teaspoon crushed dried
    red peppers
1/2 cup water
2 pounds large shrimp, peeled, deveined
1 cup pineapple chunks
vegetable oil
Coconut Ginger Rice (at left)
2 lemons, cut into quarters

Combine the peanuts, soy sauce, molasses, garlic, crushed red peppers and water in a saucepan. Bring to a boil and reduce the heat. Simmer for 5 minutes.

Thread the shrimp and pineapple alternately onto skewers. Brush generously with vegetable oil. Place the shrimp on a grill rack. Grill for 7 to 8 minutes or until the shrimp turn pink, turning once.

Spoon Coconut Ginger Rice onto each serving plate and top with the shrimp skewers. Serve the hot peanut sauce on the side for dipping. Serve with lemon quarters.

Yield: 6 servings

Vegetable Paella

$^{1}/_{2}$ cup water	$1^{1}/_{2}$ cups arborio rice
$^{1}/_{4}$ teaspoon saffron threads	3 cups chicken stock
1 red bell pepper, chopped	1 cup drained canned tomatoes
1 medium onion, chopped	$^{3}/_{4}$ teaspoon paprika
2 tablespoons olive oil	$^{1}/_{2}$ teaspoon salt
1 (14-ounce) can artichoke hearts, drained	1 (16-ounce) can black beans, rinsed, drained
2 large cloves of garlic, minced	$^{1}/_{2}$ cup petite green peas

Bring the water to a boil in a small saucepan. Add the saffron. Cover and remove from the heat. Let stand for 10 minutes. Sauté the red pepper and onion in the olive oil in a Dutch oven until the onion is golden brown. Add the artichoke hearts and garlic. Sauté for 5 minutes. Reduce the heat to low. Add the rice, stirring to coat with the olive oil. Add the chicken stock and tomatoes. Bring to a boil, stirring frequently. Add the saffron water, paprika and salt. Reduce the heat to medium-low. Cook, covered, for 15 minutes. Add the black beans and green peas and mix well. Cook, covered, for 5 minutes or until all of the liquid is absorbed and the rice is tender. Remove from the heat. Let stand for 15 minutes before serving.

Yield: 6 servings

How to Roast Peppers

For sweet, tender roasted peppers, first preheat the broiler. Place the peppers on a baking sheet lined with foil that is lightly sprayed with nonstick cooking spray. Broil the peppers 2 to 3 inches from the heat source until the skins are blistered and blackened. Remove the peppers to a paper bag. Let stand for 15 to 20 minutes. Remove the peppers from the bag and remove the blackened skin. Cut into strips, discarding the stems, seeds, and pith. Place in a sealable plastic bag. Chill until ready to use. Chile peppers can be roasted by the same method.

Garlic Cheese Grits Soufflé

1 cup quick-cooking grits
1 teaspoon salt
3 cups water
1/2 cup butter or margarine
6 ounces Gruyère cheese
3 cloves of garlic, chopped
2 eggs
1 1/2 cups milk

Cook the grits in salted water in a saucepan using the package directions. Melt the butter and cheese in a saucepan over low heat. Stir in the garlic. Beat the eggs in a 4-cup glass measure; add enough milk to equal 2 cups. Combine the grits, cheese mixture and egg mixture in a bowl and mix well. Spoon into a 2-quart casserole. Bake at 350 degrees for 35 to 45 minutes or until set.

Yield: 8 servings

Sunset Grits

2 red bell peppers, roasted
1 large onion, finely chopped
3 tablespoons unsalted butter
1 tablespoon minced garlic
1 cup quick-cooking grits
4 to 5 cups milk
1 cup grated Parmesan cheese
1/4 teaspoon Tabasco sauce or to taste
salt and pepper to taste

Purée the roasted red peppers in a food processor or blender until smooth. Cook the onion in the butter in a large heavy saucepan over medium-low heat for 5 minutes or until soft, stirring constantly. Add the garlic. Cook for 2 minutes, stirring constantly. Stir in the grits and 4 cups of the milk. Simmer for 10 minutes or until the milk is absorbed, stirring occasionally. Add the remaining milk if needed. Simmer, uncovered, for 35 minutes or until thickened, stirring occasionally. Stir in red pepper purée, Parmesan cheese, Tabasco sauce and salt and pepper. Serve immediately.

Yield: 6 servings

Mushroom Stew over Parmesan Polenta

1 ounce dried porcini mushrooms
    or other dried mushrooms

1/4 cup butter

1 tablespoon olive oil

1 yellow onion, finely chopped

2 cloves of garlic, minced

8 ounces small white mushrooms,
    sliced, coarsely chopped

4 ounces portobello mushrooms,
    sliced, coarsely chopped

1/2 teaspoon dried thyme
    leaves

salt and pepper to taste

1/2 cup chicken broth

2 tablespoons dry sherry

1 teaspoon cornstarch

2 tablespoons cold water

Parmesan Polenta
    (at right)

Place the dried porcini mushrooms in a glass bowl and cover with warm water. Let stand for 20 minutes. Drain the porcini mushrooms, reserving 1 cup of the liquid. Strain the reserved liquid and pour into a bowl. Pat the mushrooms dry and coarsely chop.

Heat the butter and olive oil in a large skillet. Add the onion and garlic. Cook over low heat for 7 to 8 minutes or until softened but not brown. Add the white mushrooms, portobello mushrooms and porcini mushrooms. Sprinkle with thyme and salt and pepper. Cook for 8 minutes, stirring frequently. Add the reserved liquid, broth and sherry. Reduce the heat. Simmer for 10 minutes. Adjust the seasonings. Stir in a mixture of cornstarch and water. Bring to a boil. Boil for 30 seconds or until the mixture clears and thickens. Spoon over the Parmesan Polenta.

Yield: 6 to 8 servings

Parmesan Polenta

2 cups water

1 quart milk

2 teaspoons kosher salt

2 cups yellow cornmeal

1/4 cup butter

1/2 cup freshly grated Parmesan cheese

salt and cracked pepper to taste

Bring the water, milk and kosher salt to a boil in a large saucepan and reduce to simmer. Add the cornmeal gradually, whisking constantly. Simmer for 10 minutes or until thickened and the mixture pulls away from the side of the saucepan, stirring constantly with a wooden spoon and crushing any lumps against the side of the saucepan. Remove from the heat. Stir in the butter and Parmesan cheese. Season with salt and pepper to taste. Serve hot.

Yield: 6 to 8 servings

Basil Couscous with Summer Squash

2 cups chicken stock
2 tablespoons olive oil
1 teaspoon salt
1 cup couscous
1 cup (¹/4-inch) diced zucchini
1 cup (¹/4-inch) diced yellow squash
1 cup slivered basil leaves

Bring the chicken stock and 1 tablespoon of the olive oil to a boil in a medium saucepan. Stir in the salt and couscous. Remove from the heat. Let stand, covered, for 5 minutes. Sauté the zucchini and yellow squash in the remaining 1 tablespoon olive oil in a skillet until tender. Add vegetables and basil leaves to the couscous and mix well. Serve immediately.

Note: An alternative serving suggestion is to carve out the centers of extra zucchini or yellow squash and steam the squash shells to the desired degree of doneness. Fill with the couscous mixture. Sprinkle with toasted sliced almonds.

Yield: 6 to 8 servings

Couscous with Raisins and Pine Nuts

1/4 cup chopped onion
1 tablespoon olive oil
2 1/2 cups chicken broth
6 tablespoons butter
1 cup couscous
1/2 cup raisins
1/2 cup toasted pine nuts
1/4 cup minced fresh basil
salt and pepper to taste

Sauté the onion in the olive oil in a skillet. Bring the broth and butter to a boil in a medium saucepan and remove from the heat. Stir in the couscous. Let stand, covered, for 5 minutes. Fluff with a fork and place in a bowl. Add the raisins, sautéed onion, pine nuts and basil and stir to mix well. Season with salt and pepper.

Yield: 8 servings

Golden Couscous

1/2 cup butter
6 cups chopped onions
3/4 teaspoon ground ginger
1/2 teaspoon turmeric
2 1/4 cups low-sodium chicken broth
1/4 cup chopped fresh mint
1/4 cup fresh lemon juice
2 cups couscous
salt and pepper to taste

Melt the butter in a large saucepan over medium-low heat. Add the onions. Cook, covered, for 35 minutes or until tender but not brown, stirring occasionally. Stir in the ginger and turmeric. Add the broth, mint and lemon juice. Bring to a simmer. Stir in the couscous. Cover the saucepan and turn off the heat. Let stand for about 5 minutes or until the couscous is tender and all of the liquid has been absorbed. Fluff with a fork and season with salt and pepper.

Yield: 8 servings

VEGETABLES

*There is nothing quite like the taste of vegetables picked fresh
from the garden or straight from the farmers' market—perfect and firm
with undeniable freshness you can see, smell and, best of all, taste.
Luminous, ivory-kerneled corn glossed with golden butter,
so good and sweet the juice drips down your chin.
Lush, fat, red vine-ripened tomatoes drizzled with olive oil and
scattered with shards of tender basil—a perfect marriage of flavors.
The old-fashioned taste and inherent creamy texture of butter beans—
petite little pouches of velvety goodness.
Vegetables should be celebrated for the diverse and magnificent array
of color, texture and taste they bring to the table. Sautéed, roasted
and grilled—the distinct flavors of the different vegetables now tend
to be enhanced and enlivened by seasonings and preparation
rather than masked or overwhelmed.
In Alabama we are blessed with some of the best nature has to offer.
Many of our roads are bordered with seemingly miles and miles of
almost uninterrupted verdant fields and farmland, resulting in a
stunning selection of vegetables to explore and enjoy.*

Photograph sponsored by Marian MacKay Pfeiffer

Fort Conde

When Fort Conde was built during the early 1700s, it was renowned as one of the finest forts of its day. The fort, originally built by the French, served at various times as the headquarters for the colonial governments of the French, British and Spanish. Under British rule, the fort was renamed Fort Charlotte for England's young queen. The partially reconstructed fort still stands in the heart of downtown Mobile, where it now serves as a unique Visitor Welcome Center.

Adjacent to Fort Conde is the Conde-Charlotte Museum House, built in the early 1800s as Mobile's first official jail. In the mid-1800s, the property was converted into a residence, but evidence of the old jail still remains today. The house has been restored and is now a fascinating museum, furnished to depict the different periods of Mobile's history under five flags.

Basil Garlic Beurre Blanc

1/2 cup dry white wine
3 tablespoons white wine vinegar
1 tablespoon minced shallot
1 tablespoon minced garlic
1/2 cup heavy cream
1/2 cup butter, cut into pieces
1/4 cup chopped fresh basil leaves

Simmer the wine, vinegar, shallot and garlic in a small saucepan until reduced by 1/2. Add the cream. Simmer until the liquid is reduced by 1/2. Add the butter. Cook over medium-low heat until the sauce is creamy, stirring constantly. Stir in the basil. Cook for 1 minute.

Yield: 3/4 to 1 cup

Grilled Artichokes

1 fresh artichoke
3 fresh lemon halves
2 cloves of garlic, coarsely chopped
salt and pepper to taste
2 tablespoons olive oil
1/4 cup water
Basil Garlic Beurre Blanc (at left)

Cut the spiny tips from the artichoke with scissors. Cut the artichoke into half lengthwise and rinse well. Scrape out the choke using a grapefruit spoon. Rub the cut surfaces immediately with 1 lemon half. Shape heavy-duty foil into 2 bowls, leaving 6 inches of overhang. Place each artichoke half into the bowls. Squeeze lemon juice from each remaining lemon half over the top of each artichoke half. Sprinkle with the garlic and salt and pepper. Drizzle with olive oil and add the water. Fold the foil over each artichoke half and seal tightly. Place on a grill rack. Grill over medium-hot coals for about 1 hour or until tender. Serve with Basil Garlic Beurre Blanc.

Yield: 2 servings

Balsamic Buttered Broccoli with Pecans

1 large bunch broccoli, rinsed, cut into florets
2 tablespoons balsamic vinegar
2 tablespoons red wine
1/4 cup butter, cut into pieces
1/4 cup chopped pecans
salt and freshly ground pepper to taste

Steam the broccoli in a steamer until tender-crisp. Combine the balsamic vinegar and red wine in a small saucepan. Cook until reduced by 1/2. Remove from the heat. Add the butter, stirring constantly until the mixture is well combined and slightly creamy. Stir in the pecans until well coated. Season with salt and pepper. Place the broccoli in a serving bowl. Pour the sauce over the top.

Yield: 4 to 6 servings

Crispy Peanut Fritters

1 cup flour
1 teaspoon minced onion
$1/2$ teaspoon crushed garlic
1 egg, lightly beaten
$3/4$ cup (or more) coconut milk
1 cup salted peanuts
vegetable oil for frying
salt to taste
Cajun seasoning to taste

Mix the flour, onion and garlic in a bowl. Add the egg and mix well. Stir in enough coconut milk to make a thin batter. Stir in the peanuts. Heat $1/2$ inch vegetable oil in a large skillet. Drop the batter by tablespoonfuls into the hot oil. Fry for 5 minutes or until light brown. Remove to paper towels to drain. Sprinkle with salt and Cajun seasoning.

Yield: 4 servings

White Beans and Red Peppers with Sage

2 tablespoons olive oil
1 red bell pepper, chopped
1 1/2 tablespoons minced fresh sage
1 clove of garlic, minced
1 (19-ounce) can cannellini beans, rinsed, drained
1 rib celery, chopped
3/4 teaspoon red wine vinegar

Heat the olive oil in a skillet. Add the red pepper and sage. Sauté until softened. Stir in the garlic. Cook for 1 minute, stirring constantly. Add the beans, celery and vinegar. Cook for 20 minutes. Serve immediately.

Yield: 4 servings

Raspberry Carrots

1 1/2 pounds carrots
1/3 cup raspberry vinegar
1/2 cup light olive oil
1 teaspoon sugar
salt and pepper to taste
2 bunches green onions, thinly sliced

Scrape the carrots and cut into thin slices. Cook the carrots in boiling water to cover in a saucepan for 5 minutes and drain. Pour the vinegar, olive oil, sugar and salt and pepper over the hot carrots. Stir in the green onions. Marinate, covered, in the refrigerator for 8 to 10 hours. Drain the carrots and adjust the seasonings before serving.
Note: May julienne the carrots and cook for 3 minutes.

Yield: 6 servings

Glazed Carrots with Ginger

1 pound carrots, peeled, sliced
2 tablespoons butter, softened
1/4 cup packed light brown sugar
1/2 teaspoon ginger
1/2 cup soy sauce
1/2 cup orange juice

Cook the carrots in boiling water to cover in a saucepan for 2 minutes and drain. Heat the butter, brown sugar and ginger in a large skillet until slightly bubbly, stirring constantly. Add the carrots, soy sauce and orange juice. Cook until the sauce turns red and the carrots are glazed.

Yield: 4 to 6 servings

Corn and Tomato Gratin with Basil

2 tablespoons olive oil
1 1/2 cups chopped onions
5 cups fresh or frozen corn kernels
salt and pepper to taste
2 1/2 cups milk
3 eggs

2 egg whites
1/4 teaspoon hot pepper sauce
2 cups drained, chopped, seeded
   tomatoes
1/2 cup chopped fresh basil

Heat the olive oil in a large heavy skillet over medium heat. Add the onions. Sauté for 4 minutes or until translucent. Add the corn. Sauté for 6 minutes or until cooked through. Season with salt and pepper. Remove from the heat and cool. Spray a 2-quart glass baking dish with nonstick cooking spray. Whisk the milk, eggs, egg whites and hot pepper sauce in a large bowl until blended. Add the corn mixture and mix well. Pour into the prepared baking dish. Bake at 350 degrees for 30 minutes or until set. Remove from the oven. Season tomatoes with salt and pepper. Sprinkle over the gratin. Return to the oven. Bake until the tomatoes are warm. Sprinkle with basil. Serve immediately.

Yield: 6 servings

Silver Queen

There are certain foods that always seem to signal the arrival of summer, and in the deep South, one of those foods is Silver Queen corn. The plump, ivory-colored kernels are so delicately sweet that they put yellow corn to shame. Silver Queen is, by and large, a Southern specialty, since it dislikes cold climates. And one of the things that makes it so special is that it doesn't linger long enough to wear out its welcome—the corn is available for only a few short weeks. It generally makes its debut during the first days of June and tends to disappear shortly after Independence Day.

The best way to enjoy Silver Queen is simply on the cob, fresh, hot, and brushed with butter. To extend the pleasures of eating Silver Queen, it can be frozen and will last in the freezer for up to a year. To freeze, the corn should be shucked and put into a large pot of water. Bring to a boil, then remove the ears and drop them into ice water. When cool, pack the corn into sealable freezer bags and store in the freezer with a temperature of at least 10 degrees below zero.

Sweet Potatoes

Sweet potatoes are a most beloved staple of Southern sideboards and the Thanksgiving table. They are often served slathered in butter, brown sugar, and crowned with melting marshmallows or spiked with orange juice. They are also divine when simply baked until the natural sugars start to caramelize, or when mashed like an ordinary potato. And as luck would have it, sweet potatoes are often called a near-perfect food because of their high nutritional value. They are loaded with vitamin A, potassium, calcium, and beta carotene.

Two main types of sweet potatoes grow in the United States. Although some folks refer to the deeper orange-fleshed variety as a yam, it's really not. The true yam, grown in Africa, is actually a much larger vegetable and is seldom available in this country.

The freshest and most moist sweet potatoes are generally available from August through October. They should be firm, heavy, and well shaped. The darker the skin, the sweeter and moister the potato.

Sweet Potato Cranberry Casserole

12 ounces fresh cranberries, chopped
1 1/4 cups packed brown sugar
1 small orange, peeled, sliced
1/4 cup orange juice
3/4 teaspoon cinnamon
1/4 teaspoon nutmeg
4 large sweet potatoes, cooked, mashed
1/2 cup chopped pecans

Mix the cranberries, brown sugar, orange slices, orange juice, cinnamon and nutmeg in a 2-quart casserole. Bake at 375 degrees for 30 minutes; stir occasionally. Stir in the sweet potatoes and pecans. Bake for 15 minutes.

Yield: 8 to 10 servings

Herbed Two-Potato Skewers

3 to 4 new potatoes (about 1 pound)
2 small sweet potatoes (about 1 1/2 pounds)
1/2 cup olive oil
2 tablespoons chopped parsley
1 tablespoon chopped fresh thyme, or 1 teaspoon dried thyme
1/4 teaspoon red pepper flakes
1/2 teaspoon freshly ground black pepper
1/2 teaspoon salt

Steam all the potatoes on a rack in a steamer over boiling water for 15 to 20 minutes or until just tender. Remove to a large bowl and cover with ice water. Let stand for 2 minutes. Drain and pat dry. Cut the potatoes into 1 1/2-inch chunks. Thread alternately onto skewers.

Whisk the olive oil, parsley, thyme, red pepper flakes, black pepper and salt in a bowl. Place the potato skewers in a sealable plastic bag. Pour the marinade over the potatoes and seal the bag. Marinate for 30 minutes. Drain the potatoes, reserving the marinade. Place the potato skewers on a grill rack. Grill 4 inches above the hot coals for 10 minutes or until the potato skins are brown, turning frequently and brushing with the reserved marinade.

Note: May wrap long rosemary pieces around the skewers before grilling.

Yield: 6 servings

Green Beans with Feta and Basil

1 pound green beans, trimmed
2 ounces feta cheese, crumbled
10 large basil leaves, chopped
1/2 teaspoon Dijon mustard
1 tablespoon red wine vinegar
3 tablespoons olive oil
salt and freshly ground pepper to taste

Steam the green beans in a steamer until tender. Place in a bowl with the feta cheese and basil. Whisk the Dijon mustard, vinegar, olive oil, salt and pepper in a small bowl. Pour over the green bean mixture and toss to mix well.

Yield: 4 servings

Garden Green Beans with Hot Bacon Dressing

1/4 cup sliced almonds
1 beef bouillon cube
1/3 cup boiling water
4 slices bacon, cut into 1/2-inch pieces
1 tablespoon sugar
1/8 teaspoon pepper
4 cups (2-inch) green bean pieces (about 11/3 pounds)
1/2 cup chopped onion
2 tablespoons red wine vinegar

Arrange the almonds on a baking sheet. Bake at 350 degrees for 10 minutes or until toasted. Watch carefully. Dissolve the bouillon cube in the boiling water. Fry the bacon in a skillet until crisp, stirring occasionally. Remove the bacon using a slotted spoon to paper towels to drain. Stir the bouillon, sugar and pepper into the bacon drippings. Stir in the green beans and onion. Cook, covered, until the green beans are tender-crisp. Remove from the heat. Stir in the vinegar. Spoon into a serving dish. Sprinkle with the bacon and sliced almonds.

Yield: 8 servings

Summer Eggplant

2 small eggplant, sliced into ¹/₂-inch circles (about 12 ounces)
1 medium red onion, thinly sliced
1 red bell pepper, thinly sliced
2 large tomatoes, cut into ¹/₂-inch slices
salt and pepper to taste
2 tablespoons sifted flour
2 tablespoons butter
³/₄ cup freshly grated Parmesan cheese
8 ounces mozzarella cheese

Layer the eggplant, red onion, red pepper and tomatoes in a deep 9x13-inch baking dish. Sprinkle with salt, pepper and flour. Dot with butter. Sprinkle with Parmesan cheese and mozzarella cheese. Bake, covered with foil, at 350 degrees for 45 minutes. Bake, uncovered, for 30 minutes longer or until the cheese is light brown.

Note: The vegetables can be layered ¹/₂ at a time if the baking dish is deep enough.

Yield: 10 to 12 servings

Grilled Corn with Shallot Thyme Butter

6 to 8 ears of corn
Shallot Thyme Butter (below)

Soak the corn in the husks in a large bowl for 30 minutes and drain. Pull the husks back but do not remove. Remove and discard the corn silk. Spread each ear of corn with about ¹/₂ teaspoon Shallot Thyme Butter. Wrap the corn with the husks. Secure with soaked butcher string or soaked pieces of corn husks. Place on a grill rack. Grill 4 to 6 inches above the hot coals for 20 to 25 minutes or until the corn is tender when pierced with a fork, turning frequently. Serve hot with remaining Shallot Thyme Butter.

Yield: 6 to 8 servings

Shallot Thyme Butter

1 cup butter, softened
1 cup chopped shallots
2 tablespoons chopped fresh thyme, or 2 teaspoons dried thyme
salt and pepper to taste

Melt 3 tablespoons of the butter in a heavy skillet over medium heat. Add the shallots. Sauté for 4 minutes or until tender and translucent. Mix the remaining butter and thyme in a bowl. Add the shallot mixture and salt and pepper to taste and mix well. Spoon into ramekins. Chill in the refrigerator. Return to room temperature before serving.

Yield: 1¹/₂ to 2 cups

Corn on the Cob

Jazz up corn on the cob by serving it dappled with butter which has been spiked with salt, pepper, and one or more of the following snazzy additions: basil, chervil, chile powder, minced chives, chopped cilantro, cumin, lemon juice, lime juice, nutmeg, oregano, chopped parsley, saffron, sage, or thyme.

Vidalia Onion Tart

1 prepared pie pastry
2 slices bacon
4 medium Vidalia onions, sliced
2 eggs
2 egg yolks
1 teaspoon chopped chives

1 teaspoon chopped parsley
2 tablespoons Dijon mustard
1/2 cup grated Parmesan cheese
salt and pepper to taste
1 cup heavy cream

Fit the pie pastry into a tart pan with a removable bottom. Trim and flute the edge. Prick the bottom of the pastry with a fork. Bake at 350 degrees until light brown. Fry the bacon in a skillet until crisp. Remove the bacon to paper towels to drain. Add the onions to the bacon drippings. Sauté until soft. Beat the eggs and egg yolks in a mixer bowl until fluffy. Add the chives, parsley, Dijon mustard, Parmesan cheese and salt and pepper. Heat the cream in a small saucepan until scalded, stirring constantly. Add heated cream to the egg mixture gradually, beating constantly. Pour into the prebaked tart shell filling 2/3 full. Layer the sautéed onions over the egg mixture. Crumble the bacon and sprinkle over the top. Place the tart pan on a baking sheet. Bake at 350 degrees for 30 minutes or until set and brown on top.

Yield: 6 to 8 servings

Onion Bread Pudding

1 1/2 pounds onions, thinly sliced
salt to taste
1/4 cup butter
8 ounces dried French bread, thinly
    sliced

6 ounces grated Parmesan cheese
6 ounces Gruyère cheese, grated
boiling salted water
Cognac to taste
2 tablespoons butter

Sprinkle the onions with salt. Cook the onions, covered, in 1/4 cup butter in an ovenproof skillet for 40 minutes. Cook, uncovered, for 10 minutes or until caramelized, stirring constantly. Spread the bread slices with the onions. Alternate layers of the bread and cheese in a 4-quart casserole until 2/3 full, ending with the cheese. Pour enough boiling salted water into the casserole to float the top layer. Simmer for 30 minutes. Sprinkle with Cognac. Dot with 2 tablespoons butter. Bake at 325 degrees for 1 hour. Serve with grilled meats and hearty game dishes.

Yield: 6 to 8 servings

New Year's Black-Eyed Peas

3 pounds dried black-eyed peas
2 ribs celery, chopped
3 large onions, chopped
6 large carrots, peeled, chopped
2 large green bell peppers, chopped
3 pounds cooked ham, cut into
    bite-size pieces
7 cloves of garlic, crushed

4 small red peppers (optional)
1/2 teaspoon thyme
5 bay leaves
2 teaspoons salt
1 teaspoon black pepper
1 teaspoon sugar
salt and black pepper to taste

Soak the peas in water to cover for 8 to 10 hours and drain. Place the peas in a large saucepan. Add the celery, onions, carrots, green peppers, ham, garlic, red peppers, thyme, bay leaves, salt, black pepper and sugar and mix well. Add enough water to cover the peas by 2 inches. Bring to a boil over high heat. Reduce the heat to low. Cook, covered, for 8 to 10 hours. Season with salt and black pepper to taste. Serve with corn bread, turnip greens and pepper sauce.

Note: May be served over rice.

Yield: 30 servings

Pickled Okra

These crisp, briny bites are the ideal accompaniment for a picnic or summer lunch on the porch. They also make a snappy and fun addition to Bloody Marys and Martinis.

1 pound small fresh okra
4 small red chile peppers
3 cloves of garlic, minced
2 tablespoons chopped fresh celery
    leaves
1 teaspoon dillseeds
1 1/3 cups water
2/3 cup white vinegar
2 1/2 tablespoons salt

Combine the okra, chile peppers, garlic, celery leaves and dillseeds in a large bowl. Bring the water, vinegar and salt to a boil in a nonaluminum saucepan, stirring until the salt dissolves. Pour over the okra mixture. Let stand until cool. Chill, covered, in the refrigerator for 3 days, stirring occasionally. Serve immediately or store in an airtight container in the refrigerator for up to 2 weeks.

Yield: about 3 pints

Herb-Cheese Stuffed Potatoes

12 small red potatoes   3 large green onions, sliced
1 small onion, chopped   2 teaspoons dried basil
2 tablespoons butter   1 large clove of garlic, minced
6 ounces cream cheese, softened   salt and freshly ground pepper
2 to 3 tablespoons sour cream   to taste
1 cup grated Swiss cheese   chopped green onions
2 tablespoons minced parsley

Scrub the potatoes. Place in a baking dish. Bake at 400 degrees for 1 hour or until tender. Cool slightly. Cut the potatoes into halves horizontally. Scoop the potato pulp into a small bowl, reserving the potato shells.

Sauté the onion in butter in a small skillet until soft. Combine the sautéed onion, cream cheese, sour cream, Swiss cheese, parsley, sliced green onions, basil, garlic and salt and pepper in a bowl and mix well. Reserve 1/3 of the cheese mixture. Add the potato pulp to remaining cheese mixture. Stuff each potato half with the potato mixture. Reassemble the potato halves together. Arrange the potatoes in a buttered large baking dish. Spoon the reserved cheese mixture over each potato. Bake at 325 degrees for 20 minutes or until heated through. Sprinkle with chopped green onions.

Note: Potatoes can be assembled and stored, covered, in the refrigerator for up to 2 days ahead. Bake just before serving.

Yield: 6 servings

Potatoes and Onions

5 pounds baking potatoes
1 Vidalia onion
salt and pepper to taste
butter

Peel the potatoes and cut into slices 2 inches thick. Peel the onion and cut into slices 1 inch thick. Place a layer of potatoes in a greased large baking dish. Place a layer of onion over the potatoes. Sprinkle with salt and pepper. Dot with butter. Repeat the layering process until all ingredients are used, ending with salt, pepper and butter. Bake at 350 degrees until the potatoes are tender.

Yield: 10 to 12 servings

Rosemary Roasted Potatoes

10 medium red potatoes, cut into quarters
8 large cloves of garlic, minced
1 1/2 tablespoons chopped fresh rosemary
1 teaspoon chopped fresh thyme
salt and pepper to taste
1/4 cup olive oil

Place the potatoes in a baking dish. Sprinkle with garlic, rosemary, thyme and salt and pepper. Pour the olive oil over the potatoes and toss to coat well. Bake at 400 degrees for 45 minutes or until the potatoes are tender and crusty, stirring occasionally.
Note: May use 20 new potatoes cut into halves.

Yield: 6 servings

Parsley Sauce

1/2 cup packed flat-leaf parsley
1 small clove of garlic, sliced
4 teaspoons balsamic vinegar
2 tablespoons water
6 tablespoons extra-virgin olive oil
salt and pepper to taste

Purée the parsley, garlic, vinegar, water, olive oil, salt and pepper in a blender. Strain through a fine sieve into a small bowl, pressing to extract all the liquid.

Note: One recipe makes enough to place on 6 plates under the terrine slices. The Parsley Sauce can be made 1 day ahead, but the bright green color will darken a little. Store in the refrigerator. Bring to room temperature before serving.

Yield: *1/2* cup

Roasted Eggplant, Red Pepper and Goat Cheese Terrine with Parsley Sauce

4 small to medium eggplant, cut lengthwise into 1/2-inch slices
    (about 31/2 pounds)
olive oil
salt and pepper to taste
1/2 cup Basil Pesto (page 109)
6 to 7 red bell peppers, roasted, cut lengthwise into 3 or 4 sections
7 ounces Montrachet cheese or other mild goat cheese, crumbled
1 to 2 recipes Parsley Sauce (at left)

Arrange the eggplant slices in a single layer on baking sheets lined with foil, brushing both sides of the eggplant with olive oil. Sprinkle lightly with salt and pepper. Broil for 4 to 5 minutes per side until golden brown. Remove with a spatula to paper towels to drain. Let stand until cool. Remove the peeling from each slice of eggplant.

Line a 5x8-inch loaf pan with plastic wrap, leaving enough overhang on each side to fold over the top. Arrange a layer of eggplant in the prepared pan. Spread with a thin layer of Basil Pesto. Next arrange a layer of pepper slices. Cover with a layer of goat cheese. Repeat the layering process, ending with eggplant. Cover with plastic wrap overhang. Weight the terrine with another loaf pan filled with canned goods. Chill for 24 hours or longer.

Unwrap and invert onto a platter. Discard the plastic wrap. Cut into slices. Spoon Parsley Sauce on individual serving plates. Place a slice of cold terrine in the Parsley Sauce. Bring to room temperature before serving. Garnish with fresh basil or parsley.

Note: Can be made 3 days in advance.

Yield: 12 servings

Baked Tomatoes Rockefeller

2 (10-ounce) packages frozen
  chopped spinach
2 cups seasoned bread crumbs
6 green onions, chopped
6 eggs, lightly beaten
3/4 cup melted butter
1/2 cup grated fresh Parmesan
  cheese

1/4 teaspoon Worcestershire sauce
1/2 teaspoon minced garlic
1 teaspoon salt
1/2 teaspoon pepper
1 teaspoon dried thyme
1/4 teaspoon Tabasco sauce
12 thick tomato slices

Cook the spinach using the butter method on the package directions
and drain. Add the bread crumbs, green onions, eggs, melted butter,
Parmesan cheese, Worcestershire sauce, garlic, salt, pepper, thyme and
Tabasco sauce and mix well. Arrange the tomato slices in a single layer in a
buttered 9x13-inch baking dish. Mound the spinach mixture on each
tomato slice. Sprinkle lightly with additional Parmesan cheese. Bake at
350 degrees for 15 minutes.

Note: May be made in advance. Freezes well.

Yield: 12 servings

Peppers

There are over 1,000 varieties of peppers, ranging from sweet and mild to fiery hot. The botanical classification for all peppers is capsicum, and they are generally grouped into two categories—sweet peppers and chile peppers. The sweet peppers include the familiar bell peppers and the elongated Italian peppers. The bells are named for their color—green, red, yellow, orange, ivory, and purple. They all start off green; but while some remain green, others ripen to their characteristic color, becoming sweeter as they do. Italian peppers look like elongated bell peppers and are a pale yellow-green. They have more flavor and less bite than green bell peppers.

The hot peppers, or chile peppers, should be handled carefully. To remove some of the heat, they should be opened and the pith and seeds removed. Most of the flavor is in the outer wall.

The most commonly available chile peppers are:

Pepperoncini—small and elongated; usually pickled; and mildly hot

Pasilla—similar to the poblano but more elongated and broader; relatively mild; often dried

Banana pepper—long tapering cones with a creamy yellow skin; usually pickled; can be mild or medium hot

Grilled Peppers and Tomatoes

15 Roma tomatoes
2 yellow bell peppers
1 cup balsamic vinegar
1³/₄ cups olive oil
2¹/₂ tablespoons minced garlic
¹/₂ cup chopped fresh basil
salt and freshly ground pepper to taste

Cut the tomatoes into halves lengthwise. Cut the yellow peppers into strips. Combine the vinegar, olive oil, garlic, basil and pepper in a bowl and mix well. Add the vegetables. Marinate for 1 hour or longer. Drain the vegetables, reserving the marinade. Place on a grill rack. Grill for 5 to 10 minutes or until cooked through. Return the vegetables to the marinade. Marinate briefly and drain.

Note: May be served over rice.

Yield: 8 servings

Tomato Tart

1 prepared pie pastry
8 ounces mozzarella cheese, shredded
3 tomatoes, peeled, cut into ¹/₂-inch-thick slices
¹/₂ cup chopped fresh basil leaves
olive oil

Fit the pie pastry into a tart pan and trim and flute the edge. Bake at 450 degrees for 5 to 10 minutes. Sprinkle the cheese in the crust. Layer the tomatoes over the cheese. Sprinkle with basil. Drizzle with olive oil. Bake at 350 degrees for 20 minutes or until golden brown.

Yield: 8 servings

Scalloped Tomatoes, Artichokes and Hearts of Palm

1/2 cup finely chopped green onions
2 teaspoons finely chopped shallots
1/4 cup butter
1 (35-ounce) can whole plum
  tomatoes, drained
1 (14-ounce) can artichoke hearts,
  drained, quartered
1 (14-ounce) can hearts of palm,
  drained, sliced

1 tablespoon chopped fresh basil
1 teaspoon dried oregano
1 teaspoon sugar
3 tablespoons lemon juice
1/2 teaspoon lemon zest
salt and pepper to taste
1/2 cup grated Parmesan cheese

Sauté the green onions and shallots in the butter in a skillet until tender. Add the tomatoes, artichoke hearts and hearts of palm. Cook for 2 to 3 minutes, stirring gently. Season with basil, oregano, sugar, lemon juice, lemon zest and salt and pepper. Spoon into a greased casserole. Sprinkle with Parmesan cheese. Bake at 325 degrees for 10 to 15 minutes or until heated through.

Yield: 6 servings

(Peppers, continued)

Anaheim—elongated with a slight twist; red or green; medium hot; canned green chiles are Anaheims

Red cherry—resemble red cherry tomatoes; usually pickled; medium hot

Poblano—cone-shaped with a long tip; shiny green or red; usually roasted; medium hot

Ancho—dried poblanos

Chimayo—shaped like slightly collapsed long cones; very hot

Jalapeño—plump little barrels with thick green skins; hot but a little milder when roasted

Chipotle—dried jalapeños

Cayenne—slim, twisted with a long point; usually dried and ground for cayenne; very hot

Serrano—fat, red or green, resembling pinky fingers; very hot; a favorite in Mexican cooking used in everything from beans to guacamole

Japone—dried serranos

Thai—extremely hot; used in Asian stir-fry dishes

Habañero—tiny, squat, and fat with a neon orange color; incredibly hot; hands should be covered when working with them

Scotch bonnet—an orange or yellow Jamaican pepper shaped like a tiny pumpkin; extremely hot; hands should be covered when working with them

Southern Greens

Making a gloriously, greasy-good mess of greens is a true Southern culinary art. Greens are hearty and delectable, with just the right snappy bite to them, and they are good for you as well. Mustard, turnip, and collard greens are all members of the cabbage family, with its potential cancer-fighting benefits. They are loaded with fiber, are a good source of vitamins A and C, and can be very low in fat, depending on how they are cooked.

All greens must first be picked over well, eliminating any yellow or brown parts. Then the hard part of the stems should be cut off up to the tender leaves. (When it comes to collards, the leaves should be cut into pieces.) Then the greens must be thoroughly washed to remove the grit. Traditional cooks suggest that greens be washed twice in salted water to remove any "critters." Then they should be washed another ten times in cold water to be absolutely sure they are clean and free from dirt and sand. Once they are completely clean, the greens can be used in a variety of recipes.

Greens are usually cooked with "boiling meat" or "fat back." But they can also be added to pasta, soups, and casseroles. Greens are great in gumbo and can be substituted for spinach. They can be used in recipes running the gamut from soul food to health food and everything in between.

Roquefort Tomatoes

8 medium tomatoes	2 tablespoons dry sherry
1/2 cup butter	salt and pepper to taste
1 1/4 pounds fresh mushrooms	dash of Worcestershire sauce
4 teaspoons flour	2 tablespoons plus 2 teaspoons
1 cup sour cream	ground almonds
1 1/2 ounces Roquefort cheese	paprika to taste
1 teaspoon chopped fresh parsley	

Cut the tops from the tomatoes. Scoop out the pulp to form shells. Invert the tomato shells onto paper towels to drain.

Melt the butter in a skillet. Add the mushrooms. Sauté until the liquid is evaporated. Stir the flour into the sour cream. Add to the mushrooms. Cook over low heat until thickened, stirring constantly. Add the cheese and stir until smooth. Add the parsley, sherry, salt, pepper and Worcestershire sauce and blend well. Remove from the heat. Let stand until cool.

Stuff the tomato shells with the stuffing. Sprinkle with the almonds and paprika. Bake at 375 degrees for 15 to 25 minutes or until bubbly.

Yield: 8 servings

Fresh Sautéed Spinach

1 pound spinach leaves
3 tablespoons olive oil
1 tablespoon minced garlic
salt and pepper to taste

Rinse the spinach and pat dry. Heat the olive oil in a large skillet. Add the spinach and garlic. Reduce the heat. Cook for 5 minutes. Season with salt and pepper.

Yield: 4 to 6 servings

Stuffed Zucchini

1 zucchini
1 tomato, seeded, chopped
1 green onion, chopped
2 tablespoons chopped fresh parsley
1 clove of garlic, minced
$1/4$ cup bread crumbs
$1/2$ cup grated Parmesan cheese
1 tablespoon olive oil
salt and pepper to taste

Cut the zucchini into halves lengthwise. Scoop out enough of the pulp to form 2 deep boats. Reserve 3 tablespoons of the pulp.

Combine the reserved pulp, tomato, green onion, parsley, garlic, bread crumbs, $1/4$ cup of the Parmesan cheese, olive oil and salt and pepper in a bowl and mix well.

Stuff the zucchini boats with the tomato mixture. Sprinkle with the remaining $1/4$ cup of Parmesan cheese. Arrange in a greased baking dish. Bake at 450 degrees for 30 minutes or until cooked through.

Yield: 2 servings

Mushrooms

A marvelous variety of mushrooms is available in most supermarkets today. And although many of the "wild" mushrooms have actually been cultivated and are not as rich as the truly wild ones, they are quite delicious nevertheless.

Fresh mushrooms should be kept dry and cold and shouldn't be rinsed until they are to be used. Then they should be wiped with a damp cloth, or, if they are particularly dirty, rinsed lightly. Some of the available mushrooms to choose from today are:

Button—white or cream in color; mild

Chanterelle—trumpet-shaped; mild; when black they are called black trumpet or horn of plenty

Cremini—cocoa-colored version of the button mushrooms and more intense

Enoki—tiny white caps with long sprout-like stems; tangy, fresh; and crunchy

Grilled Marinated Portobello Mushrooms and Fresh Vegetables

2 to 3 cloves of garlic, chopped
4 to 6 portobello mushrooms
1/4 cup olive oil
1/2 cup balsamic vinegar
2 teaspoons finely chopped garlic
1 tablespoon chopped fresh oregano
1 tablespoon chopped fresh basil
1 tablespoon chopped fresh marjoram
freshly ground pepper to taste

3 small yellow squash, cut into chunks
3 small zucchini, cut into chunks
2 red bell peppers, cut into quarters
2 yellow bell peppers, cut into quarters
1 bunch asparagus, trimmed
3 Vidalia onions, cut into quarters
3 sweet potatoes, cut into chunks
olive oil
1/2 cup crumbled Gorgonzola cheese

Insert the chopped garlic into the underside of the mushrooms. Combine 1/4 cup olive oil, vinegar, 2 teaspoons finely chopped garlic, oregano, basil, marjoram and pepper in a glass bowl and mix well. Add the mushrooms. Marinate, turning frequently. Brush the vegetables with olive oil. Drain the mushrooms. Place the mushrooms and vegetables in a grill basket. Grill until the vegetables are tender. Remove the skins from the bell peppers and sweet potatoes. Add the vegetables and mushrooms to a serving bowl. Sprinkle with cheese and toss to mix well. Serve warm.

Yield: 6 to 8 servings

Winter Vegetables

12 ounces fresh brussels sprouts
6 to 8 ounces petite carrots
7 to 9 small red potatoes
1 egg, or 1/4 cup egg substitute
2 tablespoons Dijon mustard
3 tablespoons red wine vinegar
1 tablespoon celery seeds
3/4 cup vegetable oil
salt and pepper to taste
2 green onions, finely chopped

Cook the vegetables in water to cover in 3 separate saucepans until tender and drain. Combine the egg or egg substitute, Dijon mustard, vinegar and celery seeds in a bowl and mix well. Add the oil in a fine stream, whisking constantly. Add salt and pepper. Arrange the vegetables in a shallow bowl. Pour the dressing over the top. Sprinkle with green onions.

Yield: 4 to 6 servings

(Mushrooms, continued)

Morel—cone-shaped with a spongy, beige to brown cap; rich, earthy and nut-like;.should always be cooked.

Oyster—fan-shaped and beige-colored; moist, tender, and mild; extremely perishable

Porcini—large with parasol-shaped caps and thick stems; taupe to brown; smoky and woodsy; also known as cepes

Portobello—giant cremini with large caps and thick stems; taupe to brown; deep flavor and meaty texture; serve as a good meat substitute in vegetarian dishes

Shiitake—large, tawny, parasol-shaped caps with cream-colored insides; rich and smoky flavor; dried shiitakes make a rich, intense broth when reconstituted

Wood Ear—black or brown and nearly transparent; mild and nutty; also called cloud ear and tree ear

Roasted Root Vegetables

¹/₂ cup butter
²/₃ cup vermouth
2 large sweet potatoes, peeled, cut into small to medium chunks
4 to 6 large carrots, peeled, cut into small to medium chunks
1 medium rutabaga, peeled, cut into small to medium chunks
4 medium parsnips, peeled, cut into small to medium chunks
8 to 10 shallots, peeled
2 to 4 medium beets, peeled, cut into small to medium chunks
salt and freshly ground pepper to taste

Melt the butter in a small saucepan. Add the vermouth and mix well. Place the vegetables in a large roasting pan. Add the butter mixture and toss to coat well. Season with salt and pepper. Bake, tightly covered with foil, at 325 degrees for 30 to 40 minutes. Bake, uncovered, for 1 hour longer or until the vegetables are tender and light brown.

Yield: 8 servings

Butter Bean Cakes

Justine's Courtyard and Carriageway

6 cups dried butter beans
1/2 medium onion, sliced
3 slices bacon, or 2 ham or beef
    bouillon cubes
1/2 teaspoon minced garlic
salt and pepper to taste
1 red bell pepper, chopped
2 leek bulbs, sliced
1 cup sliced shiitake mushrooms
1 cup crumbled feta cheese

1/4 cup lemon juice
2 tablespoons garlic
pinch of salt
1/4 teaspoon pepper
1/2 teaspoon Tabasco sauce
1 cup bread crumbs
vegetable oil for frying
Red Pepper and Mushroom Sauce
    (at right)

Soak the beans in water to cover in a bowl for 8 to 10 hours and drain. Place the beans in a large saucepan. Add enough water to cover. Bring to a boil. Add the onion, bacon, 1/2 teaspoon garlic and salt and pepper. Cook until the beans are tender and drain.

Place the bean mixture in a large bowl. Add the red pepper, leeks, mushrooms, cheese, lemon juice, 2 tablespoons garlic, pinch of salt, 1/4 teaspoon pepper, Tabasco sauce and bread crumbs and mix wel. Stir, crushing about 1/2 of the bean mixture. Shape into 3-inch round patties. Heat 1/4 inch vegetable oil in a large skillet. Add the bean patties. Sauté until golden brown, turning once. Drain on paper towels. Serve with Red Pepper and Mushroom Sauce.

Yield: 4 to 6 servings

Red Pepper and Mushroom Sauce

3 tablespoons butter
2 tablespoons white wine
juice of 1/2 lemon
1 red bell pepper, sliced
1 leek, sliced
1 cup sliced shiitake mushrooms

Melt the butter in a skillet. Stir in the wine and lemon juice. Add the red pepper, leek and mushrooms. Sauté until tender.

Yield: 4 to 6 servings

MEAT
POULTRY
GAME

It's an age-old tradition and a classic Southern scene—
friends and family clustered about, chatting cheerfully as seasoned,
succulent meat cooks over a crackling-hot fire. There is the distinct,
rich scent of game as it roasts to burnished perfection, dripping juicily
into the smoldering coals, the unbeatable smokey goodness
of thick lamb chops or a well-marbled steak lovingly tended on
the backyard barbeque, and the savory flavor of pork roast rubbed with
spices and slow-cooked until the meat practically melts apart. The joy of
gathering outdoors to grill is an essential part of Alabama entertaining.
The spacious, grassy pastures are flush with herds of hearty cattle
and other livestock. Fields and marshes are replete with an astounding
bevy of birds. And the thick, luxuriant woods and forests are teeming
with game and wildlife. It seems only natural, when graced with
such incredible abundance, to enjoy, and indulge in, the
flora and fauna that abound.

Photograph sponsored by The Junior League of Mobile Board of Directors

Hunting

Hunting the plentiful wildlife of the Alabama fields and woods is a time-honored tradition for many. Hunting allows its aficionados the chance to break away from busy schedules and everyday concerns to enjoy nature at its finest. The rejuvenating solitude of the majestic outdoors offers time for deep reflection and thought. It is also an opportunity to partake in a ritual passed down from generation to generation—the harvesting of bountiful game in a respectful manner.

Peppercorns

Pepper is one of the most important seasonings in the kitchen; however, prepared pepper all too often becomes rather dull and dusty tasting, so it is best to grind it fresh for each use, if possible. Green, black, white, and pink peppercorns all come from the same plant. Green peppercorns, milder than the black, are picked while they are still immature and are packed in vinegar or brine. Those berries left on the plant to mature turn red. When the mature berries are picked and dried, they shrivel and turn black. For white peppercorns, also less spicy than the black, the dried berries are soaked and their outer covering is removed. White peppercorns are ideal for pale soups and sauce. Pink peppercorns, perhaps the most subtle, are an altogether different species. They come from an island in the Indian ocean and have a faintly sweet flavor.

Roast Prime Rib with Pink and Green Peppercorn Crust

1 (7¹/2- to 8-pound) 4-rib standing rib beef roast	2 tablespoons flour
salt and pepper to taste	1 tablespoon brown sugar
2 teaspoons whole allspice berries, crushed	1 tablespoon Dijon mustard
3 tablespoons each dried pink peppercorns and dried green peppercorns, lightly crushed	1¹/2 teaspoons salt
	²/3 cup dry red wine
	2 cups low-sodium beef broth
	1¹/2 tablespoons cornstarch
	1 tablespoon Worcestershire sauce
3 tablespoons unsalted butter	1 tablespoon water

Let the beef stand at room temperature for 1 hour. Pat the beef dry and sprinkle with salt and pepper to taste. Place beef ribs side down in a roasting pan. Bake at 500 degrees for 30 minutes. Remove beef to a platter, discarding the pan drippings. Reduce the oven temperature to 350 degrees. Combine the allspice, pink peppercorns, green peppercorns, butter, flour, brown sugar, Dijon mustard and 1¹/2 teaspoons salt in a bowl and mix well to form a paste. Return the beef ribs side down to the roasting pan. Spread with the peppercorn paste. Bake for 1 to 1¹/4 hours or until a meat thermometer inserted into the thickest portion of the beef registers 140 degrees for medium-rare. Remove the beef to a cutting board and discard the strings if necessary. Let stand, loosely covered, for 20 minutes or longer before carving.

Skim the fat from the drippings in the roasting pan. Place the roasting pan over the burner. Add the wine. Bring to a boil over medium-high heat, stirring to deglaze the roasting pan. Boil until the mixture is reduced by ¹/2 and pour into a small saucepan. Add the beef broth. Return to a boil. Boil for 5 minutes. Dissolve the cornstarch in Worcestershire sauce and water in a small bowl. Add to the sauce mixture in a fine stream, whisking constantly. Bring to a boil, whisking constantly. Boil for 1 minute or until thickened, whisking constantly. Season with salt and pepper to taste.

Carve the roast and place on a serving platter. Garnish with sprigs of fresh rosemary. Serve with the sauce.

Yield: 8 to 10 servings

Marinated Pepper-Crusted Beef Tenderloin

1 cup port
1 cup soy sauce
1/2 cup olive oil
1 1/2 teaspoons pepper
1 teaspoon dried whole thyme
1/2 teaspoon Tabasco sauce
4 cloves of garlic, crushed
1 bay leaf
1 (5- to 6-pound) beef tenderloin, trimmed
2 tablespoons coarsely ground pepper

Combine the wine, soy sauce, olive oil, 1 1/2 teaspoons pepper, thyme, Tabasco sauce, garlic and bay leaf in a bowl and mix well. Place the beef in a large shallow dish. Pour the wine mixture over the beef. Marinate, tightly covered, for 8 to 10 hours, turning occasionally. Drain the beef, reserving the marinade. Bring the reserved marinade to a boil in a saucepan. Boil for 3 minutes and remove from the heat. Discard the bay leaf.

Coat the beef with 2 tablespoons pepper. Place the beef on a rack in a roasting pan. Insert a meat thermometer into the beef. Bake at 425 degrees for 45 to 60 minutes or until the meat thermometer registers 140 degrees for medium-rare or 150 degrees for medium, brushing frequently with the heated reserved marinade. Garnish with fresh parsley.

Yield: 12 servings

Hank Aaron

One of Mobile's most famous native sons is Henry Louis "Hank" Aaron. Hank Aaron was born in Mobile on February 5, 1934. At 14 years old, Aaron, already a great fan of baseball, skipped school to hear baseball great Jackie Robinson speak at a Mobile church. Before he was 17, Aaron was discovered by minor league scouts and signed to the Negro League's Indianapolis Clowns. Within months, he was scouted by, and eventually traded to, the Boston Braves. In 1952, playing for the Braves's minor league farm team in Eau Claire, Wisconsin, Aaron was chosen Northern League Rookie of the Year.

In 1954, Hank Aaron moved up to the Braves's major league team. During spring training of that year, Aaron played in an exhibition game, with Jackie Robinson on the opposing team, in front of his parents in Mobile. By 1956, just two years later, he had won the National League batting title. In 1957, Aaron's 11th inning home run won the Braves the National League pennant. "Hammerin' Hank" went on to hit .393 with 11 hits, three home runs, and seven RBIs—and the Braves beat the New York Yankees in that year's World Series.

Chianti Beef with Porcini

$1^{1}/_{2}$ ounces dried porcini mushrooms
3 cups beef stock
4 tablespoons olive oil
3 pounds stewing beef, cut into 1-inch cubes
2 ounces pancetta or bacon, finely chopped
2 cups finely chopped yellow onion
2 carrots, peeled, chopped
2 leek bulbs, finely chopped
5 cloves of garlic, minced
2 bay leaves
3 tablespoons unbleached flour
2 tablespoons tomato paste
1 cup dry red wine (chianti classico)
1 teaspoon salt
$^{1}/_{2}$ teaspoon pepper
$^{1}/_{2}$ cup finely chopped flat-leaf parsley

To reconstitute the porcini, rinse them in a strainer under cold running water. Bring the stock to a boil in a small saucepan. Combine the porcini and boiling stock in a small heatproof bowl. Let stand, covered, until cool, stirring 1 to 2 times. Drain the porcini, reserving the liquid. Let the reserved liquid stand for 5 minutes or until settled. Pour the clear liquid into a separate bowl, discarding the residue.

Heat 2 tablespoons of the olive oil in a $4^{1}/_{2}$- to 5-quart flameproof casserole or Dutch oven over medium-high heat. Pat the beef dry. Brown a small amount at a time in the preheated oil for 8 minutes, adding 1 tablespoon olive oil if needed. Remove the beef to a warm bowl.

Add the remaining 2 tablespoons olive oil to the casserole and heat over medium heat. Add the pancetta. Cook for 7 minutes or until light in color, stirring occasionally. Stir in the onion, carrots, leeks, garlic and bay leaves. Cook, covered, for 10 minutes or until the vegetables are light in color, stirring 1 or 2 times and scraping the bottom of the casserole. Sprinkle flour over the vegetables. Cook for 3 minutes, stirring frequently. Stir in the tomato paste, wine and the clear reserved liquid. Return the undrained beef to the casserole. Add salt and pepper. Bring to a simmer.

Bake, covered, at 350 degrees for 1 hour, stirring 1 or 2 times. Stir in the porcini and return to the oven. Bake, uncovered, for an additional hour or until the beef is tender and the stew is thickened. Discard the bay leaves and adjust the seasonings. Stir in the parsley. Let stand for 1 minute before serving.

Yield: 6 servings

Beef with Blue Cheese

6 slices bacon, partially cooked, drained
6 small beef filets
$1/4$ cup olive oil
$1/2$ cup dry white wine
2 cloves of garlic, crushed
2 tablespoons chopped onion
1 tablespoon cornstarch
1 (14-ounce) can beef broth
$1/4$ teaspoon rosemary
2 tablespoons butter, softened
2 tablespoons blue cheese
salt and pepper to taste

Wrap the bacon around the steaks and secure with a wooden pick. Sear on each side in the olive oil in a large skillet. Cook for 6 minutes on each side or until medium-rare. Remove to a warm plate.

Add the wine, garlic and onion to the skillet. Bring to a simmer. Dissolve the cornstarch in the beef broth in a bowl. Add to the skillet. Cook until thickened, stirring constantly. Add the rosemary, butter and blue cheese. Season with salt and pepper. Cook until melted, stirring constantly. Spoon small amounts of the sauce onto individual serving plates. Add the steak and spoon more of the sauce over the top. Garnish with parsley flakes.

Note: May also add fresh sliced mushrooms and capers to the sauce.

Yield: 6 servings

(Hank Aaron, continued)

In May of 1970, Aaron became the eighth player in baseball history to reach his 3,000th hit. And at his first time up during the 1974 season, playing against the Cincinnati Reds, Hank Aaron tied Babe Ruth's record of 714 home runs. On April 8 of that year, he hit number 715 in a game against the Los Angeles Dodgers and became baseball's new home run champion. In 1976, after 23 years in the Major Leagues, Aaron retired from baseball with 755 home runs and 2,297 RBIs. He was inducted into the Baseball Hall of Fame in Cooperstown, New York, in August of 1982.

Hank Aaron is now corporate vice president of community relations for Turner Broadcasting, a member of the TBS board of directors, and assistant to the president of the Atlanta Braves. He is also founder of the Hank Aaron Rookie League and an honorary Eagle Scout.

On April 17, 1997 the Mobile Bay Bears's Hank Aaron Stadium first opened its gates. Mobile's own Hank Aaron was there to throw the first pitch.

Herbed Tomato Chutney

Chutneys are a wonderful, all too often overlooked condiment. This savory herbed tomato chutney is especially good with lamb or other grilled meats.

1¹/₂ pounds plum tomatoes, peeled, seeded, quartered
1¹/₂ cups chopped onion
¹/₃ cup sugar
¹/₃ cup white wine vinegar
1 (1-inch) piece fresh gingerroot, peeled, minced
1 pickled jalapeño, seeded, chopped
1 teaspoon coriander seeds
1 teaspoon mustard seeds
1 teaspoon salt
1 tablespoon chopped fresh rosemary

Combine the tomatoes, onion and sugar in a large heavy saucepan and toss to coat well. Let stand for 2 hours or longer. Stir in the next 6 ingredients. Simmer for 10 minutes. Drain the tomato mixture, reserving the liquid. Place the tomato mixture in a bowl. Return the liquid to the saucepan. Boil until the liquid is reduced to about ¹/₂ cup. Pour over the tomato mixture. Add the rosemary and stir gently. Chill for 2 hours or longer. Serve at room temperature.

Yield: about 2 cups

Grilled Cubed Leg of Lamb with Herbed Tomato Chutney

¹/₄ cup olive oil
2 tablespoons lemon juice
zest of 2 lemons
¹/₄ cup chopped fresh rosemary
1 tablespoon balsamic vinegar
2 cloves of garlic, minced
1 teaspoon salt
freshly ground pepper to taste
1¹/₂ pounds boneless leg of lamb, trimmed, cut into 2-inch cubes
Herbed Tomato Chutney (at left)

Combine the olive oil, lemon juice, lemon zest, rosemary, vinegar, garlic, salt and pepper in a bowl and mix well. Add the lamb. Marinate in the refrigerator. Drain the lamb, discarding the marinade. Place on a grill screen. Grill for 8 minutes or until medium-rare, turning frequently. Serve with Herbed Tomato Chutney (at left).

Note: May add rosemary stems to the marinade for additional rosemary flavor.

Yield: 4 servings

Lamb Chops with Fresh Mint Sauce

$1/4$ cup white wine
2 tablespoons vegetable oil
$1/2$ teaspoon salt
$1/8$ teaspoon pepper
4 (1-inch-thick) lamb chops
Fresh Mint Sauce (at right)

Combine the wine, vegetable oil, salt and pepper in a bowl and whisk well until emulsified. Add the lamb. Marinate for 30 minutes or longer. Drain the lamb, reserving the marinade. Bring the reserved marinade to a boil in a small saucepan. Boil for 2 to 3 minutes and remove from the heat. Place the lamb on a rack in a broiler pan. Broil for 6 to 8 minutes on each side or until cooked through, basting every 3 to 4 minutes with the heated reserved marinade. Serve with Fresh Mint Sauce.

Yield: 2 servings

Grilled Butterflied Leg of Lamb

$1/3$ cup lightly packed mint leaves, finely chopped
$1/2$ small jalapeño, finely chopped
1 tablespoon finely chopped peeled gingerroot
2 cloves of garlic, peeled, finely chopped
2 tablespoons apricot jam
1 tablespoon soy sauce
3 tablespoons water
3 pounds butterflied leg of lamb

Combine the mint, jalapeño, gingerroot, garlic, apricot jam, soy sauce and water in a bowl and mix well. Pour into a sealable plastic bag. Place the lamb in the bag and seal. Marinate in the refrigerator for 2 to 10 hours. Drain the lamb, reserving the marinade. Bring the reserved marinade to a boil in a small saucepan. Boil for 2 to 3 minutes and remove from the heat.
Place the lamb on a grill rack. Grill over high heat for 15 minutes on each side or until the lamb tests done. Place the lamb in a roasting pan. Pour the heated reserved marinade over the lamb. Bake at 200 degrees for 15 minutes. Cut into slices and serve with the pan juices.

Yield: 4 servings

Fresh Mint Sauce

Tender young lamb and fresh mint are a match made in culinary heaven. Try this fabulous fresh mint sauce for a delightful change from the traditional, expected mint jelly. Drizzle this sauce over the lamb, and serve the extra in a gravy boat alongside.

$1/3$ cup cider vinegar
$1/4$ cup sugar
$1/4$ cup chopped mint
pinch of baking soda

Bring the vinegar and sugar to a boil in a saucepan. Remove from the heat. Add the mint and mix well. Stir in the baking soda. Chill, covered, in the refrigerator.

Yield: 10 servings

Veal Chops with Roasted Pepper Chutney

3/4 cup chopped roasted red bell peppers (page 120)
3 tablespoons olive oil
1 clove of garlic, minced
1 1/2 teaspoons balsamic vinegar
1 1/2 teaspoons drained capers
1/8 teaspoon crushed dried red pepper flakes
4 (1-inch-thick) veal loin chops
salt and black pepper to taste

Mix the red peppers, 2 tablespoons of the olive oil, garlic, vinegar, capers and red pepper flakes in a small bowl. Set aside.

Brush the veal with the remaining 1 tablespoon olive oil. Season with salt and black pepper. Place on a rack in a broiler pan. Broil for 6 minutes on each side for medium or until of the desired degree of doneness. Remove to a serving platter. Spoon the roasted pepper chutney over the veal.

Note: The chutney may be prepared 1 day in advance and stored in the refrigerator.

Yield: 4 servings

Veal Chops Supreme

1/4 cup butter
3 to 4 veal chops
1/2 cup beef broth
2 tablespoons lemon juice
1 tablespoon chopped parsley
1/2 cup heavy cream
1 tablespoon dry sherry or brandy

Melt the butter in a skillet over medium heat. Add the veal. Sauté for 3 to 5 minutes on each side. Add the broth and lemon juice. Cook, covered, for 6 minutes. Remove the veal to a warm plate. Increase the heat to high. Cook until the liquid is reduced by 1/2. Add the parsley, cream and sherry to the skillet, stirring to deglaze. Cook until thickened, stirring constantly. Return the chops to the skillet. Coat with the sauce and serve immediately.

Yield: 3 to 4 servings

Pork Tenderloin and Red Pepper Sauce

1 cup soy sauce
¹/4 cup minced garlic
2 tablespoons grated peeled fresh gingerroot
2 tablespoons vegetable oil
1¹/2 pounds pork tenderloin
Red Pepper Sauce (below)

Combine the soy sauce, garlic, gingerroot and vegetable oil in a bowl, reserving ¹/2 of the mixture for basting. Pour the remaining marinade over the pork in a sealable plastic bag and seal. Marinate in the refrigerator for 2 hours or longer. Drain the pork, discarding the marinade.

Place the pork on a grill rack. Grill over indirect heat for 45 minutes or until a meat thermometer inserted into the thickest portion registers 160 degrees, basting every 10 minutes with the reserved marinade. Serve with Red Pepper Sauce.

Yield: 4 to 6 servings

Red Pepper Sauce

1 tablespoon butter
2 teaspoons chopped garlic
¹/3 cup chopped roasted red bell peppers (page 120)
1 tablespoon flour
³/4 cup vegetable or chicken broth

Melt the butter in a small saucepan. Add the garlic. Sauté until soft. Stir in the red peppers. Cook for 1 minute, stirring constantly. Add the flour gradually, stirring until blended. Add the broth. Simmer for 5 minutes or until thickened, stirring constantly.

Note: Sauce can be made ahead and reheated.

Yield: 4 to 6 servings

Onion Conserve

This memorable onion conserve is superb served as a side dish, as a condiment for meat (especially pork tenderloins), or over cream cheese as an appetizer.

1 cup golden raisins
1 cup fresh orange juice
2 red onions
6 tablespoons unsalted butter
2 teaspoons sugar
salt and freshly ground pepper
to taste

Mix the raisins and orange juice in a bowl. Let stand for 30 minutes or until the raisins are plump. Peel the onions and cut into thin slices. Melt 4 tablespoons of the butter in a large skillet. Add the onions. Sauté over medium heat for 5 to 10 minutes or until translucent. Reduce the heat. Cook until the onions begin to caramelize and turn brown, stirring frequently. Add the undrained raisins and the remaining 2 tablespoons butter. Stir in the sugar. Season with salt and pepper.

Yield: 4 servings

Pork Tenderloins with Caramelized Pears and Brandy Cream Sauce

4 tablespoons butter
4 firm large pears, peeled, cut into $^1/_3$-inch-thick wedges
1 teaspoon sugar
$1^1/_4$ pounds pork tenderloin, trimmed, cut into 1-inch-thick slices
salt and pepper to taste
$^1/_2$ cup chopped shallots
$^3/_4$ teaspoons dried thyme
$^1/_4$ cup brandy
1 cup heavy cream
$^1/_3$ cup pear nectar

Melt 2 tablespoons of the butter in a large nonstick skillet over high heat. Add the pears and sugar. Sauté for 8 minutes or until the pears are tender and deep golden brown.

Place the pork slices between 2 pieces of plastic wrap. Pound $^1/_4$ inch thick using a meat mallet. Melt 1 tablespoon of the butter in a large nonstick skillet over high heat. Season pork with salt and pepper. Add pork in batches to the skillet. Sauté for 2 minutes on each side or until cooked through. Remove to a warm plate and cover to keep warm.

Reduce the heat to medium. Add the remaining 1 tablespoon butter to the skillet. Heat until melted. Add the shallots and thyme. Sauté for 2 minutes. Add the brandy. Boil for 2 minutes or until the liquid is reduced to a glaze consistency, stirring to deglaze the skillet. Add the cream and pear nectar. Boil for 5 minutes or until thickened, stirring constantly. Season with salt and pepper.

Spoon the caramelized pears into the center of a serving platter. Arrange the pork around the pears. Pour the sauce over the pork. Serve immediately.

Yield: 4 servings

Apple-Glazed Pork Tenderloins

1 (6-ounce) can frozen apple juice
    concentrate, thawed
1/3 cup apple jelly
1/4 cup vegetable oil
3 tablespoons bourbon
2 tablespoons Worcestershire sauce

2 tablespoons Dijon mustard
1 tablespoon ground ginger
2 teaspoons salt
1 teaspoon ground pepper
3 pork tenderloins, trimmed

Mix the apple juice concentrate, apple jelly, vegetable oil, bourbon, Worcestershire sauce, Dijon mustard, ginger, salt and pepper in a bowl. Pour over the pork in a shallow dish. Marinate, covered, in the refrigerator for 6 to 10 hours. Drain the pork. Place on a grill rack. Grill over medium-hot coals for 45 to 60 minutes or until cooked through, turning frequently.

Yield: 6 servings

Roasted Pork Loin in Horseradish Crust

1 cup fresh bread crumbs
salt and pepper to taste
2 tablespoons olive oil
2 tablespoons drained horseradish
1 pound boneless pork loin
1 1/2 tablespoons Dijon mustard

Sauté the bread crumbs and salt and pepper in 1 tablespoon of the olive oil in a skillet until golden brown. Combine with the horseradish in a bowl.

Pat the pork dry. Season with salt and pepper. Heat the remaining 1 tablespoon olive oil in a skillet until hot but not smoking. Add the pork. Cook for 5 minutes or until brown on each side. Place in a shallow baking pan. Coat the top and sides evenly with the mustard. Press the bread crumb mixture evenly into the mustard. Bake at 425 degrees for 25 to 30 minutes or until a meat thermometer inserted into the thickest portion registers 160 degrees.

Yield: 2 servings

Dry Rub

A dry rub makes a most interesting alternative to traditional barbecue sauce. The spices impart a wonderful aroma as the meat cooks, and the end result is truly delicious. Dry rub can be used on almost any grilled meat— pork, beef, chicken, even hamburgers. Store any leftovers in a jar—a dry rub will keep indefinitely.

3/4 cup paprika
1/4 cup ground black pepper
1/4 cup salt
1/4 cup sugar
2 tablespoons chili powder
2 tablespoons garlic powder
2 tablespoons onion powder
2 teaspoons cayenne

Mix the paprika, black pepper, salt, sugar, chili powder, garlic powder, onion powder and cayenne in a bowl. Store, covered, in a cool, dark pantry.

Yield: 2 cups

Pulled Roasted Pork

2 (4- to 6-pound) shoulder, butt or loin pork roasts
Dry Rub (at left)

Rub the pork with Dry Rub. Wrap each roast in heavy-duty foil and place in a baking pan. Bake at 500 degrees for 20 minutes. Reduce the oven temperature to 250 degrees. Bake for 5 hours or until cooked through. Let stand until cool enough to handle. Shred the pork, discarding the skin and bones. Serve warm with barbecue sauce, sandwich buns and coleslaw.

Note: May substitute salt and pepper for the dry rub.

Yield: 12 to 16 servings

Rosemary-Glazed Pork Chops

1 tablespoon dried rosemary, crushed
2 teaspoons finely chopped garlic
2 teaspoons salt
freshly ground pepper to taste
4 center-cut pork loin chops
2 tablespoons butter
1 tablespoon olive oil
3/4 cup dry white wine
1 tablespoon finely chopped fresh parsley, or 1 teaspoon dried rosemary

Mix the rosemary, garlic, salt and pepper in a bowl. Rub the rosemary mixture on each side of the pork chops, pressing into the pork chops. Melt the butter in olive oil in a heavy skillet over medium-high heat. Add the pork chops. Cook on each side until brown. Remove the pork chops to a heated platter. Drain the pan drippings, reserving a thin film of the drippings on the bottom of the skillet. Add 1/2 cup of the wine. Bring to a boil. Return the pork chops to the skillet. Reduce the heat. Simmer, covered, for 30 minutes or until cooked through, basting occasionally with the pan juices. Remove the pork chops to a warm platter. Add the remaining 1/4 cup wine to the skillet. Bring to a boil. Boil until the liquid is reduced to a syrupy glaze, stirring to deglaze the skillet. Reduce the heat. Stir in the parsley. Return the pork chops to the skillet. Heat until the pork chops are warm and coated with the glaze.

Yield: 4 servings

Chicken Pinot Noir

8 chicken pieces, such as breasts, thighs and drumsticks
$^1/_4$ teaspoon salt
$^1/_4$ teaspoon dry mustard
$^1/_4$ teaspoon ground mace
$^1/_4$ teaspoon ground cumin
$^1/_4$ teaspoon dried sage
$^1/_4$ teaspoon pepper
5 cloves of garlic, peeled
2 medium red or yellow bell peppers, cut into quarters
2 medium onions, peeled, cut into quarters
1 cup pinot noir
$^1/_4$ cup sherry vinegar
1 (14-ounce) can Italian stewed tomatoes

Place the chicken in a 9x13-inch baking dish sprayed with nonstick cooking spray. Mix the salt, dry mustard, mace, cumin, sage and pepper in a bowl. Rub the chicken with the spice mixture. Arrange the garlic, red peppers and onions around the chicken. Pour the wine, vinegar and undrained tomatoes over the top. Bake at 350 degrees for 50 minutes or until the chicken is cooked through.

Yield: 8 servings

Citrus Grilled Chicken with Fresh Herbs

¹/2 teaspoon coriander seeds
¹/4 teaspoon anise seeds
¹/2 cup honey
¹/4 cup fresh lemon juice
3 tablespoons fresh orange juice
3 tablespoons fresh lime juice
2 medium green onions, finely chopped
1 teaspoon finely chopped fresh thyme
1 teaspoon finely chopped fresh rosemary
1 teaspoon finely chopped fresh sage
6 boneless skinless chicken breast halves, pounded ¹/2 inch thick
salt and freshly ground pepper to taste

Sauté the coriander seeds and anise seeds in a small nonstick skillet over medium heat for 4 minutes or until toasted. Place in a mortar and grind into a powder with a pestle.

Combine the honey, lemon juice, orange juice, lime juice, green onions, thyme, rosemary, sage and ground spice mixture in a large glass dish and whisk well. Add the chicken. Marinate, covered, in the refrigerator for 4 to 10 hours. Drain the chicken, reserving the marinade. Place the reserved marinade in a small saucepan. Bring to a boil. Boil for 2 to 3 minutes, stirring constantly. Remove from the heat. Sprinkle the chicken with salt and pepper. Place on a grill rack. Grill until the chicken is cooked through, brushing occasionally with the heated reserved marinade.

Yield: 6 servings

Chicken Breasts Stuffed with Herbed Goat Cheese

3 to 4 ounces goat cheese, softened
1 tablespoon finely chopped fresh thyme
1 tablespoon finely chopped fresh parsley
1 tablespoon finely chopped fresh basil
1 egg
1 cup fresh bread crumbs
1 tablespoon chopped fresh parsley
4 boneless skinless chicken breast halves
4 to 6 slices bacon, partially cooked

Combine the goat cheese, thyme, 1 tablespoon finely chopped parsley and basil in a small bowl and mix well. Beat the egg in a shallow dish. Mix the bread crumbs and 1 tablespoon chopped parsley in a shallow dish.

Cut a pocket in each chicken breast. Stuff 1/4 of the cheese mixture into each pocket. Wrap 1 slice of bacon around each stuffed chicken breast. Roll in the beaten egg and then in the bread crumb mixture. Place in a nonstick baking dish. Bake at 350 degrees for 35 to 45 minutes or until the chicken is cooked through.

Note: To partially cook the bacon, place the bacon in a microwave-safe dish. Microwave on High for 45 to 60 seconds.

Yield: 4 servings

Too Hot to Handle

When handling all but the mildest of peppers, use rubber gloves. Some of the hotter varieties can cause burning pain just by coming in contact with unbroken skin. Never touch your eyes or other sensitive areas after handling peppers.

What to do if you get burned? If it's your skin that is burning, try a little vegetable oil. If it's your mouth that's aflame, try milk, sour cream, yogurt, or ice cream. Tomato juice also works, as do lemon and lime juice, as well as bread and rice. Water, surprisingly, can actually fan the flame by distributing the capsaicin (the heat-causing compound) to more areas of the mouth.

Southwestern Chicken over Black Beans

4 boneless skinless chicken breast halves (about 6 ounces each)
4 ounces mild goat cheese, softened
2 medium jalapeños, minced (about 1 tablespoon)
3 sun-dried tomatoes, minced
salt and freshly ground black pepper to taste
2 cups cooked black beans

1 small red onion, finely chopped (about ¹/₂ cup)
3 tablespoons olive oil
¹/₃ cup chopped cilantro
1 teaspoon ground cumin
1 teaspoon red wine vinegar
pinch of cayenne
paprika to taste
lime wedges

Make a cut about 3 inches long and 2 inches deep in the middle of the thick side of each breast to create a pocket.

Combine the goat cheese, jalapeños and sun-dried tomatoes in a small bowl and mix well. Spoon ¹/₄ of the filling into each pocket. Press the edges to seal. Season generously with salt and black pepper. Place in a dish. Chill for 15 minutes.

Combine the black beans, onion, olive oil, 3 tablespoons of the cilantro, cumin, vinegar, cayenne, salt and black pepper in a bowl and mix well.

Cut baking parchment into four 15-inch squares. Fold each square into halves on the diagonal and crease. Spoon about ¹/₂ cup of the black bean mixture onto 1 triangle of each square. Top with a stuffed chicken breast and sprinkle with paprika. Fold the remaining triangle of parchment over the chicken to cover. Fold edges of the parchment together to seal. Place on 2 baking sheets. Bake at 375 degrees for 30 to 35 minutes or until the packets are puffed and light brown. Serve immediately with the remaining cilantro and lime wedges.

Yield: 4 servings

Spicy Peanut Chicken

1 (4-pound) chicken
salt to taste
2 tablespoons butter or vegetable oil
1 cup chopped onion
1 cup chopped green bell pepper
6 cloves of garlic, crushed
1 cup peanut butter
2 cups diced peeled tomatoes
2 cups cubed eggplant
Tabasco sauce or cayenne to taste
paprika to taste
3 cups cooked white rice

Boil the chicken in salted water to cover in a large saucepan for 45 to 50 minutes. Drain the chicken, reserving 4 cups of the stock. Cut the chicken into pieces, discarding the skin and bones.

Melt the butter in a small skillet. Add the onion, green pepper and garlic. Sauté until the onion is translucent.

Reheat the reserved chicken stock in a small saucepan. Add gradually to the peanut butter in a large saucepan, stirring constantly until smooth. Add the sautéed vegetables, tomatoes and eggplant. Simmer until the eggplant is nearly cooked through. Add the chicken. Simmer for awhile longer; do not boil. Stir in Tabasco sauce or cayenne. Sprinkle with paprika. Serve over rice.

Yield: 8 to 10 servings

Fooling with Phyllo

Phyllo, phylo, fillo, filo. Any way you spell it, it means the same thing—leaf, as in fragile, sheer pastry leaf. Phyllo, pronounced "fee-loh not filoh," is a staple in Greek and Middle Eastern cooking and is used to make baklava and a multitude of other culinary delights. Unfortunately, a lot of folks grit their teeth at the mere thought of wrangling with delicate phyllo leaves. Here are some tips to make working with phyllo an easier feat:

• You must allow the dough to thaw gradually in the refrigerator overnight. (If you try to thaw the dough too quickly, it becomes sticky and the sheets fuse together.)

• When working with phyllo, it is important to keep the individual sheets from drying out. Unroll the package of phyllo sheets and place them on a piece of heavy plastic. Cover them with another piece of plastic. Then while working with individual phyllo sheets, keep the others covered at all times. The unused phyllo can be rewrapped and refrozen.

Individual Wrapped Stuffed Chicken Breasts

1/2 cup shredded Monterey Jack cheese (about 3 ounces)
1/2 cup shredded Cheddar cheese (about 3 ounces)
2 tablespoons butter, softened
2 tablespoons chopped parsley
2 teaspoons chopped fresh tarragon, or 1/2 teaspoon dried tarragon
1/2 teaspoon pepper
1/4 teaspoon salt
4 boneless skinless chicken breast halves (4 to 5 ounces each)
salt and pepper to taste
8 sheets phyllo dough
1/4 cup melted butter

Combine the Monterey Jack cheese, Cheddar cheese, 2 tablespoons of butter, parsley, tarragon, 1/2 teaspoon pepper and 1/4 teaspoon salt in a bowl and mash until a stiff paste forms. Shape the cheese mixture into 4 logs, 3 inches long.

Place the chicken between 2 sheets of waxed paper. Pound with a meat mallet until 1/4 inch thick and 5 inches wide. Season with salt and pepper to taste. Place a cheese log in the center of each chicken breast. Roll up and fold the ends under to enclose the cheese log completely.

Place 1 sheet of phyllo dough on a clean work surface, keeping the remaining covered with a damp towel. Top with another sheet of phyllo dough and brush lightly with butter. Place a chicken breast in the center. Roll up to enclose the chicken, folding and tucking the ends under. Repeat with the remaining chicken and phyllo dough.

Arrange the packets in a 9x13-inch baking dish sprayed with nonstick cooking spray. Brush the packets with the remaining butter. Bake at 350 degrees for 45 to 50 minutes or until the chicken is cooked through and the tops are brown.

Yield: 4 servings

Chicken and Spinach
Packaged in Phyllo

1 onion, chopped
2 tablespoons olive oil
1 pound fresh spinach, shredded, or
    1 (10-ounce) package
      frozen chopped spinach,
      thawed, squeezed dry
1 pound fontina cheese, grated

1/4 cup dry white wine
1 large egg, beaten
salt and pepper to taste
4 cups chopped cooked chicken
1 pound phyllo dough, thawed
1 cup melted butter
paprika to taste

Sauté the onion in the olive oil until translucent. Add the spinach. Sauté for 3 minutes. Remove from the heat and let cool slightly. Add the cheese, wine, egg and salt and pepper and mix well. Stir in the chicken. Chill for 1 hour or longer.

Place 1 sheet of phyllo dough on a sheet of waxed paper and brush with melted butter, keeping the remaining phyllo dough covered with a damp towel. Stack another sheet of phyllo dough on top and brush with melted butter. Continue the stacking process until there are 6 layers. Spoon 1/2 of the chicken mixture on one end of the stack and roll up and tuck ends under to enclose the filling. Brush with melted butter. Cut diagonal vents on the surface and sprinkle with paprika. Repeat with the remaining phyllo dough, butter and chicken mixture. Place the phyllo packages on a greased baking sheet. Bake at 375 degrees for 20 minutes.

Yield: 6 to 8 servings

(Fooling with Phyllo, continued)

• *It is almost inevitable that at least a few of the sheets will tear. When tears occur, simply place the tattered pastry leaf in or on top of your culinary creation and cover with a good sheet. (This can actually work to your advantage; it makes the pastry for whatever you're creating lighter and fluffier.)*

• *It is best to use clarified butter (see page 189) when at all possible. Clarified butter makes phyllo creations crisp instead of gummy. (Using clarified butter will also help your creations keep longer as there are no milk solids to spoil.)*

Mama Dot's Sauce for Grilled Chicken

This tangy, lip-smacking, lemon-laced sauce has been enchanting Mama Dot's guests along with her children, grandchildren, and now great-grandchildren for more than half a century.

1 (32-ounce) bottle of catsup
1/2 cup vinegar
1/2 cup butter
1/4 cup prepared mustard
1/4 cup Worcestershire sauce
2 medium onions, grated
zest and juice of 2 lemons
6 tablespoons sugar
salt and pepper to taste

Bring the catsup, vinegar, butter, mustard, Worcestershire sauce, onions, lemon zest, lemon juice, sugar and salt and pepper to a boil in a saucepan. Boil for 1 minute.

Yield: 6 to 6 1/2 cups

Marinated Grilled Chicken with Mama Dot's Sauce

1/2 cup soy sauce
1/4 cup vegetable oil
1/4 cup red wine vinegar
1 teaspoon dried oregano
1/2 teaspoon dried basil
1/2 clove of garlic, minced
1/2 teaspoon pepper
1 (3-pound) chicken, cut up

Combine the soy sauce, vegetable oil, vinegar, oregano, basil, garlic and pepper in a bowl and mix well. Place the chicken in a nonmetal dish. Pour the marinade over the chicken. Marinate, covered, in the refrigerator for 6 to 8 hours, turning the chicken occasionally. Drain the chicken, reserving the marinade. Bring the reserved marinade to a boil in a small saucepan. Boil for 3 minutes, stirring constantly. Remove from the heat. Place the chicken on a grill rack. Grill until the chicken is cooked through, brushing with the heated reserved marinade.

Yield: 4 to 6 servings

Chicken Delight

 Buie's

4 boneless chicken breast halves
salt and pepper to taste
1/4 cup olive oil
8 ounces sliced fresh mushrooms
1/2 cup chopped green onions
1/4 teaspoon garlic powder
1 cup heavy cream

Season the chicken with salt and pepper. Cook in the olive oil in a skillet until brown, turning once. Add the mushrooms, green onions and garlic powder. Cook until the chicken is cooked through. Add the cream. Simmer over medium-high heat until thickened, stirring constantly. Serve over pasta.

Yield: 4 servings

Spinach and Prosciutto Stuffed Turkey

1 boneless turkey breast
1 tablespoon olive oil
1/2 cup chopped onion
salt and pepper to taste
1 bunch fresh spinach, torn
4 ounces prosciutto, chopped

1/4 cup grated Parmesan cheese
2 tablespoons olive oil
1/4 teaspoon dried thyme
2 teaspoons cornstarch
1/2 cup dry white wine
3/4 cup chicken broth

Butterfly the turkey by holding the knife parallel to the turkey and cutting 3/4 of the way through. Spread the turkey open like a book. Place between 2 sheets of plastic wrap. Pound until 1/2 inch thick.

Heat 1 tablespoon olive oil in a large skillet. Add the onion. Sauté until golden brown. Season with salt and pepper. Add the spinach. Cook until the spinach is wilted and all the liquid is evaporated. Stir in the prosciutto and Parmesan cheese. Spread the mixture along the center of the turkey, leaving a 1-inch border. Roll up to enclose the filling beginning at the narrow end. Tie with string in 1-inch intervals.

Place the turkey on a rack in a roasting pan. Brush with a mixture of 2 tablespoons olive oil, thyme and salt and pepper. Bake, covered, at 325 degrees for 1 hour. Bake, uncovered, for 30 minutes or until a meat thermometer inserted into the center registers 170 degrees. Remove the turkey to a serving platter and keep warm.

Dissolve the cornstarch in the wine in a glass measure. Add the broth to the roasting pan. Bring to a boil, stirring to deglaze the pan. Add the wine mixture. Cook for 1 minute or until thickened, stirring constantly. Cut the turkey into slices and serve with the gravy.

Note: May substitute one 10-ounce package frozen chopped spinach, thawed and squeezed dry, for the fresh spinach.

Yield: 4 to 6 servings

Cranberry Sauce

This Cranberry Sauce is sure to become a holiday tradition. It is a wonderful accompaniment for poultry or fowl. The preparation of this sauce fills the kitchen with the most wonderful aroma.

12 ounces fresh cranberries
3/4 cup orange juice
2 tablespoons grated orange peel
1/2 cup sugar
1 tablespoon lemon juice
1/8 teaspoon cinnamon
1/8 teaspoon ground cloves
1 tablespoon Grand Marnier

Mix the cranberries, orange juice, grated orange peel and sugar in a 2-quart saucepan. Simmer over medium heat for 10 minutes or until thickened, stirring occasionally. Add the lemon juice, cinnamon and cloves. Simmer a few minutes longer. Remove from the heat. Stir in the Grand Marnier.

Yield: 2¹/2 cups

Turkey with Madeira

5 tablespoons madeira
1/4 cup unsalted butter, softened
4 ounces cream cheese, softened
4 to 5 tablespoons chopped fresh
   herbs, such as thyme, sage
   and parsley
1 (10- to 12-pound) fresh
   turkey
salt and pepper to taste
1 small apple, quartered
1 carrot, peeled, cut into 1-inch pieces
1 rib celery, cut into 1-inch pieces
2 tablespoons flour
1/3 cup heavy cream
2 tablespoons butter

Combine 2 tablespoons madeira, 1/4 cup butter, cream cheese and herbs in a bowl and mix well. Season the turkey cavity with salt and pepper. Place the apple, carrot and celery in the cavity. Spread the butter mixture underneath the skin of the turkey. Sprinkle the turkey with salt and pepper. Place breast side up on a rack in a roasting pan.

Bake at 425 degrees for 20 minutes. Reduce the oven temperature to 350 degrees. Cover the turkey with foil. Bake for 20 minutes per pound or until cooked through. Uncover the turkey. Increase the oven temperature to 425 degrees. Bake the turkey for 5 to 10 minutes longer or until the skin is crisp. Remove the turkey to a serving platter. Cut into slices.

Drain the roasting pan, reserving 2 cups of pan juices. Dissolve the flour in the cream and 3 tablespoons madeira in a bowl. Heat the reserved pan juices and 2 tablespoons butter in a saucepan until the butter is melted. Stir in the cream mixture. Cook until thickened, stirring constantly. Serve over the sliced turkey.

Yield: 16 to 20 servings

Nana's Doves

10 to 12 doves, dressed
1/2 cup vegetable oil
2 cups beef broth
2 cups white wine

Sear the doves in the vegetable oil in a large Dutch oven until brown. Add 1 cup of the beef broth and 1 cup of the wine. Simmer until the liquid is reduced, basting the doves occasionally. Add the remaining beef broth and wine. Simmer until the doves are tender and cooked through.

Note: Total cooking time is about 3 to 3½ hours. May make gravy to serve with the doves by thickening the pan juices with a small amount of flour.

Yield: 5 to 6 servings

Curried Peanut Duck

6 ducks, dressed
salt and pepper to taste
1 cup ground roasted peanuts
2 teaspoons chopped fresh oregano
1/2 cup olive oil
1 (6-ounce) jar Dijon mustard
1 (12-ounce) jar orange marmalade
2 to 3 tablespoons curry powder, or to taste

Season the ducks with salt and pepper. Pierce the skin with a knife. Place in a glass baking dish. Combine the peanuts, oregano, olive oil, mustard, marmalade and curry powder in a bowl and mix well. Spread over the ducks. Marinate, covered, in the refrigerator for 6 to 8 hours. Bake, uncovered, at 350 degrees for 1 hour or until the ducks are nearly cooked through. Drain the ducks, reserving the marinade. Place the reserved marinade in a saucepan. Bring to a boil. Boil for several minutes. Remove from the heat. Place the ducks on a grill rack. Grill for 10 minutes longer or until cooked through, basting with the heated marinade.

Yield: 6 servings

Cranberry Chutney

This Cranberry Chutney offers a tasty twist on the traditional. Serve as you would a classic cranberry sauce. It is perfect for holidays.

2¹/₂ cups fresh cranberries
2 cups white raisins
1 lemon, thinly sliced
¹/₂ cup thinly sliced onion
1 cup packed brown sugar
2 cups unpasteurized apple cider
¹/₂ cup cider vinegar
6 tablespoons candied ginger, cut
   into small pieces
1 teaspoon dry mustard
1 teaspoon chili powder
¹/₂ teaspoon salt

Combine the cranberries, raisins, lemon, onion, brown sugar, apple cider, vinegar, ginger, dry mustard, chili powder and salt in a large saucepan. Bring to a boil and reduce the heat. Simmer for 35 to 45 minutes or until of the desired consistency, stirring occasionally. Cool. Spoon into an airtight container. Chill, covered, until serving time.

Note: May store in the refrigerator for several weeks.

Yield: 4 to 5 cups

Duck with Blackberry Sauce

3 tablespoons butter
3 tablespoons sugar
¹/₃ cup dry white wine
¹/₃ cup orange juice
2 tablespoons raspberry vinegar
1¹/₄ cups blackberries

1 cup beef broth
³/₄ cup chicken broth
2 tablespoons Cognac
1 tablespoon pure maple syrup
4 boneless duck breast halves with skin
salt and pepper to taste

Melt 2 tablespoons of the butter in a skillet. Add the sugar. Cook for 5 minutes or until the sugar dissolves and turns a dark amber color. Add the wine, orange juice and raspberry vinegar. Boil until the caramel dissolves, stirring constantly. Add the blackberries, beef broth and chicken broth. Boil until reduced to 1 cup. Strain into a small heavy saucepan. Stir in the Cognac and maple syrup.

Pierce the skin of the duck and season with salt and pepper. Heat an ovenproof skillet until hot. Add the duck skin side down. Sear for 5 minutes or until brown. Turn over the duck. Cook for 3 minutes. Place the skillet in the oven. Bake at 400 degrees for 3 minutes or until cooked through.

Bring the sauce to a simmer over low heat. Add the remaining 1 tablespoon butter. Whisk until the butter is melted. Spoon the sauce onto individual serving plates. Cut the duck into slices. Arrange the sliced duck in the sauce.

Yield: 4 servings

Roasted Quail

10 quail, dressed
salt and pepper to taste
$^1/_2$ cup butter
2 tablespoons pressed garlic
1 tablespoon flour
1 pound sliced mushrooms
2 cups white wine
4 chicken bouillon cubes

Season the quail with salt and pepper. Brown the quail in the butter in a heavy cast-iron skillet. Remove the quail to a warm platter. Add the garlic and flour to the skillet. Cook for a few minutes, stirring constantly. Add the mushrooms, wine and bouillon cubes. Cook until the bouillon cubes dissolve, stirring constantly. Return the quail to the skillet. Bake, tightly covered, at 350 degrees for $1^1/_2$ to 2 hours or until very tender.

Yield: 8 to 10 servings

Quail and Rice Casserole

12 quail, dressed
salt and pepper to taste
$^1/_2$ cup butter
$^3/_4$ cup finely chopped celery
$^1/_4$ cup chopped celery leaves
$^1/_3$ cup chopped onion
2 teaspoons chopped parsley
1 teaspoon salt

$^1/_2$ teaspoon dried sage
$^1/_4$ teaspoon dried marjoram
$^1/_8$ teaspoon pepper
$^3/_4$ cup (or more) sauterne
$^1/_4$ cup butter
$1^1/_2$ cups cooked rice
$1^1/_2$ cups chicken stock

Season the quail with salt and pepper to taste. Melt $^1/_2$ cup butter in a skillet. Add the quail. Simmer, covered, for 30 minutes. Sauté the celery, celery leaves, onion, parsley, 1 teaspoon salt, sage, marjoram and $^1/_8$ teaspoon pepper in sauterne and $^1/_4$ cup butter in a skillet until tender-crisp. Add the rice and chicken stock to vegetables. Spoon into a casserole. Add the quail and cover with foil. Bake at 350 degrees for 45 minutes or until the liquid is absorbed and the quail is cooked through.

Note: May substitute 2 chicken bouillon cubes dissolved in $1^1/_2$ cups boiling water for the chicken stock.

Yield: 5 servings

Spring Hill

Spring Hill is just seven miles from downtown Mobile. The area, named for its many springs, first became popular as a summer retreat during the Spanish regime of colonial Mobile. Spring Hill offered a respite from the heat and yellow fever of the city. A resort hotel and several summer homes were subsequently built to take advantage of the lovely atmosphere of this country village.

During the early 1800s, Spring Hill became home to a number of pre-Civil War families. These newcomers built palatial antebellum homes, many of which have been restored and are still standing today. Spring Hill is also home to Spring Hill College, established in 1830. The college is the oldest operating institution of higher learning in Alabama and the oldest Roman Catholic campus in the South.

In the 1930s and 40s, Spring Hill became a popular homesite for many permanent residents. No longer considered the country, Spring Hill was annexed by the city of Mobile in 1956. Expansion and development have continued at a steady pace and today Spring Hill is a vibrant and popular area of Mobile.

Shrimp-Stuffed Quail

 Martha Rutledge Catering

1 medium onion, chopped	2 teaspoons salt
3/4 cup butter	2 teaspoons coarsely ground pepper
9 cups soft bread crumbs	1/2 cup chicken stock
1 cup chopped dried parsley	1/2 cup cream sherry
2 tablespoons chopped fresh rosemary	1/2 cup peeled fresh shrimp, chopped
	6 boneless quail
1 teaspoon chopped fresh sage	6 slices bacon
1 1/2 teaspoons dried summer savory	seasoned salt to taste
	chopped dried rosemary to taste

Sauté the onion in the butter in a large skillet until the onion is opaque. Combine the sautéed onion, bread crumbs, parsley, 2 tablespoons rosemary, sage, summer savory, salt, pepper, chicken stock and sherry in a large bowl and mix well. Add the shrimp and mix well. Spoon into the cavity of the quail. Wrap each quail with a slice of bacon. Sprinkle with seasoned salt and dried rosemary to taste. Place in a greased baking dish. Bake at 350 degrees for 25 to 30 minutes or until the quail are cooked through.

Note: If boneless quail are unavailable, remove the backbone from the quail by cutting through the bottom of the quail using sharp scissors, and leaving the legs intact.

Yield: 3 servings

Venison Medallions in Tomato Mustard Cream

1/4 cup red wine vinegar

1/4 cup red wine

2 tablespoons brandy

2 cloves of garlic, crushed

8 (1-inch-thick) slices venison
    backstrap tenderloin

2 tablespoons olive oil

1 small onion, minced

4 ounces fresh mushrooms, finely
    chopped

1/2 cup chicken stock

1 teaspoon Creole mustard

1 teaspoon tomato paste

1/2 teaspoon dried thyme

1/4 teaspoon dried basil

1 tablespoon minced fresh parsley

1/4 cup heavy cream

2 tablespoons butter, softened

salt and freshly ground pepper
    to taste

Combine the red wine vinegar, red wine, brandy and garlic in a glass dish. Add the venison. Marinate, covered, in the refrigerator for 8 to 10 hours, turning the venison over 1 to 2 times. Drain the venison, reserving 1/2 of the marinade. Remove the venison and pat dry.

Heat the olive oil in a large heavy skillet. Add the venison. Cook over high heat for 2 to 3 minutes on each side or until done to taste. Remove to a warm platter and keep warm.

Add the onion and mushrooms to the skillet. Sauté for 5 minutes. Strain the reserved marinade into the skillet. Add the chicken stock. Bring to a boil. Cook until the mixture is reduced by half. Add the mustard, tomato paste, herbs and cream. Reduce the heat. Cook for 1 to 2 minutes, whisking constantly. Add the butter a small amount at a time, whisking constantly. Season with salt and pepper.

Yield: 4 servings

An Alabama Sportsman's Calendar

January: Deer hunting is in full swing. Avid wingshooters are hunting duck and quail.

February: Deer season is over so die-hard hunters switch to small game, such as squirrel and rabbit. This is also the favorite month for quail hunting, which is considered by some to be the most majestic of all the game birds.

March: Hunters perform "Honey Do's" and wait around until the end of March when turkey season begins.

April: This is "the month" for dedicated turkey hunters, and it is hard to get these folks to do anything or think about anything unless it is related to turkey hunting. (This is very difficult for normal non-turkey hunters to understand.)

May: This is the month most hunters reserve for getting reacquainted with their families—although there are more than a few hunters who get their golf clubs out as soon as their hunting equipment is cleaned and put away. May is also the month when the bream start bedding in the lakes and the cobia start showing up on the coast—so many hunters make an overnight

Pineapple Venison Kabobs

1 cup soy sauce
2 cups pineapple juice
1/2 cup balsamic vinegar
1 cup olive oil
1/4 cup corn syrup
1 tablespoon chopped fresh
   rosemary
2 teaspoons chopped fresh basil
4 cloves of garlic, minced

3 pounds venison tenderloins, cut into
   chunks
1 pineapple, cut into chunks
1 1/2 onions, cut into quarters
12 fresh whole mushrooms
1 1/2 green bell peppers, cut
   into quarters
cooked wild rice

Combine the soy sauce, pineapple juice, vinegar, olive oil, corn syrup, rosemary, basil and garlic in a sealable plastic food storage bag and mix well. Add the venison and seal the bag. Marinate in the refrigerator for 8 to 10 hours. Drain the venison, discarding the marinade.

Alternate the venison, pineapple, onions, mushrooms and green peppers onto 6 skewers, being sure to place the pineapple chunks next to the venison. Place on a grill rack. Grill over medium-high heat until the venison is medium-rare to medium. Do not overcook. Serve over wild rice.

Yield: 6 servings

Venison Steaks with Black Currant Sauce

3 tablespoons vegetable oil
1 tablespoon freshly grated lemon
    peel
2 tablespoons fresh lemon juice
1/2 teaspoon chopped fresh thyme
    leaves, or 1/4 teaspoon
    crumbled dried
    thyme leaves
8 (1/4-pound) boneless venison
    loin steaks

salt and pepper to taste
1/4 cup unsalted butter
1/2 cup red wine vinegar
1 cup fruity red wine, such as beaujolais
    or zinfandel
1/4 cup black currant jam
2 cups rich beef stock
1/4 cup unsalted butter, softened

Whisk the vegetable oil, lemon peel, lemon juice and thyme in a shallow baking dish. Place the venison steaks between 2 sheets of waxed paper. Pound with a meat mallet until the steaks are 1/2 inch thick. Place in a single layer in the marinade, turning to coat well. Marinate, covered, in the refrigerator for 2 to 10 hours, turning occasionally.

Drain the steaks, discarding the marinade. Pat the steaks dry. Season with salt and pepper. Melt 1/2 of the 1/4 cup butter in each of 2 large heavy skillets over high heat. Heat until the foam subsides. Place the steaks in the skillets. Cook for 5 minutes for medium-rare, turning once. Remove to a warm platter and cover to keep warm.

Add half of the vinegar and the wine to each skillet. Cook over high heat, stirring to deglaze the skillets. Combine all the deglazing liquid into 1 of the skillets. Bring to a boil. Boil until the liquid is reduced to 2/3 cup. Whisk in the jam and beef stock. Boil for 2 minutes. Reduce the heat to low. Whisk in 1/4 cup butter 1 tablespoon at a time and any venison juices that have accumulated on the platter. Do not boil. Strain the sauce into a serving bowl. Season with salt and pepper.

Place the venison on heated individual serving plates. Spoon some of the sauce over the venison. Garnish with fresh sprigs of parsley.

Yield: 8 servings

(An Alabama Sportsman's Calendar, continued)

transformation from hunter to fisherman.

June: Freshwater and saltwater fishing is excellent.

July: Saltwater fishing is good. Freshwater fishing slows down due to hotter weather.

August: It is too hot to fish, but most fishermen continue to go anyway just to get outdoors.

September: Hunting season returns! Early season duck hunters get a chance to take blue- or green-winged teal (a marvelous and beautiful duck that tastes out of this world). This is the month dove season opens. Dove season is enjoyed by all, serious wingshooters and ordinary people alike. (The latter seem to go more for the social aspect of the sport.)

October: Dove hunting continues. Deer bowhunting begins, enabling the primitive hunters to get an early shot at harvesting deer before the woods get crowded with gun hunters. Squirrel hunting begins. Wild hogs are also hunted.

November: Deer hunting with guns starts—this is "big game hunting" in the South and perhaps the most popular hunting sport. Quail season also opens, bringing much joy to the fowl hunters.

December: Deer hunting is in full swing and duck season opens, which brings more joy to fowl hunters.

SEAFOOD

Seafood at its finest is shimmering and ultra fresh.
Plump, perfect, pink shrimp straight from the shell or splashed with
a snappy citrus-laced sauce. The sensational smokey flavor of oysters
grilled over glowing, crackling embers until their rocklike shells
pop open, yielding succulent interiors to be gilded lightly with butter.
Lump crabmeat, alabaster-hued, delicate and sweet. Sheer, savory bliss.
The plentiful waters surrounding Mobile are virtually brimming
with glorious seafood. And, as if the exceptional natural abundance was
not fortune enough, there is also the unique phenomenon we call a Jubilee.
It is an astonishing event that occurs along the shores of Mobile Bay—
a joyous, exuberant occasion for both locals and visitors alike.
It happens when the tide turns, most often during the hushed
feltlike darkness of night or the pale, pink-tinged dawn of early morning.
The crabs, shrimp and fish come in droves to the beach and shallow water.
Then the shouts of "Jubilee" resound all around as people scramble
to harvest the copious bounty offered up by the sea.

Photograph sponsored by The Bay Tables *Cookbook Development Committee*

Sunset Suppers on the Wharf

Entertaining, especially during the sultry months of summer, often means a casual supper on the wharf (the name locals use for the private piers built out onto the water). Hot boiled crabs or shrimp, fresh grilled fish and steaming one-pot suppers are all staples of the season. It's a glorious time for friends and family to gather to savor the spectacular evening sunsets. It's an incredible sight to behold— the sky painted in luminous, pastel-swirled hues of cantaloupe, violet and pink as the sun slowly melts into the lapping waves of the Bay. Delicious, balmy breezes whispering off the water make for an enchanting atmosphere in which to indulge in the pleasures of good food and good company.

Photograph sponsored by Alicia Ormond Anderson, Diane Anderson Ireland and Karen Anderson Williams

Fish Facts

There are generally three types of fish: lean, white fish; oily, dark-fleshed fish; and flat fish. White fish are generally interchangeable in recipes as their relative oil content does not vary too much. This group includes snapper, sea bass, trout, grouper, cod, hake, and orange roughy. These fish are generally prepared either whole or filleted.

The dark-fleshed fish are not as easily substituted for one another due to their varying levels of oil content. This group includes mackerel, tuna, salmon, shark, swordfish, mahimahi (dolphin), and pompano. The fish that can typically be interchanged within this group are swordfish and tuna or possibly salmon (which, while it can be prepared in a similar manner, will give a different, yet usually good result). These fish are generally prepared either filleted or in steaks.

The flat fish family is white, has a low oil content, and includes flounder, sole, and turbot. These fish are either prepared whole or filleted and are easily interchangable.

When it comes to cooking fish, there is a general rule that fish steaks should be cooked about 10 minutes per inch of thickness to be cooked through; however, many people prefer their tuna simply seared on each side with the middle remaining rare.

Grilled Red Snapper with Mango Salsa

1/4 cup fresh lime juice
4 tablespoons chopped fresh cilantro
2 teaspoons olive oil
4 red snapper fillets
1/4 teaspoon each salt and pepper
Mango Salsa (below)

Combine the lime juice, 2 tablespoons of the cilantro and olive oil in a large shallow dish and mix well. Place the fish in the marinade, turning to coat. Marinate, covered, in the refrigerator for 30 minutes, turning once.

Drain the fish, discarding the marinade. Sprinkle with salt and pepper. Place in a grilling basket sprayed with nonstick cooking spray. Grill over medium-hot (350- to 400-degree) coals for 10 minutes on each side or until the fish flakes easily.

Place the fish on a serving platter. Spoon Mango Salsa evenly over the top. Sprinkle with the remaining 2 tablespoons cilantro.

Note: Grouper, mahimahi or your favorite fish may be used instead of red snapper.

Yield: 4 servings

Mango Salsa

1 cup chopped Roma tomatoes
1 cup chopped mango
1 tablespoon chopped red onion
1 tablespoon chopped fresh cilantro
1/2 teaspoon each sugar and cumin
1/8 teaspoon each salt and pepper
dash of hot sauce
2 tablespoons fresh lime juice

Mix the tomatoes, mango, red onion, cilantro, sugar, cumin, salt, pepper, hot sauce and lime juice in a medium bowl. Serve at room temperature.

Yield: 2 cups

Baked Flounder with Shrimp

2 pounds small to medium flounder fillets
salt and pepper to taste
$^{1}/_{2}$ pound small shrimp, cooked, peeled, deveined
1 cup thinly sliced leek bulbs
2 tablespoons butter
1 cup heavy cream
2 tablespoons tomato paste
1 tablespoon Dijon mustard
1 teaspoon cornstarch

Season the fish with salt and pepper. Arrange the shrimp on the fish.
Roll up to enclose the shrimp. Place seam side down close together in a
shallow baking dish. Sauté the leeks in the butter in a skillet until softened.
Spoon over the fish. Whisk the cream, tomato paste, Dijon mustard,
cornstarch and salt and pepper in a bowl. Pour over the leeks and fish.
Bake at 350 degrees for 30 minutes.

Note: This dish can be prepared and refrigerated before cooking.

Yield: 6 to 8 servings

The Joy of a Jubilee

"Jubilee" is a popular word in Mobile. It is a biblical term that originally referred to a Hebrew festival held at 50-year intervals to celebrate the deliverance from Egypt. To Roman Catholics, it denotes a year of special indulgence.

Along the shores of Mobile Bay, "Jubilee" refers to another sort of celebration—an exciting phenomenon when a myriad of crab, shrimp, eel, flounder, and other sea creatures head toward the beach, climbing the pilings of piers or, in the case of flounder, swimming to the water's edge. A Jubilee takes place when the oxygen level drops in the water, causing the ocean's bottom-dwellers to head to shore. Jubilees generally occur in June, July and August, but sometimes as late as September. Harbingers of a Jubilee are an overcast day, calm water, running tide, and gentle east wind.

Once folks become aware of the happening, the shouts of "Jubilee" ring out and the news quickly spreads from household to household. Before long a crowd gathers and everyone busily scoops up crab, shrimp, and fish by the hundreds. It's an exhilarating, joyous occasion that brings people together to reap and revel in the bounty of Mobile Bay.

Baked Orange Roughy with Crabmeat Dressing

4 orange roughy fillets
salt and pepper to taste
1/2 cup lemon juice
lemon slices
paprika to taste
Crabmeat Dressing (below)

Rinse the fish and pat dry. Sprinkle with salt and pepper. Place on a greased baking sheet. Pour the lemon juice over the fish. Arrange lemon slices over the fish. Sprinkle with paprika. Bake at 400 degrees or until the fish flakes easily. Arrange the fish on individual serving plates. Spoon the Crabmeat Dressing on top of each fish.

Yield: 4 servings

Crabmeat Dressing

1/4 cup chopped green bell pepper
1/4 cup finely chopped celery
1 cup chopped mushrooms
1/4 cup finely chopped green onions
2 tablespoons butter
1 pound fresh lump crabmeat
1/4 cup dry white wine

Sauté the green pepper, celery, mushrooms and green onions in the butter in a skillet until tender. Add the crabmeat and white wine. Cook until heated through, stirring occasionally. Remove from the heat and keep warm.

Note: May sauté the vegetables in a skillet sprayed with nonstick cooking spray instead of butter to lower calories.

Red Snapper in Tomato Herb Broth

2 cups dry white wine
2 cups water
2 onion slices
2 cloves of garlic, cut into halves
2 (¹/4-inch-thick) fresh ginger
    slices
2 bay leaves

2 fresh thyme sprigs, or 2 pinches of
    crumbled dried thyme
4 (6-ounce) red snapper fillets
salt and pepper to taste
²/3 cup drained, chopped, seeded
    tomatoes
2 tablespoons chopped fresh chives

Bring the first 7 ingredients to a boil in a large deep skillet. Reduce the heat to medium-low. Simmer for 5 minutes. Season the fish with salt and pepper. Add the fish to the broth. Simmer, covered, for 8 minutes or until the fish is opaque in the center. Remove fish to shallow soup bowls. Cover with foil and keep warm. Strain the liquid in the skillet into a saucepan. Bring to a boil. Boil for 8 minutes or until the liquid is reduced to 1¹/2 cups. Stir in the tomatoes and chives. Pour over the fish in the bowls.

Yield: 4 servings

Red Snapper and Pesto Phyllo Packages

³/4 cup Basil Pesto (page 109)
6 (6-ounce) red snapper fillets, cut into quarters
¹/2 cup butter
12 frozen phyllo sheets, thawed

Spread I tablespoon of the Basil Pesto on 1 fish fillet. Top with another fish fillet. Repeat with the remaining fish and Basil Pesto, forming 12 fish sandwiches. Clarify the butter in a small saucepan over medium heat. Place 1 phyllo sheet on a work surface so the long side is parallel to the edge of the work surface, keeping the remaining phyllo sheets covered with a damp towel. Brush lightly with butter. Fold in half from the short side like a book and brush with butter. Place 1 fish stack 2 inches from the bottom edge. Fold the 2-inch border over the fish. Fold in the long sides and roll up to enclose the fish. Place seam side down on a large baking sheet. Brush with butter. Repeat with the remaining ingredients to form 12 packets. Bake at 425 degrees for 15 to 20 minutes or until the fish is firm and the pastry is golden brown. Arrange 2 packets on each individual serving plate.

Yield: 6 servings

How to Clarify Butter

To clarify butter, melt the butter in a small saucepan over low heat until it foams. Remove from the heat and let stand until the milk solids settle to the bottom of the saucepan and the salt crystals settle on the top. Skim off the salt crystals and carefully pour the butter oil into a separate container. Discard the milk solids that have settled to the bottom. Voilà!

Flounder with Lobster, Corn and Cream Sauce

1 lobster tail	$^1/_2$ teaspoon pepper
$^3/_4$ cup white wine	$^1/_2$ teaspoon onion powder
1 tablespoon butter	$^1/_2$ teaspoon garlic powder
4 flounder fillets	1 cup cream
4 green onions, chopped	$^1/_4$ cup cooked fresh corn, slightly cooled
$^1/_2$ teaspoon salt	

Boil the lobster tail in $^1/_2$ cup of the wine in a saucepan. Reduce the heat. Simmer, covered, for 10 minutes. Drain and peel the lobster, reserving 2 tablespoons of the lobster stock. Cut the lobster into medallions and keep warm.

Spread the butter in a baking dish. Arrange the fish in the buttered dish. Pour the remaining $^1/_4$ cup wine over the fish and sprinkle with $^1/_4$ of the green onions. Bake at 400 degrees for 15 minutes. Drain the baking liquid into a saucepan. Reduce the oven temperature to 300 degrees. Turn over the fish and sprinkle with salt, pepper, onion powder and garlic powder. Return to the oven. Bake for 5 minutes. Keep warm.

Add the reserved lobster stock to the baking liquid. Stir in the cream. Boil until the mixture is reduced to a sauce consistency. Add the lobster and corn. Stir in the remaining green onions. Pour over the flounder fillets.

Yield: 4 servings

Battles Wharf Trout Amandine

2 eggs	1 cup melted butter
1/2 cup milk	vegetable oil for frying
6 trout fillets	2 lemons, cut into halves
1 1/2 cups self-rising flour	1/2 to 1 cup sliced almonds, toasted
1 teaspoon salt	1/3 cup minced fresh parsley

Beat the eggs with a fork in a large bowl until fluffy. Add the milk and beat well with a fork. Place the fish in the egg mixture. Let soak for a few minutes. Mix the flour and salt together on a sheet of waxed paper. Remove the fish from the egg mixture 1 at a time and dredge in the flour mixture. Shake off the excess flour mixture. Dredge in the flour mixture again, making sure the fillets are well coated and the excess is shaken off. Place the floured fillets on a sheet of waxed paper.

Heat 6 small serving platters in the oven. Pour a small amount of the melted butter onto each platter and keep warm. Heat 1 1/2 inches of vegetable oil in a cast-iron skillet. Add 2 to 3 of the fillets at a time to the skillet. Do not overcrowd the skillet. Fry until the fillets are golden brown. Place the fried fillets on the warm buttered platters. Squeeze the lemons over the fillets. Sprinkle with toasted almonds. Drizzle with the remaining melted butter and sprinkle with parsley.

Yield: 6 servings

Grilled Catfish with Mustard Sauce

1/4 cup chopped onion	3/4 cup white wine
3 tablespoons butter	1 tablespoon green onion tops
3 tablespoons flour	1/2 teaspoon salt
1/4 teaspoon dry mustard	1/4 teaspoon white pepper
1 1/2 cups milk	10 large catfish fillets
1 1/4 cups shredded cheese	

Sauté the onion in the butter in a skillet until translucent. Stir in the flour and dry mustard. Cook for 1 minute, stirring constantly. Add the milk. Cook until thickened, stirring constantly. Add the cheese. Cook until the cheese melts, stirring constantly. Add the wine, green onion tops, salt and white pepper and mix well. Spray a grill rack or fish basket with nonstick cooking spray. Place the fish on the grill rack or in the fish basket. Grill for 5 to 8 minutes or until the fish flakes easily. Serve with the sauce.

Yield: 8 to 10 servings

The Battle of Mobile Bay

In August, 1864, the Civil War Battle of Mobile Bay ended in a sound defeat for the South and for the future of wooden warships as well. The entrance of Mobile Bay was guarded on the west by Fort Gaines at Dauphin Island and by Fort Morgan on the east. The Southern fleet, under the leadership of Franklin Buchanan, consisted of one ironclad and three wooden ships. David Farragut was the Union commander of 30 ships, both ironclad and wooden, that were poised to strike from the Gulf of Mexico.

As the attack began, Farragut suffered an early loss when the ironclad "Tecumseh" hit an underwater Confederate mine at the mouth of Mobile Bay and quickly sunk. This incident prompted Farragut's famous battle cry, "Damn the torpedoes! Full speed ahead!" The heavily outnumbered Southern fleet was quickly defeated and naval history was made.

The South's last port and link with Europe was lost, and the battle proved that wooden ships were no match for the new ironclads. After his victory in Mobile Bay, Farragut was named the navy's first full admiral.

Weeks Bay Estuary

Weeks Bay is a shallow subestuary of Mobile Bay and is a critical nursery for fish and shellfish. It is also a research and learning facility for interested students. Estuaries come in all shapes and sizes, each unique to its location and climate. Bays, sounds, marshes, swamps, inlets, and sloughs are all examples of estuaries. The community of life found on the land and in the water includes mammals, birds, fish, reptiles, shellfish, and plants, all interacting within a complex food web. Estuaries serve as nature's water treatment facilities, flood control areas, buffers against storm damage, and protection against shoreline erosion. Today more than two-thirds of the commercially important fish and shellfish spawn, grow up, or feed in estuaries.

Pecan-Encrusted Trout

3 cups pecan halves	1 tablespoon Creole seasoning
1 tablespoon walnut oil	6 (7- to 9-ounce) trout fillets
2 tablespoons Creole seasoning	1 1/2 cups flour
2 eggs	1 1/2 cups ground pecans
2 cups heavy cream	1 cup canola oil
2 tablespoons Dijon mustard	Tomato Butter Sauce (below)

Mix the pecan halves, walnut oil and Creole seasoning in a bowl. Place on a baking sheet. Bake at 350 degrees for 10 minutes or until light brown.

Blend the eggs, cream, Dijon mustard and Creole seasoning in a blender until smooth. Pour over the fish in a shallow glass dish. Marinate, covered, in the refrigerator for 30 minutes.

Mix the flour and 1 1/2 cups ground pecans together on a sheet of waxed paper. Dredge the fish in the flour mixture until well coated and shake off the excess. Place 2 fillets at a time in hot oil in a skillet. Fry for 2 to 3 minutes on each side until the fish flakes easily. Remove from the skillet and place on a baking sheet in a warm oven until serving time. Arrange the trout on a serving plate. Top with Tomato Butter Sauce. Sprinkle with the toasted pecans.

Yield: 6 servings

Tomato Butter Sauce

2/3 cup dry white wine
1/2 cup white wine vinegar
1/4 cup minced shallots
2 tablespoons heavy cream
1 1/3 pounds tomatoes, peeled, seeded, chopped, drained
1 1/2 cups cold butter, chopped
1/4 cup fresh lemon juice
salt and pepper to taste

Boil the wine, vinegar and shallots in a saucepan for 5 minutes or until most of the liquid is evaporated. Add the cream and 1/2 of the tomatoes. Return to a boil. Reduce the heat to low. Add the butter 1 piece at a time, cooking until the butter melts before adding any more butter and stirring constantly. Stir in the remaining tomatoes and lemon juice. Season with salt and pepper. Remove from the heat and keep warm until ready to serve.

Yield: 2 1/2 to 3 cups

Dixie Bar Trout

8 to 12 trout fillets
milk
1 teaspoon salt
salt to taste
2/3 cup flour

1 cup butter
1/2 teaspoon Tabasco sauce
1/2 cup finely chopped green onions
1/2 cup finely chopped green pepper
2/3 cup dry white wine

Place the fillets in a shallow dish. Add enough milk to cover and sprinkle with 1 teaspoon salt. Marinate in the refrigerator for 1 hour. Remove the fish and pat dry. Sprinkle generously with salt. Dredge in the flour on waxed paper and shake off the excess. Place 1/2 cup of the butter and Tabasco sauce in a glass baking dish and place on the middle oven rack in a broiler oven. Broil on low until the butter begins to bubble. Remove from the oven. Sprinkle the green onions and green pepper in the butter. Arrange the fillets over the vegetables. Dot with the remaining butter. Return to the broiler oven. Broil for 15 to 20 minutes or until the fillets flake easily and are golden brown, basting 2 times. Remove to a platter and keep warm until serving time. Pour the pan drippings into a saucepan. Add the wine. Bring to a boil over medium heat. Boil for 3 to 4 minutes, stirring constantly. Spoon the sauce over the fillets and serve immediately.

Yield: 8 to 12 servings

Five-Pepper Tuna

5 tablespoons five-pepper blend
4 (8-ounce) tuna steaks
salt to taste
1 tablespoon butter
1 tablespoon olive oil

1/4 cup Cognac
1/2 cup chicken broth
2 tablespoons Dijon mustard
1 cup heavy cream

Crush the pepper blend and spread on a plate or cutting board. Press the tuna steaks into the crushed pepper, turning to coat both sides. Sprinkle steaks with salt. Melt the butter in the oil in a sauté pan over high heat. Add the steaks. Cook for 3 minutes on each side for rare or until the steaks flake easily. Remove the steaks to a warm platter.

Drain the excess oil from the pan. Add the Cognac. Cook over high heat, stirring to deglaze the pan. Add the broth, mustard and cream. Cook until the sauce is reduced by 1/2. Spoon over the tuna steaks and serve.

Yield: 4 servings

Crab Cakes with Mustard Creole Sauce

1 pound fresh lump crabmeat	white pepper to taste
2 tablespoons finely chopped green onions	1 egg white, slightly beaten
1 tablespoon white wine	3 to 4 tablespoons finely crushed saltine crackers
1 tablespoon Dijon mustard	vegetable oil or butter for sautéing
1 tablespoon lemon juice	Mustard Creole Sauce (below)
3 tablespoons mayonnaise	lemon wedges

Combine the crabmeat, scallions, white wine, Dijon mustard, lemon juice, mayonnaise and white pepper in a bowl and mix gently. Add the egg white and enough of the cracker crumbs to hold the mixture together and mix gently. Shape into 4 patties. Sauté in vegetable oil or butter in a skillet for 3 to 4 minutes on each side or until golden brown. Serve with Mustard Creole Sauce and lemon wedges.

Yield: 4 servings

Mustard Creole Sauce

$^1/_4$ cup dry white vermouth	$^1/_2$ teaspoon minced fresh tarragon
1 teaspoon white wine vinegar	$1^1/_2$ teaspoons Creole mustard
1 teaspoon chopped shallot	$^1/_2$ teaspoon Dijon mustard
$^1/_2$ cup heavy cream	1 tablespoon unsalted butter
1 tablespoon chopped, peeled, roasted red bell pepper	salt to taste
	cayenne to taste

Boil the vermouth, white wine vinegar and shallot in a small heavy saucepan until the mixture is reduced to 2 tablespoons. Add the cream, red pepper and tarragon. Boil until thickened and reduced to about $^1/_3$ cup, stirring constantly. Reduce the heat to medium-low. Whisk in the Creole mustard and Dijon mustard. Cook for 30 seconds. Whisk in the butter. Season with salt and cayenne. Keep warm until ready to serve.

Yield: $^1/_2$ cup

Sautéed Soft-Shell Crabs with Macadamia Lime Butter

8 soft shell crabs, cleaned
1 cup flour
1 tablespoon paprika
1 1/2 teaspoons coarse salt
1/2 teaspoon white pepper
4 to 6 tablespoons butter
Macadamia Lime Butter (below)

Rinse the crabs and pat dry. Combine the flour, paprika, salt and white pepper in a shallow bowl and mix well. Dredge the crabs in the flour mixture until well coated. Melt the butter in a large skillet over medium-high heat. Do not burn the butter. Sauté the crabs in batches of 2 or 3 at a time for about 3 minutes on each side or until browned. Remove to a heated platter. Serve with Macadamia Lime Butter.

Yield: 4 servings

Macadamia Lime Butter

1/2 cup butter
1 cup chopped macadamia nuts
2 tablespoons lime juice

Melt the butter in a medium saucepan. Add the nuts. Cook for 2 minutes or until the nuts are light brown. Stir in the lime juice. Remove from the heat.

Yield: 1 1/2 cups

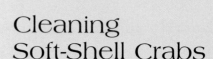

Cleaning Soft-Shell Crabs

Soft-shell crabs are simply the familiar blue crabs that have molted, or shed their shells, and are in the process of growing new ones. Since the entire process takes little more than an hour, the crabs have to be gathered within 15 to 20 minutes after shedding and put on ice to prevent the shell from hardening.

To clean a soft-shell crab, turn the crab on its back with its underside up. Then using kitchen shears, cut across the crab about 1/4 of an inch behind the eyes and mouth. Scoop out and discard the soft material just behind this cut and rinse lightly. Next lift the pointed apron and twist or cut it off. Turn the crab right side up, lift the shell at each point, and remove and discard the spongy, gray gills "dead man's fingers." Replace the top shell. Rinse lightly in cold water and pat dry. Everything left is edible. Cook and enjoy.

Rémoulade Sauce

Rémoulade sauce made its way to the Southern table via France. The French mayonnaise-based sauce was adapted and refashioned by Creole cooks, who added a medley of their own signature ingredients—such as Creole mustard, horseradish, and the occasional dash of Tabasco sauce. This piquant sauce for seafood has many variations, and some recipes have been tightly guarded secrets for generations. It is a great match for crispy-fried soft-shell crabs, and perfect paired with boiled shrimp. It is also terrific on crab claws, and any other seafood.

Fried Soft-Shell Crabs with Rémoulade Sauce

8 soft shell crabs, cleaned
1 egg, beaten
1/2 cup milk
1/2 cup cornmeal
1/2 teaspoon coarse salt
1/2 teaspoon fresh ground pepper
1/4 cup vegetable oil
Rémoulade Sauce (below)

Rinse the crabs and pat dry. Combine the egg and milk in a shallow bowl and beat well. Mix the cornmeal, salt and pepper in a shallow bowl. Dip the crabs in the egg mixture, soaking thoroughly and draining off the excess. Dredge the crabs in the cornmeal mixture until thoroughly coated. Heat the vegetable oil in a large skillet. Add the crabs. Fry for 3 minutes on each side or until crispy golden brown and cooked through. Serve with Rémoulade Sauce.

Yield: 4 servings

Rémoulade Sauce

1/2 cup chili sauce
1/2 cup mayonnaise
3 tablespoons Dijon mustard
2 tablespoons fresh lemon juice
2 tablespoons minced green onions

2 tablespoons drained chopped capers
1 tablespoon prepared horseradish
Tabasco sauce to taste
freshly ground pepper to taste

Combine the chili sauce, mayonnaise, Dijon mustard, lemon juice, green onions, capers, horseradish, Tabasco sauce and pepper in a bowl and mix well. Adjust the seasonings to taste. Store in the refrigerator.

Yield: 3 1/4 cups

Crabmeat Florentine

4 (10-ounce) packages frozen
    spinach
chopped green onions to taste
2 cloves of garlic, minced
1/4 cup butter
1/4 cup flour

2 cups milk
1/4 cup white wine
chopped fresh parsley to taste
2 tablespoons grated Parmesan cheese
salt and white pepper to taste
1 pound jumbo lump crabmeat

Cook the spinach in a saucepan using the package directions and drain
well. Place in a greased 3 quart casserole. Sauté the green onions and garlic
in a small skillet sprayed with nonstick cooking spray until the green onions
are tender. Melt the butter in a saucepan. Stir in the flour. Add the milk
gradually, stirring constantly. Cook until thickened, stirring constantly. Add
the wine, parsley, sautéed green onions, Parmesan cheese, salt and white
pepper. Stir in the crabmeat. Pour over the spinach. Bake at 350 degrees for
45 minutes or until bubbly.

Note: Can also add sautéed mushrooms or artichokes to the
cream sauce.

Yield: 6 to 8 servings

West Indies Salad

1 medium onion, finely chopped
1 pound fresh lump crabmeat
salt and pepper to taste
4 ounces vegetable oil
3 ounces cider vinegar
4 ounces ice water

Spread half the onion over the bottom of a large bowl. Cover with
separated crab lumps and then remaining onion. Season with salt and
pepper. Pour oil, vinegar and ice water over all. Cover and marinate in the
refrigerator for 2 to 12 hours. Toss lightly before serving.

Yield: 4 servings

West Indies Salad

This incredible, cold, crabmeat
creation is a summer specialty in Mobile.
It is sensational served on fresh, ripe
tomato slices or with crackers as an
appetizer. It is outlandishly easy, yet
elegant and truly addicting. The recipe
originated at Bayley's Steak House in
Belle Fontaine, Alabama just outside of
Mobile. The proprietor, William Bayley
(better known as Bill), concocted this
beloved taste treat after traveling through
the Cayman Islands. During his time in
the tropics, he tasted what he thought was
the best salad he had ever eaten but felt it
was missing something—fresh crabmeat.
So upon his return, Bayley worked up his
version of the salad using local blue crabs
and dubbed the dish after the British West
Indies islands of the Caymans. (West
Indies Salad is not Bayley's only claim
to culinary fame; he is also credited
with creating another local favorite, fried
crab claws.)

At left is the recipe Bill Bayley
submitted to Recipe Jubilee, the Junior
League of Mobile's first cookbook, back in
the early 1960s.

Oysters

Oysters are a luxury you either love or loathe. Originally a food of the poor, oysters became fashionable and expensive as they became scarce. They might have disappeared altogether in Europe if a French marine biologist had not developed the means to raise them artificially.

Most American oysters, unlike those in Europe, are harvested in the wild. They are usually named for the area where they are caught—Blue Point, Wellfleet, Chincoteague, Appalachicola, and Bon Secour, for example. On the West Coast, the Pacific, or Japanese oyster, is the most common. The Olympia, another Pacific oyster, is the only one native to the West Coast.

European oysters are all farmed by aquaculture. The best British oysters include the Whitstable, the Colchester, and the Helford. They all have rounded shells and a subtle flavor. In France, this type is known as Belon, a

Broiled Oysters in Parsley Sauce

1 quart oysters
1 bunch fresh parsley, stems removed
3 cloves of garlic
8 ounces sliced fresh mushrooms
1 cup butter, softened
1 teaspoon salt
1 teaspoon pepper
$1/4$ teaspoon nutmeg
1 cup bread crumbs

Sauté the undrained oysters in a saucepan until the edges curl. Remove from the heat and drain well. Place the drained oysters in a large shallow gratin dish.

Blend the parsley, garlic and mushrooms in a food processor until the parsley is finely chopped. Add the butter, salt, pepper and nutmeg and blend well. Add the bread crumbs and blend well.

Spread the sauce over the oysters. Broil until brown and bubbly.

Yield: 6 to 8 servings

Oysters Johnny Reb

$1/2$ cup finely chopped parsley
$1/2$ cup chopped green onions
2 tablespoons lemon juice
Tabasco sauce to taste
$1/2$ cup melted butter or margarine
1 tablespoon Worcestershire sauce
2 cups fine cracker crumbs
salt and pepper to taste
2 quarts oysters, drained
6 tablespoons half-and-half
6 tablespoons milk
paprika to taste

Combine the parsley, green onions, lemon juice, Tabasco sauce, butter, Worcestershire sauce, 2 cups cracker crumbs, salt and pepper in a bowl to make a crumb mixture.

Alternate layers of oysters and crumb mixture in a greased shallow 2-quart baking dish.

Pour a mixture of the half-and-half and milk over the top. Sprinkle with paprika. Bake at 375 degrees for 30 minutes.

Yield: 10 to 15 servings

Baked Oysters

1/4 cup butter
1/4 cup olive oil
1 cup Italian bread crumbs
1/2 teaspoon salt
1/2 teaspoon pepper
pinch of cayenne
1/2 teaspoon dried tarragon
1/2 teaspoon dried oregano
2 tablespoons minced parsley
2 teaspoons minced garlic
1/4 cup sliced green onions
1 pint oysters, drained

Melt the butter in a small heavy saucepan over low heat. Add the olive oil and blend well. Add the bread crumbs, salt, pepper, cayenne, tarragon, oregano, parsley, garlic and green onions and mix well. Remove from the heat. Place the oysters in a 9-inch round gratin dish. Cover the oysters evenly with the bread crumb mixture. Bake at 425 degrees for 20 to 25 minutes or until the edges of the oysters curl and the topping is brown.

Note: May place in individual ramekins and bake for 15 to 20 minutes or until the edges of the oysters curl and the topping is brown.

Yield: 2 to 3 servings

(Oysters, continued)

relative of the American Olympia oyster. The second type eaten in France, known as the rock oyster, is the Pacific Oyster in America. These have elongated shells and a sharper, more oceanic flavor. In Portugal, the Portuguese oyster is being supplanted by the Pacific or Japanese oyster, which is thought to be finer.

Oysters come in many sizes, and not everyone prefers the largest ones. There are stringent regulations to keep oysters safe from pollution.

Oysters on the half-shell can be accompanied by a few drops of Tabasco sauce, a standard horseradish-tinged cocktail sauce, or red wine vinegar with a few chopped shallots afloat in it, and a generous supply of lemon wedges.

Oysters are at their best during the colder months. In the summer, as the sea warms, they may start breeding and can be milky, fat, and soft. This accounts for the admonition to avoid oysters during the months with names that do not contain an "r".

Scallops in Parchment

60 to 80 sea scallops

2 large Vidalia onions, peeled, cut
    into 6 wedges

2 small red bell peppers, cut into
    $^1/_4$-inch strips

2 small yellow bell peppers, cut
    into $^1/_4$-inch strips

60 sugar snap peas, trimmed

12 medium cloves of garlic, minced

12 tablespoons butter

12 tablespoons dry white wine

4 tablespoons fresh lemon juice

$1^1/_4$ teaspoons Old Bay
    seasoning

12 sprigs of fresh thyme

Rinse the scallops under cold running water. Remove any adjoining tendons and discard. Pat the scallops dry with paper towels.

Cut baking parchment into 12 equal squares. Fold the parchment squares in half crosswise forming a triangle. Divide the onions, red peppers, yellow peppers, sugar snap peas, scallops and garlic into 12 equal portions.

Arrange 1 portion of each of the vegetables, scallops and garlic near the fold of each triangle. Place 1 tablespoon of the butter on top of each. Sprinkle each with 1 tablespoon of the wine and 1 teaspoon of the lemon juice. Sprinkle the scallops with Old Bay seasoning. Top each with a sprig of thyme. Fold the edges together, sealing the package. Spread the parchment packages well with additional butter. Place seam side down on baking sheets sprayed with nonstick cooking spray.

Bake at 400 degrees for 12 to 15 minutes or until the parchment puffs. Garnish each packet with a sprig of parsley and a lemon slice.

Yield: 12 servings

Jumbo Sea Scallops Cajun-Marsala

 Bienville Bistro

1 tablespoon olive oil
1 tablespoon peanut oil
3 fresh jumbo sea scallops
1/3 cup scallop juice
2 cloves of garlic, minced
1/2 teaspoon Seafood Magic
    seasoning

1/2 teaspoon flour
2 ounces marsala
juice of 1/2 lemon
1/3 cup heavy cream
1 sprig of parsley, chopped

Heat the olive oil and peanut oil in a medium sauté pan over medium heat. Add the sea scallops and scallop juice. Sauté for 3 minutes. Add the garlic. Sauté for 1 minute. Sprinkle with Seafood Magic and toss to coat. Sprinkle with flour and toss to coat. Add the wine. Simmer for 1 minute. Add the lemon juice. Cook for 1 minute, stirring constantly. Add the cream. Simmer for 2 minutes or until the liquid is reduced, stirring constantly. Remove from the heat. Pour into a shallow bowl. Sprinkle with parsley.

Yield: 1 appetizer serving

Scallops Niçoise

1 pound tomatoes (2 or 3)
3 tablespoons unsalted butter
1 1/2 teaspoons peeled crushed
    garlic
1/2 cup dry white wine

1 teaspoon salt
1/2 teaspoon freshly ground pepper
1 1/2 pounds medium sea scallops
1 cup shredded basil leaves

Plunge the tomatoes into a saucepan of boiling water. Let stand submerged for 15 to 20 seconds. Drain and cool under cold water. Peel the tomatoes. Cut the tomatoes into halves horizontally. Squeeze gently, pressing out the seeds and excess juice. Cut the tomatoes into 1/2- to 1-inch pieces.

Melt the butter in a large saucepan. Add the garlic. Sauté for 5 to 10 seconds. Add the wine, salt and pepper. Cook, covered, for 1 minute. Add the scallops and tomatoes. Bring to a boil over high heat, shaking the saucepan occasionally. Cook for 1 1/2 minutes or until the scallops are cooked through. Add the basil and toss to coat. Serve immediately on warm individual serving plates.

Yield: 6 servings

Crawfish Divine

1 medium onion, chopped
1 bunch green onions, chopped
1 green bell pepper, chopped
1 cup butter
1 tablespoon Creole seasoning
$^{1}/_{2}$ tablespoon cayenne
$^{1}/_{2}$ tablespoon white pepper
1 pound crawfish tails
1 cup white wine
1 cup heavy cream

Sauté the onion, green onions and green pepper in the butter in a skillet until the onion is translucent. Add the Creole seasoning, cayenne and white pepper. Cook for 1 minute. Add the crawfish tails and white wine. Simmer, covered, for 25 minutes. Add the cream. Simmer for 5 minutes, stirring constantly. Serve over hot cooked rice.

Yield: 4 servings

Shrimp Creole

1 1/2 tablespoons bacon drippings
1 1/2 tablespoons flour
1 onion, finely chopped
1/2 green bell pepper, finely chopped
2 ribs celery, finely chopped
1 (8-ounce) can tomato sauce
1 (16-ounce) can Italian plum
    tomatoes with basil
1 clove of garlic, minced

3 dashes of Tabasco sauce
2 tablespoons Worcestershire sauce
1 teaspoon sugar
2 teaspoons salt
1/4 teaspoon pepper
1/2 cup chopped fresh parsley
1 bunch chopped green onions
2 1/2 pounds fresh, peeled shrimp

Heat the bacon drippings in a skillet. Add the flour, stirring constantly. Cook until the mixture is a dark golden brown, stirring constantly. Add the onion, green pepper and celery. Cook until the vegetables are tender. Add the tomato sauce and tomatoes and mix well. Add the garlic, Tabasco sauce, Worcestershire sauce, sugar, salt and pepper. Simmer for 30 minutes. Add the parsley and green onions. Simmer for 30 minutes. Add the shrimp. Cook for 3 minutes or until the shrimp turn pink. Serve over hot cooked rice.

Yield: 4 to 6 servings

Shrimp

The number of ways to prepare shrimp is limited only by one's imagination—and there are several varieties of shrimp with which to be creative. Most common on the Gulf Coast are Gulf brown, Gulf white, and royal reds. There is not much difference between the brown and white varieties, but some believe the white peel more easily. Gulf white shrimp also have longer whiskers, tend to be larger, and are a tad more expensive. The royal reds are big, light maroon-colored shrimp which come from the deep Gulf waters and have large heads. Despite subtle differences, most would be hard-pressed to tell them apart by taste alone.

Shrimp are high in vitamins and minerals, and are a natural source of iodine. They are low in saturated fats and contain omega-three fatty acids, known to be good for a healthy heart.

The most common mistake made in cooking shrimp is overcooking them, which makes shrimp tough and hard to peel. To properly boil shrimp, bring the water and seasonings to a boil, add the shrimp, and watch for the shrimp to float to the top or the water to return to a boil. Then remove from the heat, add ice to prevent further cooking, and let the shrimp soak in the cooled water, absorbing the flavors, for about 10 minutes.

Champagne Shrimp with Ginger

4 cloves of garlic, finely chopped
3 tablespoons freshly grated gingerroot
6 tablespoons butter
pinch of fine sea salt
pinch of sugar
2 cups Champagne
1 pound (20-count) large shrimp, peeled, deveined
steamed jasmine rice or white rice
2 tablespoons finely chopped basil
2 tablespoons green onion curls

Combine the garlic, ginger, butter, sea salt and sugar in a large skillet and mix well. Cook over medium heat for 4 minutes or until the garlic is tender. Add the Champagne. Bring to a simmer. Simmer for 10 minutes or until the mixture is reduced to 1 cup. Add the shrimp in a single layer. Cook for 4 minutes or until the shrimp turn pink, stirring occasionally. Spoon shrimp and sauce over the jasmine rice in shallow bowls. Sprinkle with basil and green onion curls.

Note: For green onion curls, cut the green onions into 2-inch-long pieces. Slice each piece into thin slivers. Place in a bowl of ice water for 15 minutes. The green onion slivers will curl by themselves.

Yield: 4 servings

C.J.'s Shrimp

1/4 cup olive oil
2 pounds fresh shrimp, peeled, deveined
2 bay leaves
1 teaspoon salt
1/2 tablespoon chopped fresh rosemary
6 to 8 cloves of garlic, crushed
1 teaspoon freshly ground pepper
2 teaspoons chopped fresh oregano
1/4 cup dry white wine

Heat the olive oil in a sauté pan. Add the shrimp, bay leaves, salt, rosemary, garlic, pepper and oregano. Sauté over low heat for 5 minutes or until the shrimp turn pink. Add the wine. Simmer for 10 minutes. Remove the bay leaves and discard. Serve with crusty French bread or focaccia to dip in the sauce.

Yield: 4 servings

Loretta's Shrimp and Grits

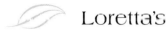 Loretta's

3 slices bacon
1 pound peeled shrimp
1 teaspoon chopped garlic
1/4 cup white wine or sherry
1/2 cup cream
cooked grits

Fry the bacon in a skillet until crisp-fried and crumbly. Remove the bacon to paper towels to drain. Crumble the bacon. Remove the excess bacon drippings from the skillet. Add the shrimp, garlic and crumbled bacon to the skillet. Cook for 3 minutes, stirring occasionally. Add the wine, stirring to deglaze the skillet. Cook for 3 minutes. Add the cream. Cook until thickened, stirring constantly. Serve over hot cooked grits.

Yield: 2 to 4 servings

Blessing of the Fleet

Bayou La Batre, the seafood capital of Alabama, is located just south of Mobile near the Gulf of Mexico. Each May the fishermen gather for the "Blessing of the Fleet" celebration. Shrimp trawlers, oyster boats, and other crafts are decorated with colorful flags and pennants for the festive occasion. The Archbishop offers prayers for the protection of the fishermen and their boats and for a bountiful harvest. Following the annual blessing, the boats join in a parade down the bayou.

The celebration continues on land with seafood cooking contests, live music and entertainment, arts and crafts, and childrens' activities.

Jazz Up Your Boiled Shrimp Dinners

To add depth to a typical Mobile boiled shrimp meal, add your favorites to the same pot in which the shrimp are to be cooked. Various ingredients must be added according to how long they need to cook. Possibilities include small new potatoes, corn on the cob, a variety of smoked sausages, hot dogs for the children, crawfish, and blue crabs. Piling it all in a huge bowl in the center of a cloth- or paper-covered table makes an attractive, festive, and abundant meal.

One-Pot Boil

2 packages crab boil
1/2 cup olive oil
2 pounds small red potatoes
10 ears of corn, shucked
4 pounds Conecuh County smoked
    sausage
5 pounds large shrimp

Add the crab boil and olive oil to a large stockpot of boiling water. Add the potatoes. Boil for 10 minutes. Add the corn on the cob and sausage. Boil for 5 minutes. Add the shrimp. Boil for 5 minutes or until the shrimp turn pink. Drain and serve.

Yield: 10 servings

Sautéed Shrimp with Artichoke Sauce

 The Pillars

28 extra-large shrimp, peeled,
    deveined
Creole seasoning to taste
2 cups extra-fine cracker meal
1/4 cup olive oil
1/4 cup butter
3 green onions, thinly sliced
12 canned artichoke hearts,
    chopped, drained

1/2 cup dry white wine
1 cup heavy cream
dash of cayenne
salt and freshly ground black pepper
    to taste
2 tablespoons chopped fresh
    parsley

Sprinkle the shrimp with Creole seasoning. Dredge the shrimp in the cracker meal on waxed paper. Heat the olive oil in a skillet over medium-high heat. Add the shrimp in batches to the skillet. Sauté each batch until golden brown on each side. Remove to a platter and keep warm until the last batch of shrimp has been sautéed.

Heat the butter in a skillet. Add the green onions. Sauté until the green onions are soft, but not brown. Add the artichoke hearts and wine. Simmer for 5 minutes or until heated through. Stir in the cream. Season with cayenne, salt and black pepper.

Arrange the shrimp on individual serving plates. Spoon the sauce over the shrimp. Sprinkle with parsley.

Yield: 4 servings

Citrus Grilled Shrimp

1 1/2 pounds fresh jumbo shrimp	1/4 cup chopped fresh cilantro
1/3 cup fresh grapefruit juice	1/4 cup chopped fresh mint
1/4 cup fresh orange juice	1/4 teaspoon salt
2 tablespoons fresh lime juice	1/4 teaspoon pepper

Peel and devein the shrimp, leaving the tails intact. Combine the grapefruit juice, orange juice, lime juice, cilantro, mint, salt and pepper in a shallow glass dish. Add the shrimp and toss well. Marinate, covered, in the refrigerator for 30 minutes. Drain the shrimp, discarding the marinade.

Arrange the shrimp evenly on 4 metal skewers. Spray the grill rack with nonstick cooking spray. Place the skewers of shrimp on the grill rack. Grill, with the grill lid down, over medium-hot (350 to 400 degrees) coals for 3 minutes per side or until the shrimp turn pink. Serve over hot cooked rice.

Yield: 4 servings

Coconut Beer Shrimp

1 pound medium shrimp, peeled, with tails on	1 (12-ounce) can beer
2 tablespoons lemon juice	1 cup shredded coconut
2 cups flour	vegetable oil for frying
1 tablespoon paprika	1/2 cup orange marmalade
1 teaspoon salt	1/2 cup honey
1 tablespoon salt	lemon wedges

Pat the shrimp dry and place in a shallow bowl. Drizzle with the lemon juice. Let stand for 15 minutes. Mix 1 cup of the flour, paprika and 1 teaspoon salt in a shallow bowl. Combine the remaining 1 cup flour, 1 tablespoon salt, beer and coconut in a bowl and mix well. Dredge the shrimp in the flour mixture. Dip the floured shrimp in the batter and coat well. Fry in hot oil in a skillet until golden brown. Combine the orange marmalade and honey in a bowl and mix well. Spoon into a small serving bowl. Serve shrimp with orange honey mixture and lemon wedges.

Yield: 2 to 4 servings

Jimmy Buffett

Jimmy Buffett, songwriter, popular musician, novelist, environmentalist, sailor, and pilot, is one of Mobile's favorite sons. He was born as William James Buffett on Christmas Day in 1946 in Pascagoula, Mississippi. Reared in Mobile, Buffett attended Catholic Schools. In addition to playing in the school band, he also served as a varsity cheerleader. He began his musical career by playing guitar and singing in the bars in downtown Mobile. Buffett attended Auburn University and graduated from the University of Southern Mississippi in 1969 with a degree in history.

While waiting for his big break, Buffett worked in Nashville writing articles for Billboard Magazine. *About the same time that he signed a recording contract with Barnaby Records, Buffett was appearing with a group called "The New Generation." He later formed what is now known as the "Coral Reefer Band."*

Buffet released his first album in 1970. He hit the pop charts in 1974 with the hit single "Come Monday" from his second album, but perhaps his best known song is "Margaritaville." From there, he went on to release 24 more albums and is still recording today. Of these albums, four went gold and of these, three went platinum. And while the rest of the world may have their infamous Elvis sightings, Mobilians are more satisfied with real-life Jimmy Buffett sightings.

Hurricanes

Hurricanes, or the impending threat thereof, are an annual occurrence in Mobile and along the Gulf Coast. Hurricane season begins June 1 and is heralded with a flurry of free hurricane-tracking charts and other related paraphernalia. The season ends November 1. Today, thanks to modern technology, we are able to follow hurricanes on television from their birth off the coast of Africa until they, with any luck, fade away in the cold waters of the north Atlantic.

Hurricanes come to be known by names and each grows to have an individual personality. Some are unpredictable, dancing on and off the shore, changing direction on a whim. Others are more focused, gaining strength and speed as they crash onto shore, their path never varying.

Before the days of meticulous, Doppler-aided tracking, the hurricanes of 1906, 1916, and 1926 roared into Mobile without much warning. Many people drowned, buildings were destroyed, and many low-lying areas were cut off from fresh water, food,

Sautéed Shrimp with Lemon Sauce

1 pound shrimp, peeled, deveined
3 tablespoons olive oil
2 cloves of garlic, finely minced
1/4 cup fresh lemon juice
1 tablespoon finely chopped parsley
1/2 to 1 teaspoon salt
1/8 teaspoon white pepper, or 1/4 teaspoon black pepper

Rinse the shrimp. Drain and pat dry. Heat the olive oil in a large skillet over low heat. Increase the heat to high. Add the shrimp. Cook until the shrimp turn pink. Reduce the heat to medium. Add the garlic, lemon juice and parsley. Cook for 1 minute. Sprinkle with salt and white pepper. Remove to a warm platter. Serve warm with pita or French bread.

Yield: 2 to 4 servings

Shrimp with Crabmeat and Blue Cheese

2 pounds large shrimp, peeled, deveined
1/2 cup butter, softened
3 ounces cream cheese, softened
1 ounce blue cheese, softened
1/2 pound fresh lump crabmeat
1 tablespoon lemon juice
1 1/2 teaspoons fresh parsley
1 tablespoon grated onion
5 drops of Tabasco sauce
dash of pepper

Rinse the shrimp. Drain and pat dry. Cut the shrimp into halves lengthwise. Arrange the shrimp in individual ramekins. Beat the butter, cream cheese, blue cheese and crabmeat in a bowl until creamy. Add the lemon juice, parsley, onion, Tabasco sauce and pepper and mix well. Spoon over the shrimp. Bake at 375 degrees for 15 to 20 minutes or until the shrimp turn pink. Serve with French bread.

Yield: 8 servings

Crab-Stuffed Pastry Shrimp with Plum Relish

 Adam's Mark Hotel

1/2 sheet frozen puff pastry
6 (16- to 20-count) shrimp
1 ounce lump crabmeat
juice of 1/2 lemon
salt and pepper to taste
2 smoked Gouda cheese slices, cut into 1/2x1-inch strips
Plum Relish (below)

Let the puff pastry stand at room temperature for 5 minutes or until thawed. Cut the pastry into 3/4x4-inch strips.

Peel and devein the shrimp, leaving the tails intact. Butterfly the shrimp to form a pocket.

Combine the crabmeat, lemon juice and salt and pepper in a bowl and mix well.

Spoon the stuffing into the shrimp pocket. Arrange the cheese over the stuffing. Wrap a puff pastry strip around each stuffed shrimp to enclose. Arrange on a baking sheet sprayed with nonstick cooking spray. Bake at 350 degrees for 10 minutes or until golden brown. Serve with Plum Relish.

Yield: 2 servings

Plum Relish

2 medium plums
3 tablespoons orange marmalade
3 tablespoons brandy

Cut the plums into halves and remove the pit. Chop the plums coarsely. Sauté the plums in a skillet over medium heat until heated through. Add the orange marmalade. Cook until the marmalade is melted. Add the brandy, stirring to deglaze the skillet. Do not overcook. Spoon into a serving bowl.

Yield: about 1/2 cup

(Hurricanes, continued)

and aid for weeks. The most powerful storms of recent years to affect Mobile were Hurricane Camille in 1969, which hit near Biloxi, Mississippi but flooded Mobile, Hurricane Frederic in 1979 which did extensive damage to all parts of the city, and Hurricane Danny in 1997 which dropped over 40 inches of rain in two days.

DESSERTS

Sumptuous sweets have long been a staple of Southern hospitality.
It can be something as simple as fresh, dew-dappled blackberries dashed
with cream or sweet, plump figs gobbled greedily from a backyard tree.
Or it can be as opulent as a great-grandmother's heirloom gâteau
or an exceedingly elegant, involved chocolate confection.
Dessert means many things to many people—and everyone has
his or her own favorite memories. The first frosty lick of the dasher lifted
from the homemade, hand-cranked ice cream—cold, lush and creamy.
The unforgettable fragrance of warm, rich cake fresh from the oven.
The joy of coupling just-baked cookies with a great big glass
of ice-cold milk.
And if you close your eyes you can almost envision the
hulking mahogany sideboard dressed with lacy doilies and heirloom silver
all laden with desserts of every description—pies, cakes, custards
and candies—it's the timeless setting for countless family gatherings
and special occasions.
Dessert is the proverbial icing on the cake. It's that little something extra
that sweetens life and brings a smile to every face.

Photograph sponsored by Ann Blackburn Faulkner, Chairman, One of a Kind, *1977-1981*

Photograph sponsored by Kate Blanton Dempsey, Lynn Mosher Fondren, Betty Hyder Stone and Cynthia Sconyers Tindell

Oakleigh

The stately Oakleigh mansion is a fine example of the Greek Revival style of architecture. The elegant and imposing house was built by James W. Roper, a Mobile merchant, in 1833—a time when Mobile was fast becoming a great cotton port.

The house once sat in the midst of a generous 33-acre parcel of land; however, much of the land was developed after the Civil War. Oakleigh is now surrounded by the well-kept houses of the Oakleigh Garden Historic District. Since 1955, Oakleigh has been owned by the City of Mobile. It is leased to the Historic Mobile Preservation Society as their headquarters and is open to the public. Oakleigh is at its most enchanting during the holiday season when the Preservation Society holds "Candlelight Christmas at Oakleigh," a festive event that lasts several days, and during the spring when all the magnificent azaleas are abloom.

Strawberry Pecan Shortcakes

$1^1/_2$ cups flour

$^1/_3$ cup sugar

$2^1/_4$ teaspoons baking powder

$^1/_2$ teaspoon baking soda

$^1/_4$ teaspoon salt

6 tablespoons chilled unsalted
    butter, chopped

1 cup pecan halves

$^3/_4$ cup plus 3 tablespoons buttermilk

$^3/_4$ teaspoon vanilla extract

sugar to taste

3 pints strawberries, sliced

6 tablespoons sugar

sweetened whipped cream

Mix the flour, $^1/_3$ cup sugar, baking powder, baking soda and salt in a food processor. Add the butter and process until coarse crumbs form. Add the pecans and process until chopped. Place in a large bowl.

Mix $^3/_4$ cup buttermilk and vanilla in a glass measure. Add to the flour mixture, mixing with a fork until a moist dough forms, adding the remaining 3 tablespoons buttermilk only if needed. Drop the dough by rounded $^1/_3$ cupfuls 3 inches apart onto a baking sheet lined with parchment paper. Sprinkle the top of each biscuit with sugar. Bake at 375 degrees for 15 minutes or until golden brown. Remove to a wire rack to cool.

Combine the strawberries and 6 tablespoons sugar in a large bowl and mix gently. Let stand for 15 minutes or longer. Split the warm biscuits into halves. Place the biscuit bottoms in individual shallow bowls. Spoon $^1/_2$ of the strawberry mixture over the biscuit bottoms. Spoon a dollop of sweetened whipped cream over each and top with the biscuit tops. Spoon the remaining strawberry mixture over the tops. Serve immediately.

Yield: 6 servings

Phyllo Baskets with Lemon Curd and Raspberries

1/2 teaspoon unflavored gelatin
1 to 2 tablespoons cold water
1 cup sugar
3 eggs
1 egg yolk
1/2 cup butter
6 tablespoons fresh lemon juice
Phyllo Baskets (below)
1 pint fresh raspberries

Sprinkle the gelatin over the cold water in a cup. Let stand for 10 minutes or until softened. Combine the sugar, eggs, egg yolk, butter and lemon juice in a medium saucepan. Cook over low heat until the butter melts, whisking constantly. Cook for 5 minutes or until thickened to the consistency of lightly whipped cream, whisking constantly. Pour into a bowl. Stir in the gelatin. Chill, covered, for 4 hours or until set.

Spoon the lemon curd into Phyllo Baskets. Top with fresh raspberries. Note: The lemon curd can be prepared up to 2 days ahead.

Yield: 12 servings

Phyllo Baskets

4 sheets frozen phyllo dough
1/4 cup melted butter

Place 1 sheet of phyllo on a work surface and brush with butter, keeping the remaining sheets covered with a damp towel. Top with another sheet of phyllo and brush with butter. Repeat the layering and stacking process with the remaining phyllo sheets and butter. Cut the layered stack into twelve 4-inch squares. Brush every other muffin cup in two 12-cup muffin pans with butter. Place 1 phyllo square into each buttered muffin cup. The corners can stick up. Bake at 350 degrees for 10 minutes or until golden brown and crisp.

Note: Phyllo baskets can be made up to 2 days ahead and stored in an airtight container.

Yield: 12 servings

Meringues

Meringues are elegant, ultra easy, and fat-free! They are delicious all by themselves or for an extra-special dessert—crush the tops and fill with whipped cream or ice cream and fresh fruit.

> 4 egg whites
> 1 cup sugar
> 1 teaspoon white vinegar
> 1 teaspoon vanilla extract

Beat the egg whites at high speed in a large bowl until stiff but not dry. Add the sugar gradually, beating constantly at low speed. Fold in the vinegar and vanilla. Drop by spoonfuls onto a baking sheet lined with parchment paper. Bake at 275 degrees for 50 to 60 minutes. Remove from the paper at once.

Note: May make 1 large circle or oval ring.

Yield: 20 meringues

Chocolate Kahlúa Cheesecake

1 cup graham cracker crumbs	1 cup sour cream
1 tablespoon sugar	2 tablespoons heavy cream
1 tablespoon baking cocoa	1 cup sugar
1 teaspoon cinnamon	3 eggs
1/2 teaspoon instant coffee	1 cup semisweet chocolate chips
1/4 cup melted unsalted butter	1/2 cup Kahlúa
24 ounces cream cheese, softened	2 teaspoons vanilla extract

Combine the graham cracker crumbs, 1 tablespoon sugar, baking cocoa, cinnamon and coffee powder in a bowl and mix well. Add the butter and mix well. Press into a 3x8-inch springform pan.

Beat the cream cheese and sour cream in a mixer bowl until light and fluffy. Blend in the cream. Add 1 cup sugar and beat until fluffy. Add the eggs 1 at a time, beating at low speed until blended after each addition.

Melt the chocolate chips in a double boiler over hot water. Cool slightly. Add the Kahlúa gradually, stirring constantly. Add to the cream cheese mixture gradually, beating constantly. Stir in the vanilla. Pour into the prepared pan. Bake at 325 degrees for 50 minutes. Turn off the oven. Let the cheesecake stand in the oven with the oven door ajar for 1 hour. Cool to room temperature. Chill in the refrigerator.

Yield: 12 servings

Pumpkin Cheesecake

$^1/_3$ cup butter, softened

$^1/_3$ cup sugar

1 egg

$1^1/_4$ cups flour

16 ounces cream cheese, softened

$^3/_4$ cup sugar

2 cups mashed cooked pumpkin

1 teaspoon cinnamon

$^1/_4$ teaspoon ginger

$^1/_2$ teaspoon nutmeg

dash of salt

2 eggs, beaten

Beat the butter and $^1/_3$ cup sugar in a bowl until light and fluffy. Add the egg and beat well. Beat in the flour. Reserve 1 to 2 tablespoonfuls of the dough. Spread the remaining dough over the bottom and 2 inches up the side of a 9-inch springform pan. Bake at 400 degrees for 5 minutes. Remove from the oven. Decrease the oven temperature to 350 degrees.

Beat the cream cheese and $^3/_4$ cup sugar in a bowl until smooth. Add the pumpkin, cinnamon, ginger, nutmeg and salt and mix well. Beat in the eggs. Pour into the prepared pan. Shape the reserved dough into a leaf and arrange on top of the filling. Bake for 50 minutes or until set.

Yield: 8 to 10 servings

Individual Chocolate Lava Cakes

1 cup unsalted butter

8 ounces semisweet chocolate

4 egg yolks

5 eggs

1 cup sugar

1 cup (slightly heaping) flour, sifted

Microwave the butter and chocolate in a glass bowl for 2 minutes or until melted. Remove and stir until smooth.

Whip the egg yolks, eggs and sugar in a bowl until tripled in volume. Add the chocolate mixture gradually, whisking constantly. Whisk in the flour until smooth.

Butter eight 6-ounce metal or ceramic molds. Add the batter filling $^1/_4$ inch from the top of the molds. Bake at 500 degrees for 7 to 8 minutes. Remove from the oven. Let stand for 2 minutes to cool slightly. Unmold onto individual serving plates. Garnish with confectioners' sugar or whipped cream.

Yield: 4 servings

Peaches in Wine

4 cups sliced fresh peaches
2 cups dry red wine
3 tablespoons sugar
fresh mint, garnish

Mix the peaches, wine and sugar in a glass bowl. Chill, covered, for 6 hours or longer. Garnish with sprigs of fresh mint before serving.

Yield: 6 servings

Chocolate Espresso Pots de Creme

 ## Bienville Bistro

2¹/₂ cups whipping cream, chilled
4 teaspoons instant espresso powder
5 ounces bittersweet chocolate, finely chopped
6 egg yolks
2 tablespoons sugar
1 teaspoon vanilla extract
pinch of salt
chocolate coffee bean candies

Combine 2 cups of the cream and espresso powder in a heavy medium saucepan. Bring to a simmer, whisking constantly. Remove from the heat. Add the chocolate and whisk until smooth. Whisk the egg yolks, sugar, vanilla and salt in a large bowl until blended. Whisk in the chocolate mixture gradually. Strain the mixture into a large glass measure.

Fit six ³/₄-cup soufflé dishes or custard cups with foil collars. Place in a large roasting pan. Pour the mixture into the soufflé dishes. Pour enough hot water into the roasting pan to come halfway up the sides of the soufflé dishes. Bake at 325 degrees for 20 to 25 minutes or until the custards are set around the edges, but still soft in the centers. Remove the dishes from the hot water and cool. Chill, covered, for 2 hours. Beat the remaining ¹/₂ cup cream in a bowl until soft peaks form. Spoon into a pastry bag fitted with a large star tip. Pipe 1 large rosette in the center of each custard. Sprinkle with candies.

Note: The custard can be prepared 1 day ahead and refrigerated.

Yield: 6 servings

Heavenly Crème Brûlée

4 cups heavy cream
1 vanilla bean, split lengthwise
pinch of salt
8 egg yolks
³/4 cup plus 2 tablespoons sugar

Combine the cream, vanilla bean and salt in a saucepan. Heat over low heat until heated through. Combine the egg yolks and sugar in a large bowl and mix well. Add the hot cream gradually, stirring constantly. Strain into a pitcher and skim off any bubbles.

Place eight ³/4-cup ramekins in a roasting pan. Pour the custard into the ramekins, filling to the rim. Add enough hot water to the roasting pan to fill halfway up the sides of the ramekins. Cover the roasting pan loosely with foil. Bake at 300 degrees for 1¼ hours or until set. Remove from the oven and let stand until cool. Cover each ramekin individually with foil. Chill for 3 hours or up to 2 days.

Sprinkle each ramekin with enough additional sugar to cover the top. Heat the sugar with a blow torch or under the broiler until the sugar caramelizes. Serve immediately.

Variations: The following are splendid versions of the classic recipe.

1. Chocolate Crème Brûlée: Add 4¹/2 ounces melted bittersweet or semisweet chocolate to the custard along with 2 tablespoons Grand Marnier and mix well. Divide among the ramekins.

2. Raspberry Crème Brûlée: Place 4 to 6 raspberries on the bottom of each ramekin. Stir 2 tablespoons raspberry liqueur into the custard. Divide among the ramekins.

3. Coconut Crème Brûlée: Divide ²/3 cup toasted golden coconut between the ramekins and pour the custard over the top.

4. Coffee Crème Brûlée: Add 1¹/2 tablespoons instant espresso powder and 2 tablespoons Kahlúa to the milk or cream during the preparation stage and then prepare as usual.

Yield: 8 servings

Crème Brûlée

Crème Brûlée is a much-loved, classic dessert that is always a crowd-pleaser. It is the dessert's bronze-colored crystalline sugar layer that sets Crème Brûlée apart from its cousins custard and flan. Here are two tried-and-true techniques for achieving that splendid hard-sugar shell.

Method 1: Top the crème brûlée with brown sugar and place it under the broiler until it turns a wonderful deep caramel color. (Watch carefully as this takes only a few moments.)

Method 2: Top the crème brûlée with raw sugar and apply heat from a small handheld blow torch. While you do need the proper equipment, this method provides greater control and often superior results.

Lemon Mousse

2 eggs, separated
1 (15-ounce) can sweetened condensed milk
1 tablespoon grated lemon peel
1/2 cup lemon juice
1/2 teaspoon almond extract
3 chocolate wafer cookies, crushed

Add the egg yolks 1 at a time to the condensed milk in a large bowl, beating well after each addition. Fold in the lemon peel, lemon juice and almond extract. Beat the egg whites at high speed in a bowl until stiff peaks form. Fold into the lemon mixture. Pour into individual ramekins or demitasse cups, filling to the rim. Chill in the refrigerator. Sprinkle with crushed cookies just before serving.

Yield: 6 to 8 servings

Orange Mousse with Toasted Almonds

1 tablespoon unflavored gelatin
1/4 cup cold water
1 cup sugar
3 tablespoons grated orange peel
1/2 cup water
1 cup orange juice
1/4 cup lemon juice
3/4 cup whipping cream, whipped
1 cup slivered almonds, toasted

Soften the gelatin in 1/4 cup cold water in a bowl for 15 minutes. Bring the sugar, orange peel and 1/2 cup water to a boil in a saucepan. Boil for 1 minute. Add to the gelatin mixture, stirring constantly until dissolved. Stir in the orange juice and lemon juice. Chill for 30 minutes or until thickened. Fold in the whipped cream. Pile high into sherbet glasses. Chill for 6 hours. Sprinkle with toasted almonds just before serving.

Yield: 8 servings

White Chocolate Bread Pudding

1 loaf French bread
8 egg yolks
2 eggs
1/2 cup sugar
2 tablespoons vanilla extract

3 cups heavy cream
1 cup milk
pinch of salt
10 ounces white chocolate
Brandy Sauce (at right)

Cut the French bread into 1 1/2-inch slices. Place on a baking sheet. Bake in a warm oven until dry.

Combine the egg yolks, eggs, sugar, vanilla, cream, milk and salt in a double boiler and mix well. Cook over hot water until heated through. Add the white chocolate. Cook until melted, stirring constantly.

Place 1 to 2 pieces of dried French bread in the bottom of individual glass custard cups. Pour the white chocolate mixture into the cups. Cover the cups with foil. Place in a large glass baking dish. Add enough water to the large baking dish to come halfway up the sides of the custard cups. Bake at 275 degrees for 1 hour. Bake, uncovered, for 15 minutes longer.

Invert onto individual serving plates. Serve with Brandy Sauce.

Yield: 10 to 12 servings

White Chocolate Ice Cream

4 cups half-and-half
6 egg yolks
1/2 cup sugar
6 ounces white chocolate, chopped

Bring 3 cups of the half-and-half to a simmer in a saucepan over medium heat. Remove from the heat. Whisk the egg yolks and sugar in a large bowl until blended. Add the hot half-and-half gradually, whisking constantly. Return to the saucepan. Cook over medium heat until thickened, stirring constantly. Do not boil. Strain into a large bowl. Add the white chocolate and stir until melted. Stir in the remaining 1 cup half-and-half. Chill for 1 hour. Pour into an ice cream freezer container. Freeze using the manufacturer's directions. Spoon into an airtight container and freeze until firm.

Yield: 8 servings

Brandy Sauce

Nothing could be more perfect with bread pudding than the classic brandy sauce. This rich warm sauce can also be poured over pound cake, fruit tarts, or cobblers.

1/2 cup sugar
2 egg yolks
3 tablespoons brandy
1/4 cup heavy cream
1/4 cup butter, chopped

Combine the sugar, egg yolks and brandy in a saucepan and mix well. Heat over medium heat until the sugar is dissolved, stirring constantly. Add the cream, stirring constantly. Cook until thickened, stirring constantly. Add the butter. Cook until the butter melts, stirring constantly. Cook for 1 minute longer, stirring constantly. Serve hot.

Yield: 1 cup

Buttermilk

Buttermilk is highly treasured in the South by the many who love to drink it and cook with it. The beverage may not be as popular as it once was when it was being churned on the farm, but buttermilk's many fans know the benefits of having it on hand in the refrigerator. Southern cooks put buttermilk in biscuits and cakes, and even freeze it to make ice cream. The best bakers know that in cake making you can substitute the same amounts of baking soda and buttermilk for the baking powder and milk and always produce a successful cake—dense, sweet, and delicious.

Buttermilk, a by-product of making butter, is kin to sour cream and yogurt. It is naturally low in fat and will keep in the refrigerator for quite a long time.

Ginger Ice Cream

2 tablespoons finely minced crystallized ginger
3 eggs, beaten
1 cup sugar
2 cups milk
2 cups half-and-half
1 teaspoon vanilla extract

Combine the ginger, eggs, sugar and milk in a heavy saucepan and mix well. Cook over medium-low heat for 7 to 10 minutes or until thickened, stirring constantly. Remove from the heat. Let stand until cool. Add the half-and-half and vanilla and mix well. Chill for 4 or 5 hours to overnight. Pour into an ice cream freezer container. Freeze using the manufacturer's directions.

Yield: 8 servings

Lemon Buttermilk Ice Cream

1 quart buttermilk
$^1/_2$ cup lemon juice
2 teaspoons lemon peel
$1^1/_2$ cups white corn syrup
$^1/_2$ cup sugar
$^1/_8$ teaspoon salt

Combine the buttermilk, lemon juice, lemon peel, corn syrup, sugar and salt in a bowl and beat well. Pour into a container. Freeze until partially frozen. Place in a bowl and beat well. Return to the container. Freeze until firm. Serve with strawberries and fresh mint.

Note: May pour into an ice cream freezer container and freeze using the manufacturer's directions.

Yield: 8 servings

Peachy Peach Sherbet

4 cups chopped peeled peaches
2 cups sugar, or to taste
2 cups buttermilk

Process the peaches and sugar in a blender until puréed. Add the buttermilk and process until well blended. Pour into an ice cream freezer container. Freeze using the manufacturer's directions until firm.

Yield: 10 servings

Molasses Cookie Baskets

Turn a simple scoop of ice cream into an incredibly elegant finale by tucking it into a crisp lacy cookie basket.

¹/4 cup unsalted butter
¹/4 cup sugar
¹/4 cup light molasses
¹/2 teaspoon grated lemon peel
¹/2 teaspoon ground ginger
1 teaspoon vanilla extract
¹/2 cup flour, sifted

Combine the butter, sugar, molasses, lemon peel and ginger in a small heavy saucepan. Bring to a simmer over medium heat, stirring constantly. Remove from the heat. Whisk in the vanilla and flour. Cool for 10 minutes.

Drop by level tablespoonfuls 6 inches apart onto 2 buttered nonstick cookie sheets, forming 3 cookies on each sheet. Press each round into a 4¹/2-inch circle using buttered fingertips.

Place 1 cookie sheet in the oven. Bake at 325 degrees for 8 minutes or until the cookies are golden brown. Cool on the cookie sheet for 2 minutes or until the cookies are just firm enough to lift without breaking. Lift 1 cookie from the sheet and drape top side up over an inverted ³/4-cup custard dish. Flatten the cookie gently on the dish bottom and crimp the side to form a fluted cup. Repeat with the remaining baked cookies, returning to the oven briefly if the cookies harden. Let stand until cool. Remove the baskets gently from the dishes.

Repeat the baking and molding process with the remaining cookie sheet.

Yield: 6 servings

Brown Sugar and Cinnamon Ice Cream

2 cups half-and-half
6 egg yolks
1 cup packed light brown sugar
3 tablespoons dark corn syrup
2 cups sour cream
1 teaspoon vanilla extract
1/4 to 1/2 teaspoon cinnamon

Bring the half-and-half to a simmer in a heavy saucepan over medium heat. Remove from the heat. Whisk the egg yolks, brown sugar and corn syrup in a large bowl. Add the hot half-and-half gradually, whisking constantly. Return to the saucepan. Cook over medium-low heat until thickened, stirring constantly. Do not boil. Strain into a large bowl. Add the sour cream and vanilla and whisk until smooth. Chill for 1 hour. Pour into an ice cream freezer container. Freeze using the manufacturer's directions. Spoon into a container and freeze until firm.

Yield: 8 servings

Fresh Blackberry Sherbet

3 cups fresh blackberries
2/3 cup confectioners' sugar
1 1/3 cups sweetened condensed milk
1/4 cup fresh lime juice
4 egg whites, stiffly beaten

Mix the blackberries and confectioners' sugar in a bowl. Let stand for 15 minutes. Press the mixture through a sieve or strainer into a bowl. Add the condensed milk and lime juice and mix well. Chill until the mixture just begins to thicken. Fold in the beaten egg whites. Freeze until partially frozen. Remove from the freezer and beat until smooth. Spoon into a serving dish or mold. Freeze, covered, for 8 to 10 hours or until firm.

Note: Can use drained thawed frozen blackberries instead of fresh.

Yield: 6 servings

Whipping Cream Pound Cake

1 1/2 cups melted butter
3 cups (heaping) sugar
6 eggs
3 1/2 cups sifted flour
2 cups heavy cream
1 teaspoon vanilla extract
confectioners' sugar

Combine the butter and sugar in a bowl and beat well. Add the eggs 1 at a time, beating until smooth after each addition. Do not overbeat. Add the flour alternately with the cream, beating well after each addition. Stir in the vanilla. Spoon into a greased and floured bundt pan or two 5x9-inch loaf pans. Bake at 300 degrees for 1 1/2 hours or until the cake tests done. Cool in the pan for a few minutes. Invert onto a wire rack to cool completely. Place on a cake plate. Sift confectioners' sugar over the cooled cake.

Note: Do not use unsalted butter in this recipe.

Yield: 16 servings

Marinated Fruit

Marinated fruit has the most marvelous flavor, sweet and tart. It is divine served over pound cake, meringues, or over romaine lettuce as an intriguing salad dressing.

1/4 cup balsamic vinegar
1/2 cup packed brown sugar
1 cup sliced strawberries, peaches or
  cantaloupe

Mix the vinegar and brown sugar in a bowl. Add the fruit and toss to mix well. Marinate in the refrigerator for 30 minutes or longer, stirring occasionally.

Yield: 1 cup

Chocolate Snowflakes and Shavings

Chocolate Snowflakes: Chocolate snowflakes are an ethereal addition to many delicious desserts. The snowflakes should be small, and so light and thin that they instantly melt in your mouth. Make them by scraping a hard piece of chocolate, one that has been refrigerated, with a melon-baller onto a piece of waxed paper. (Use white chocolate if you really want it to look like snow.) Keep the snowflakes in the refrigerator or the freezer until you are ready to use them.

Chocolate Shavings: Delicate chocolate shavings are just as simple to make. Again, use a cool block of bittersweet or white chocolate, one that has been refrigerated. With a sharp vegetable peeler, shave off paper-thin bits, as small or large as you'd like, onto a piece of waxed paper. These will often curl and are very fragile. Keep the shavings in the refrigerator or freezer until you are ready to use them.

Chocolate Mousse Cake

1 1/2 cups cake flour
3/4 teaspoon baking soda
3/4 teaspoon salt
1 cup sugar
6 tablespoons baking cocoa
2 extra-large eggs, separated
1/2 cup buttermilk

1/3 cup vegetable oil
1/4 cup Grand Marnier or framboise
* (optional)*
Chocolate Mousse (page 227)
Ganache (page 227)
1 cup chocolate shavings

Grease and flour a 9-inch springform pan. Line the pan with parchment paper or waxed paper. Butter and flour the paper. Sift the cake flour, baking soda, salt, 3/4 cup of the sugar and baking cocoa together.

Beat the egg whites at high speed in a bowl until soft peaks form. Add the remaining 1/4 cup sugar gradually, beating until stiff peaks form. Combine the buttermilk and egg yolks in a bowl and beat well. Add the flour mixture gradually, beating well after each addition. Add the vegetable oil and beat until the batter is shiny. Fold in the stiffly beaten egg whites. Pour into the prepared pan. Bake at 350 degrees for 20 to 30 minutes or until a cake tester inserted in the center comes out clean. Remove to a wire rack to cool. Release the side of the pan. Cut the cake into 3 horizontal layers.

Line a baking sheet with parchment paper or waxed paper. Top with the ring from the springform pan. Place 1 cake layer in the ring and brush with liqueur. Top with 1 1/2 inches of Chocolate Mousse. Repeat the layers. Place the remaining cake layer on top. Brush with remaining liqueur. Freeze, tightly covered, for 8 hours or longer. Remove from the freezer and run a sharp knife around the edge. Place on a serving plate. Place a hot towel around the ring to loosen and remove the side. Cover the top and side of the cake with Ganache. Chill for 20 minutes or longer. Cover with chocolate shavings. Chill until serving time.

Yield: 12 servings

Chocolate Mousse

8 ounces semisweet or bittersweet chocolate
8 ounces milk chocolate
7 large eggs, separated
3/4 cup sugar
2 cups whipping cream, whipped
1/4 cup Grand Marnier, framboise or rum (optional)

Melt the semisweet chocolate and milk chocolate in a double boiler over hot water. Remove from the heat. Beat the egg whites at high speed in a bowl until soft peaks form. Add 1/2 cup of the sugar gradually, beating constantly until stiff peaks form. Beat the egg yolks and remaining sugar in a bowl for 10 minutes or until pale yellow. Add the chocolate mixture gradually, beating constantly. Fold in the stiffly beaten egg whites. Fold in the whipped cream and liqueur. Chill in the refrigerator.

Yield: 6 to 7 cups

Ganache

1 cup heavy cream
20 ounces semisweet chocolate, chopped
1/4 cup unsalted butter, softened
2 tablespoons sugar

Bring the cream to a boil in a nonaluminum saucepan and remove from the heat. Beat in the chocolate, butter and sugar.

Note: May be made in advance and chilled in the refrigerator. Bring to room temperature before using.

Yield: about 3 cups

Chocolate Curls

Chocolate Curls: For elegant chocolate curls, it is best to have a warm, but not melted, block of the finest bittersweet chocolate. It can be warmed by short bursts of High power in the microwave, 2 or 3 seconds at a time, or by leaving the chocolate under a warm light for a few minutes. Use a sharp vegetable peeler and go slowly. The longer the bar of chocolate, the longer the curl. Greater pressure makes thicker, open curls. A lighter touch produces thinner, tighter curls. Experiment with different widths until you've got just what you want. Keep the curls in the refrigerator or freezer, on a piece of waxed paper, until you are ready to use them.

The Azalea City

Spring arrives each year in Mobile with a blaze of blooming azaleas. The gorgeous pink, purple, red, coral, and white blossoms produce a spectacular show of color that usually peaks in March. It all began in 1929, when the Mobile Jaycees began promoting a city beautification project by encouraging businesses and homeowners to plant azaleas. Today thousands of azaleas grace the city's streets, parks, yards, and neighborhoods, earning Mobile its nickname "The Azalea City."

"The Azalea Trail" is a driving route that winds through the city, highlighting many of the most abundant azalea plantings. The trail threads through the historic districts as well as the newer suburbs, offering a unique tour of many of Mobile's neighborhoods.

Chocolate Almond Soufflé Torte

1 cup whole almonds, toasted, cooled	6 eggs, separated
2 tablespoons sugar	1/3 cup sugar
2 tablespoons vegetable oil	1 cup whipping cream, chilled
3/4 cup unsalted butter	2 tablespoons amaretto, or
1/2 cup whipping cream	1 teaspoon almond extract
1 pound bittersweet or semisweet chocolate, finely chopped	2 tablespoons sugar
	confectioners' sugar
	1/2 cup sliced almonds, toasted

Butter and flour a 9-inch springform pan. Shake out the excess flour. Line the bottom of the pan with parchment paper and butter the paper.

Process 1/2 cup of the whole almonds and 2 tablespoons sugar in a food processor until finely ground. Spoon into a large bowl. Combine the remaining 1/2 cup whole almonds and vegetable oil in a food processor. Process for 3 minutes or until a smooth paste forms, stopping to scrape the side of the container frequently.

Combine the butter and 1/2 cup cream in a large heavy saucepan. Cook over medium heat until the butter melts and the mixture is simmering, stirring constantly. Remove from the heat. Add the chocolate and whisk until smooth. Stir in the ground almonds and the almond paste. Cool slightly.

Beat the egg whites at high speed in a large bowl until soft peaks form. Add 1/3 cup sugar gradually, beating until stiff peaks form. Beat the egg yolks in a large bowl for 5 minutes or until thick and pale yellow. Beat in the chocolate mixture gradually. Fold in the stiffly beaten egg whites 1/3 at a time.

Pour into the prepared pan. Bake at 350 degrees for 35 minutes or until the sides crack and puff and a cake tester inserted in the center comes out with moist batter attached. Remove to a wire rack. Let stand for 2 hours or until cool. The center of the cake will fall slightly.

Beat the chilled whipping cream, amaretto and 2 tablespoons sugar in a large bowl until soft peaks form. Run a sharp knife around the edge of the pan to loosen the side. Release the side of the pan. Place on a cake plate. Sprinkle the cake with confectioners' sugar. Sprinkle the toasted almond slices around the top edge of the cake. Serve with the whipped cream.

Yield: 12 to 14 servings

Chocolate Raspberry Squares

$1^1/4$ cups finely chopped bittersweet
    chocolate (7 ounces)

$^1/4$ cup plus 2 tablespoons heavy
    cream

1 cup plus 2 teaspoons unsalted
    butter, softened

1 teaspoon vanilla extract

1 tablespoon raspberry liqueur

1 cup flour

$^1/4$ teaspoon salt

$1^1/4$ cups sugar

3 eggs

$^1/2$ cup seedless raspberry jam

Place $^3/4$ cup of the chocolate in a medium bowl. Bring the cream and 2 teaspoons of the butter to a boil in a small saucepan. Pour over the chocolate. Let stand for 30 seconds and whisk until smooth. Whisk in $^1/2$ teaspoon of the vanilla and the raspberry liqueur. Let stand until cool. Chill for 30 to 60 minutes or until of a desired spreading consistency.

Melt the remaining $^1/2$ cup chocolate in a double boiler over simmering water, stirring occasionally. Remove from the heat.

Mix the flour and salt together. Beat the remaining 1 cup butter and sugar in a bowl until light and fluffy. Beat in the eggs 1 at a time. Add $^1/4$ cup of the jam and beat well. Beat in the melted chocolate and remaining $^1/2$ teaspoon vanilla. Add the flour mixture $^1/2$ at a time, beating at low speed after each addition until blended. Pour into a lightly greased 9x13-inch cake pan.

Bake at 350 degrees for 20 to 25 minutes or until the cake tests done. Remove to a wire rack to cool. Spread the frosting over the cooled cake. Chill for 1 hour. Place the remaining $^1/4$ cup jam in a sealable plastic bag. Cut $^1/8$ inch from one corner. Squeeze decorative stripes on top of the cake. Cut into $1^1/2$-inch squares.

Note: The frosting may be prepared and chilled, covered, for up to 5 days in advance. Bring to room temperature before using.

Yield: 15 servings

Cranberry Upside-Down Cake

2 cups chopped cranberries
1/2 cup chopped pecans
1 1/2 cups sugar
2 eggs
3/4 cup melted butter
1 cup flour
1/4 teaspoon salt
1/4 teaspoon almond extract

Mix the cranberries, pecans and 1/2 cup of the sugar in a bowl. Spoon into a buttered 10-inch springform pan. Combine the eggs, remaining 1 cup sugar and butter in a bowl and mix well. Add the flour, salt and almond extract and stir until smooth. Pour over the cranberry mixture. Bake at 350 degrees for 40 minutes or until a cake tester inserted in the center comes out clean. Serve with whipped cream or vanilla ice cream.

Yield: 12 to 14 servings

Lemon Easter Gâteau

4 egg yolks	2 tablespoons flour
2/3 cup sugar	1/4 cup fresh lemon juice
grated peel of 2 lemons	4 egg whites, stiffly beaten
2 tablespoons ground almonds	Lemon Mousse (below)
2 tablespoons fine semolina flour	confectioners' sugar

Grease an 8-inch springform pan. Line the bottom with parchment paper or waxed paper. Grease the paper and sprinkle with flour and sugar.

Whisk the egg yolks, sugar and lemon peel in a bowl until thick and pale yellow. Beat in the ground almonds, semolina flour, flour and lemon juice. Fold in the stiffly beaten egg whites. Spoon into the prepared pan and smooth the top. Bake at 350 degrees for 20 to 25 minutes or until the cake tests done. Remove to a wire rack to cool completely.

Release the side of the springform pan. Cut the cake into halves horizontally. Wash the springform pan and pat dry. Line the pan with parchment paper or waxed paper. Place the bottom half of the cake in the prepared pan. Pour the Lemon Mousse over the cake layer. Chill for 1 hour. Press the top half of the cake over the Lemon Mousse. Chill, covered, for 8 to 10 hours. Sprinkle with confectioners' sugar. Garnish with lemon geranium leaves and raspberries, or rose petals.

Yield: 8 to 10 servings

Lemon Mousse

juice from 2 lemons	1 tablespoon heavy cream
1 tablespoon water	grated peel of 2 lemons
1 envelope unflavored gelatin	1 cup whipping cream, whipped
1/2 cup sugar	2 egg whites, stiffly beaten

Mix 3 tablespoons of the lemon juice and water in a small bowl. Sprinkle with the gelatin. Let stand for 10 minutes.

Whisk the sugar, 1 tablespoon cream and lemon peel in a bowl until thick and pale yellow. Beat in the remaining lemon juice gradually.

Pour the gelatin mixture into a double boiler. Cook over simmering water until clear and liquified. Cool. Add the lemon mixture and beat well. Fold in the whipped cream immediately. Fold in the stiffly beaten egg whites.

Yield: about 4 cups

Azalea Trail Maids

Mobile's Azalea Trail Maids serve as official hostesses for the city. Dressed in pastel-hued antebellum costumes, they add a special charm to the many occasions in which the city extends hospitality to visitors. The many roles and responsibilities of the young ladies include greeting VIPs upon their arrival to Mobile, posing for pictures in Bellingrath Gardens, and accompanying guests on the battleship U.S.S. Alabama.

A panel of judges selects the 50 Azalea Trail Maids from among the city's outstanding high school seniors. In addition to representing Mobile both locally and nationally, the girls also compete for college scholarships.

Edible Flowers

A remarkable number of flowers are actually edible, with flavors ranging from delightfully peppery to slightly sweet. Blossoms and petals have been used for culinary purposes since Roman times. In the Orient, flowers have long been used for both cooking and, of course, for making teas. The English have cooked them into delicate-flavored jellies and jams and made candied tiny flowers for garnishing sweets.

Among those that taste best in salads are arugula flowers, chive flowers, chrysanthemums, dandelions, geraniums, marigolds, mustard flowers, violets, and nasturtiums.

Good in teas and other drinks are rose petals, borage, chamomile, and daisy petals.

Delicious stuffed and sautéed or deep-fried are hollyhocks, and squash blossoms.

Good choices for jams and jellies are lavender, pansies, and rose petals.

Beautiful as garnishes and decorations for cakes and other desserts are daylilies, geraniums, lavender, pansies, roses, and violets.

Particularly attractive when candied or crystallized are pansies, violets, and rose petals.

(Note: Not all flowers are edible—some are poisonous. Eat only those flowers that you can positively identify as safe.)

Banana Cake

3 cups flour	2 eggs
1 1/2 teaspoons baking powder	1 teaspoon vanilla extract
1 1/2 teaspoons baking soda	1 cup plus 2 tablespoons buttermilk
1/2 teaspoon salt	1 1/2 cups mashed ripe bananas
3/4 cup margarine	2 bananas, sliced
2 cups sugar	Banana Cake Frosting (below)

Sift the flour, baking powder, baking soda and salt together. Beat the margarine and sugar in a bowl until light and fluffy. Add the eggs 1 at a time, beating well after each addition. Beat in the vanilla. Add the flour mixture alternately with the buttermilk, beating well after each addition. Stir in the bananas. Spoon into 3 greased and floured 8-inch cake pans. Bake at 325 degrees for 30 minutes or until the layers test done. Do not overbake. Remove to a wire rack to cool. Spread Banana Cake Frosting over bottom layer. Top with sliced bananas. Add next layer and repeat. Add the top layer. Frost top and side of cake.

Yield: 12 to 16 servings

Banana Cake Frosting

1/2 cup butter, softened
8 ounces cream cheese, softened
2 teaspoons vanilla extract
1 (16-ounce) package confectioners' sugar
1 cup chopped pecans (optional)

Beat the butter and cream cheese in a bowl until smooth. Add the vanilla and mix well. Beat in the confectioners' sugar. Stir in the pecans.

Yield: 4 cups

Pumpkin Roll Cake

3 eggs
2/3 cup mashed cooked pumpkin
1 cup sugar
1 teaspoon salt
1 teaspoon baking soda
1/2 teaspoon cinnamon

1/4 teaspoon nutmeg
3/4 cup flour
1/3 cup chopped nuts
confectioners' sugar
Cream Cheese Filling (below)

Grease a jelly roll pan and line with waxed paper. Beat the eggs in a bowl until fluffy. Add the pumpkin, sugar, salt, baking soda, cinnamon and nutmeg and mix well. Add the flour, beating until smooth. Spread in the prepared pan. Sprinkle with nuts. Bake at 375 degrees for 15 minutes. Invert onto a towel sprinkled liberally with confectioners' sugar. Remove the waxed paper. Roll up the cake in the towel as for a jelly roll. Chill for 1 hour. Unroll the cake. Spread with Cream Cheese Filling. Roll up the cake as for a jelly roll. Wrap in foil. Chill until serving time.

Yield: 8 to 10 servings

Cream Cheese Filling

8 ounces cream cheese, softened
2 tablespoons butter, softened
1 teaspoon vanilla extract
1 cup confectioners' sugar

Beat the cream cheese and butter in a bowl until smooth and creamy. Add the vanilla and mix well. Add the confectioners' sugar, beating constantly.

Yield: 2 cups

Mobile Novelist Augusta Evans Wilson

Augusta Evans Wilson was the most famous and successful Alabama novelist of the nineteenth century. She belonged to the school of writing that has been characterized as the "domestic sentimentalists," which was extremely popular from the 1850s to the turn of the century. Augusta Evans reputedly made $100,000 from the sale of her books. She was one of the early challengers of the traditional view that a woman had no place outside the home and she helped prove that women writers could indeed be the intellectual equals of men.

Augusta Evans began writing when she was 14. By 1859, her third book, Beulah, sold over 20,000 copies in the first nine months—she was 24. She wrote about the kind of poverty that plagued her family during her youth, depicting the hardships she had known intimately. In 1866, she published St. Elmo, which proved to be the most popular of her novels. Steamships, hotels, cigars, and even a town were named after it.

In 1868, Augusta Evans met and married one of Mobile's wealthiest citizens, Colonel Lorenzo Madison Wilson, and became mistress of Ashland, one of the showplaces of Mobile. As was the case with two of her heroines, Evans was much younger

Peanut Butter Chocolate Bonbons

2 cups sifted confectioners' sugar
1 cup graham cracker crumbs
3/4 cup chopped pecans
1/2 cup grated coconut
1/2 cup butter or margarine, softened
1/2 cup peanut butter
1 1/2 cups semisweet chocolate chips
3 tablespoons shortening

Combine the confectioners' sugar, cracker crumbs, pecans and coconut in a large bowl. Melt the butter and peanut butter in a small saucepan. Pour over the coconut mixture and blend until moistened. Shape into 1-inch balls. Spear with wooden picks.

Melt the chocolate chips and shortening in a small saucepan. Dip the coconut balls into the chocolate mixture to coat. Place on waxed paper. Chill until set. Store between sheets of waxed paper in a tightly covered container in the refrigerator.

Yield: 4 dozen

Chocolate Rum Balls

1 (16-ounce) package vanilla wafers, finely crushed
2 cups confectioners' sugar
1/4 cup baking cocoa
2 cups finely chopped pecans
1 cup light corn syrup
1/2 cup rum
confectioners' sugar

Combine the vanilla wafers, 2 cups confectioners' sugar and baking cocoa in a large bowl and mix well. Add the pecans, corn syrup and rum and stir until stiff. Coat hands with some confectioners' sugar. Roll the mixture into 1-inch balls and place on waxed paper. Let stand for 1 hour. Roll the balls in confectioners' sugar. May keep for several weeks between sheets of waxed paper in a tightly covered container.

Yield: 1 1/2 to 2 dozen

Truffles

$^1/_4$ cup heavy cream
3 ounces bittersweet chocolate
$^1/_4$ cup baking cocoa

Bring the cream just to a boil in a small saucepan over medium heat. Remove from the heat. Add the chocolate and stir until smooth and glossy. Pour into a bowl and let stand until cool. Chill in the refrigerator until the consistency of soft fudge.

Sift the baking cocoa into a shallow bowl. Roll the chocolate mixture $^1/_2$ to $^3/_4$ teaspoonfuls at a time into a ball. Roll in the baking cocoa. Store between sheets of waxed paper in a tightly covered container in the refrigerator. Let stand at room temperature for 20 minutes before serving.

Yield: 16 to 20 servings

Almond Squares

1 to 2 cups sliced almonds
4 teaspoons sugar
4 eggs
2 cups sugar
1 cup melted butter
2 cups flour
$^1/_4$ teaspoon salt
4 teaspoons almond extract

Mix the almonds with 4 teaspoons sugar in a small bowl. Beat the eggs in a bowl. Add 2 cups sugar and beat until light and fluffy. Add the butter, flour, salt and almond extract and mix until smooth. Spoon into a greased 9x13-inch baking pan. Sprinkle with the almond mixture. Bake at 325 degrees for 35 minutes. Cool on a wire rack. Cut into squares.

Yield: 2 dozen

(Mobile Novelist, Augusta Evans Wilson, continued)

than her husband; he was 60 and she was 33 at the time of their marriage. After her marriage, she continued to publish, receiving a $15,000 advance on her next novel, Vashti. Her books promoted themes of moral regeneration and the sanctity of marriage.

When Colonel Wilson died at the age of 83, the despondent Augusta, decided that she could no longer live at Ashland and moved to Mobile. She bought a large house on Government Street, and there she and her brother Howard lived for the rest of their lives. She died in 1909. She and her brother are both buried in Magnolia Cemetery.

Although Augusta Evans Wilson's literary style was demanded by the public of her day, she was criticized and parodied by her literary contemporaries. But the tremendous sales of her books reassured the author of her popularity with her readers, and gave her a place in history.

Cappuccino Squares

1 cup butter or margarine	1³/4 cups flour
8 ounces unsweetened chocolate	1/2 teaspoon salt
1/4 cup instant espresso coffee powder	2 teaspoons vanilla extract
	1/2 teaspoon cinnamon
6 eggs	2 cups chopped walnuts
3¹/2 cups sugar	confectioners' sugar

Heat the butter and chocolate in a 4-quart heavy saucepan over low heat until melted and smooth. Add the espresso powder and stir until dissolved. Remove from the heat. Whisk in the eggs and sugar until well blended. Add the flour, salt, vanilla and cinnamon and mix well. Stir in the walnuts. Spread evenly in a greased 9x13-inch baking pan. Bake at 350 degrees for 35 minutes. Cool completely in the pan on a wire rack. Cut into 24 squares. Sprinkle with confectioners' sugar.

Yield: 2 dozen

Oatmeal Crisps

2¹/2 cups rolled oats
1 cup packed brown sugar
2 teaspoons baking powder
1/4 teaspoon cinnamon
1/2 cup melted butter
1 egg, beaten

Combine the oats, brown sugar, baking powder and cinnamon in a bowl and mix well. Add the butter and mix well. Beat in the egg. Drop by teaspoonfuls onto a greased cookie sheet. Spread each one into a thin round. Bake at 350 degrees for 8 to 10 minutes or just until the edges start to brown. Cool on the cookie sheet for 1 to 2 minutes. Remove to a wire rack to cool completely.

Yield: 2 dozen

Pistachio White Chocolate Chip Cookies

2 1/2 cups flour
1 teaspoon baking powder
1 teaspoon baking soda
1/2 cup old-fashioned oats
1 1/2 cups butter, softened

2 cups packed brown sugar
2 eggs
2 teaspoons vanilla extract
2 cups white chocolate chips
1 1/2 cups chopped pistachios

Mix the flour, baking powder, baking soda and oats in a bowl. Beat the butter and brown sugar in a bowl until light and fluffy. Add the eggs and vanilla and mix well. Add the flour mixture gradually, beating well after each addition. Stir in the white chocolate chips and pistachios. Drop by teaspoonfuls onto ungreased cookie sheets. Bake at 350 degrees for 10 to 12 minutes or until golden brown. Cool on the cookie sheets for 2 minutes. Remove to a wire rack to cool completely.

Yield: 5 dozen

Homemade Vanilla Extract

To make delicious vanilla extract, slice 2 vanilla beans down the center so that the seeds are exposed. Drop them into a pint bottle of good brandy and cover and shake. Marinate for several weeks, shaking every few days. This homemade version is much better than the store-bought extracts and can last for years.

Raspberry Chocolate Divine Sandwich Cookies

3/4 cup butter, softened
2/3 cup sugar
2 teaspoons vanilla extract
2 eggs
3/4 cup plus 2 tablespoons flour, sifted
1 jar seedless raspberry jam
8 ounces semisweet chocolate, melted

Beat the butter, sugar and vanilla in a bowl until creamy. Beat for 2 to 3 minutes longer. Add the eggs. Beat for 2 minutes. Add the flour and beat until smooth. Drop by rounded teaspoonfuls 3 inches apart onto a greased cookie sheet. Bake at 350 degrees for 12 to 15 minutes or until the edges are light brown. Cool on a wire rack. Spread 1/2 of the cookies with raspberry jam. Top with the remaining cookies. Dip the sandwich cookies halfway into the chocolate. Place on waxed paper and cool in the refrigerator. Store between waxed paper in an airtight container in the refrigerator.

Yield: 2 dozen

Strawberry Cookies

1/2 cup margarine, softened
1/4 cup packed brown sugar
1 egg yolk
1 teaspoon vanilla extract
1 cup sifted flour
1/4 teaspoon salt
1 egg white, lightly beaten
finely chopped pecans and strawberry preserves

Beat the margarine and brown sugar in a bowl until light and fluffy. Add the egg yolk and mix well. Add the vanilla. Beat in the flour and salt until smooth. Roll into 1/2-inch balls. Dip in the egg white and roll in the pecans. Place 1 inch apart on an ungreased cookie sheet. Bake at 375 degrees for 5 minutes. Remove from the oven. Make an indention in the top of each cookie using a thimble. Return to the oven. Bake for 10 minutes. Cool on a wire rack. Fill the centers with strawberry preserves.

Yield: 3 dozen

Apple Blackberry Crisp

2 cups flour
1 cup sugar
1/2 cup yellow cornmeal
1 1/2 teaspoons ground cinnamon
1 cup chilled unsalted butter,
    chopped
2 cups fresh or frozen blackberries

3 1/2 pounds Granny Smith apples,
    peeled, thinly sliced
3/4 cup sugar
2 tablespoons lemon juice
1 tablespoon flour
2 1/2 teaspoons grated lemon peel

Mix the 2 cups flour, 1 cup sugar, cornmeal and cinnamon in a bowl. Cut in the butter until coarse crumbs form. Mix the blackberries, apples, 3/4 cup sugar, lemon juice, 1 tablespoon flour and lemon peel in a large bowl. Pour into a buttered 9x13-inch glass baking dish. Sprinkle with the butter mixture. Bake at 375 degrees for 1 hour or until the apples are tender. Cool slightly before serving. Serve with ice cream.

Yield: 6 to 8 servings

French Country Apple Tart

1/4 cup sugar
1 tablespoon flour
1 tablespoon cornstarch
1 egg
1 cup milk

1/2 teaspoon vanilla extract
1 (16-ounce) package puff pastry,
    thawed
6 Granny Smith apples, peeled,
    cut into 1/4-inch slices

Combine the sugar, flour, cornstarch and egg in a bowl and whisk until light. Bring the milk and vanilla to a boil in a saucepan over medium heat. Remove from the heat. Stir 1/4 cup of the hot milk mixture into the egg mixture. Stir the egg mixture into the hot milk mixture. Return the saucepan to medium heat. Bring to a boil, whisking constantly. Cook until thickened, whisking constantly. Ladle through a strainer into a bowl. Cover with plastic wrap. Chill in the refrigerator.

Place a puff pastry rectangle on a baking sheet lined with parchment paper. Flute the edges of the puff pastry to create a 1/4-inch border. Spread the pastry cream evenly over the pastry. Layer the apples over the pastry cream in a circular pattern, covering the top fully. Bake at 375 degrees for 30 to 40 minutes or until golden brown and bubbly. Serve hot with whipped cream, crème fraîche or ice cream.

Yield: 6 to 8 servings

Devonshire Cream

Thick snowy Devonshire cream is the classic capper for a bowl of sweet, juicy, fresh berries. Try it on any number of desserts, including pies, cakes, and crisps. This recipe is easy and unforgettable.

3 ounces cream cheese, softened
2 tablespoons sugar
1 tablespoon Cointreau or Grand
    Marnier
1 cup whipping cream
fresh whole strawberries with stems

Beat the cream cheese and sugar in a bowl until light and fluffy. Add the liqueur and 2 tablespoons of the cream. Whip the remaining cream in a bowl until stiff peaks form. Fold into the cream cheese mixture. Spoon into a serving bowl and place on a platter. Surround the bowl with whole strawberries.

Yield: 2 cups

Pie, Pan Dowdy, Crisp, or Cobbler?

What do you get when you combine sweetened fruit with a handful of dough? Perhaps a pie or a pan dowdy? Could be a cobbler, crumble, or crisp? Better yet, a betty or a buckle? The answer is any of the above.

Depending on the recipe, its region, and whether the dough is on top, underneath, in between, or all over the fruit filling, the dessert may have several names. But any way you spell it or make it, you have a satisfying sweet.

Pies: Pie is a generic term for just about anything and everything that consists of a filling and a crust. Pies may have a top or bottom crust or both.

Cobblers: Cobblers are topped with dollops of a sweet pastry or biscuitlike dough and then baked. The origin of the name, according to one theory, comes from the phrase "cobble up," meaning to put something together in a hurry. The name is also commonly believed to be a commentary on the appearance of the dessert—as in lumpy and bumpy like cobblestones.

Crumbles and crisps: Depending on who's doing the cooking and the naming, these two terms are fairly interchangeable. Both consist of lightly sweetened fruit capped with a crumbly, shortbread-style pastry. Some say that a crumble is a crisp that uses rolled oats as the flour mixture, while others say the exact opposite.

Blueberry Pie

5 cups fresh blueberries
3/4 cup sugar
1/4 cup flour
2 prepared pie pastries
3 tablespoons butter or margarine

Rinse the blueberries and drain. Place in a large bowl. Mix the sugar and flour in a bowl. Add to the blueberries evenly, being careful not to crush the blueberries.

Fit 1 of the pie pastries into a glass pie plate. Add the blueberry mixture. Dot with butter. Top with the remaining pie pastry, trimming and fluting the edge and cutting 5 vents. Bake at 425 degrees for 15 minutes. Reduce the oven temperature to 350 degrees. Bake for 35 to 40 minutes or until brown. Cool before serving.

Yield: 8 servings

Peanut Butter Pie

3/4 cup creamy peanut butter
1/2 cup unsalted butter
1 cup sugar
1 cup packed light brown sugar
3 eggs
2 tablespoons flour

1/3 cup light corn syrup
1/3 cup milk or evaporated milk
1 teaspoon vanilla extract
pinch of salt
1 (9-inch) pie shell, partially baked

Melt the peanut butter and butter in a small heavy saucepan over low heat, stirring occasionally. Remove from the heat. Combine the sugar, brown sugar, eggs, flour, corn syrup, milk, vanilla and salt in a large bowl and mix well. Blend in the peanut butter mixture. Pour into the partially baked pie shell. Bake at 325 degrees for 1 hour and 20 minutes or until the filling is puffed and soft. Cool to room temperature before serving.

Yield: 6 to 8 servings

Chocolate Mousse Pie

4 egg whites
1/2 teaspoon cream of tartar
1/8 teaspoon salt
1 cup sugar
1 teaspoon vanilla extract
1/4 cup blanched sliced almonds
Chocolate Mousse Filling (below)
bittersweet chocolate shavings (page 226)

Spray a 10-inch pie plate with nonstick cooking spray. Beat the egg whites, cream of tartar and salt at high speed in a bowl until foamy. Add the sugar 2 tablespoons at a time, beating constantly until stiff peaks form. Fold in the vanilla. Spread in the prepared pie plate. Sprinkle with almonds. Bake at 300 degrees for 1 hour. Let stand until cool. Fill with Chocolate Mousse Filling. Chill for 8 to 10 hours. Sprinkle with chocolate shavings just before serving.

Yield: 8 to 10 servings

Chocolate Mousse Filling

6 ounces German chocolate
1/2 cup semisweet chocolate chips
1/4 cup water
2 tablespoons Cointreau (optional)
2 cups whipping cream
2 to 3 tablespoons confectioners' sugar
1 teaspoon vanilla extract

Melt the German chocolate and chocolate chips in the water in a double boiler over hot water. Remove from the heat and let stand until cool. Stir in the liqueur.

Beat the whipping cream in a bowl. Add the confectioners' sugar gradually, beating until soft peaks form. Fold in the vanilla. Fold in the chocolate with a wire whisk.

Yield: about 4 cups

(Pie, Pan Dowdy, Crisp, or Cobbler?, continued)

Bettys: Kin to the crisps and the crumbles, bettys are usually made of apples that have been sweetened and seasoned with spices, then covered with buttered crumbs. The name of the dessert reportedly comes from the tradition of Christmas minstrel shows popular in pre-Civil War Virginia, featuring Father Christmas, who handed out gifts, and Old Bett (or Betty) who dished out a special cobblerlike confection.

Pan dowdies: This dessert dates back to late 18th-century New England, where it started as a breakfast dish. A pan dowdy is baked in a rectangular pan with fruit fillings on the bottom and a single layer of biscuit dough or pie crust on the top. Often during the baking process and just before serving, the crust is broken up and stirred down into the filling. It is believed that it was this cooking term, dowdying, that led to the word dowdy, meaning frumpy or disheveled in appearance.

Slumps and grunts: Some say that slumps and grunts are basically the same, with each requiring stove-top preparations of stewed fruit and light steamed dumplings. Grunts were prepared in a cast-iron skillet, usually with blueberries, whereas slumps use any variety of fruit and are cooked in a saucepan or skillet.

Buckles: Buckles are basically like berry-laden coffee cake, usually cut into squares before serving. The name probably comes from the rather buckled appearance of the cake after baking.

Special Thank You List

Special thanks to these members of our community who helped make Bay Tables a success through generous donations of food, opening their homes or lending us their beautiful items to use as props for the photographs. Many thanks also to our sidebar contributors. Finally, we wish to thank all the people who helped guide us along the way.

Lee Rutherford Adams
Atchison Imports
Ruth Sullivan Austill
Faye Carrington Brady
Lucy Bowman Brady
Martha King Ballard
Mr. and Mrs. F. McKinley Bell, III
Bellingrath Gardens
Mr. and Mrs. James C. Bledsoe
Dr. and Mrs. Gerhard Boehm
Anne Blake Murray Brooks
Mary Courtney Cane
Joy Downey Cave
Claude Moore Jewelers
Jeanene Quimby Cockrell
Kara Coley Coats
BryAnne Little Collier
Phyllis Mull Creel
Mr. Michael Creech
Fort Conde
Elizabeth Roberts English
Ann Blackburn Faulkner
Bradley Clark Forster
Mrs. Emmett B. Frazer
Fruit Distributing
Lillian Riddle Gilley
Gillettes
The Giving Tree
Mr. and Mrs. Robin Herndon
Mr. and Mrs. Zebulon M.P. Inge
Cammie Dunson Israel
Carolyn Stephenson Jeffers
Helen Davis Kennedy
Beth Travis Lapeyrouse
Paula Miller Levi
Livin' Southern
Austill Samford Lott
Camille Levi Luscher
Mr. and Mrs. B.J. Lyons
Marriott's Grand Hotel
Sara Megginson McDonald

Cathy Waller McGowin
Ann Murray Meador
Melissa Cope Morrissette
Vaughan Inge Morrissette
Thomas C. McGehee
Mr. and Mrs. John T. Murray, Jr.
Mr. and Mrs. J. Manson Murray
Oakleigh Historic Mansion
Joy Blackwell Nash
Mr. and Mrs. J.C. O'Neill, Jr.
Michele Fundinger Nolen-Schmidt
The Pavilion
Poodle Casey Pipes
Port City Rentals
Mr. and Mrs. Ben M. Radcliff, Jr.
Jean Faulk Radcliff
Robbin Rhodes
Mr. and Mrs. Thomas Sharp, Jr.
Barkley Byrd Shreve
Sarah Irvine Slater
Mr. and Mrs. E. Bailey Slaton
H. Crawford Slaton
Selwyn Turner Slaton
William Edward Slaton
Betty Hyder Stone
Donna Childree Sutherlin
Carolyn Webb Thomas
Mr. and Mrs. Vester Thompson, Jr.
Tideline Outfitters
Cynthia Sconyers Tindell
Karen Neely Travis
Elizabeth Hood Turner
Marietta Murray Urquhart
Trisha Donaghey Valleé
Malinda Feaster Vollmer
Sally Smith Wall
Barbara Waller Wells
Mr. and Mrs. John H. Wright, Jr.
Mr. and Mrs. Ferd Zundel
Zundel's Jewelry

Restaurant Contributor List

Adam's Mark Hotel
Chef: Brent Perszyk
Crab Stuffed Pastry Shrimp with Plum Relish, page 209

Bienville Bistro
Owner and Chef: Chakle Diggs
Chocolate Espresso Pots de Creme, page 218
Jumbo Sea Scallops Cajun-Marsala, page 201

The Bubble Lounge
Owners: Mary Elizabeth Kimbrough and Lori Hunter
Lemon Drop, page 36
Loretta's Mint Julep, page 36

Buie's
Owners and Chefs: Buie Mayes and Chuck Csehoski
Chicken with Shallots and Mushrooms, page 172

Eats of Eden
Owner: Betty Lou Pierce
Chefs: Harmony Thomas and Keith Jeznach
Asparagus Soup, page 42

Guido's
Owners and Chefs: Chatman Ellis and Kristopher Conlon
Gnocchi with Gorgonzola Sauce, page 129

Justine's Courtyard and Carriageway
Owner and Chef: Matt Shipp
Butter Bean Cakes, page 129

Loretta's
Owners and Chefs: Christopher and Lori Hunter
Loretta's Shrimp and Grits, page 205

Martha Rutledge Catering
Chef and Owner: Martha Rutledge
Quail Stuffed with Shrimp, page 178

Michael's Midtown Cafe
Owner and Chef: Michael Ivey
Grapefruit and Avocado Vinaigrette, page 51

The Pillars
Owner and Chef: Filippo Milone
Sautéed Shrimp with Artichoke Sauce, page 206
Ziti Napolitana, page 109

Recipe Contributors

*The Junior League of Mobile would like to recognize and thank all of the people
in the community who graciously shared their fabulous recipes with us.*

Mary Jane Taylor Abercrombie
Adams Mark Hotel
Stephanie Adkins Alexander
Donna Smith Ames
Leslie Smith Anderson
Cindy Wallace Angelette
Pamela Johnson Angerholzer
Anne Kaiser Apple
Susan Kight Armbrecht
William Taylor Armbrecht
Ellen Jones Armistead
Beth Shelley Armstrong
Suzanne Otts Ashurst
Patti Deen Aubey
Kristin Mendenhall Babington
Cissy Klotz Bacon
Leslie Gruenewald Baggett
Leslie Gingles Baker
Agnes Lott Bancroft
Cathy Watson Barbato
Robin Meijer Barnett
Ginny Moss Behlen
Lynda Garstecki Bell
Andie Rogers Bender
Candace Gantt Bennett
Bienville Bistro
Wendy Biggerstaff Bigler
Susan Marshall Bixler
Colleen Ball Blackwell
Sage Morrissette Bolt
Pam Copeland Bostick
Mabel Shields Botts
April Brister Boudreaux
Harriet Turner Boughton
Lil Shedd Bowab
Ann Simmons Bowers
Angela Case Bowman
Faye Carrington Brady
Lucy Bowman Brady
John David Brady, Jr.
Barbara White Brewster
Tootsie Johns Bridges
Heather Chandash Brock
Mary Anne Thurston Brown

Peyton Phillips Bryars
Bubble Lounge
Buie's Restaurant
Goldie Grubbs Burkholder
Patti Denney Burkholder
Alice Brewster Byrd
Annette McDermott Carwie
John Carwie
Ann Bodden Carwie
Glynn Botts Case
Allison Moran Castle
Joy Downey Cave
Wanda Edenfield Chalhub
Juli Frost Chambliss
Karen Zoghby Charnock
Troy Joseph Chenoweth
Susan Hybart Childers
Julie Joseph Chunn
Laura Morrissette Clark
Kara Coley Coats
Jeanene Quimby Cockrell
Judy Pierce Coggin
BryAnne Little Collier
Evelyn Dietze Cooksey
Deborah Arnold Cope
Gloria Gayden Corona
Laura Miller Courtney
James Vickers Courtney
Mildred Starke Cowan
Lindsey Bennett Crawford
Eva Sumlin Creel
Amy Simmons Cummings
Cele Lile Cushing
Sylvia Sargent Cushing
Pat Konnersman D'Olive
Fran Aldridge Danley
Stephanie Toomey Daves
Ashley McDonough DeMouy
Lenae Cleveland Denson
Anne-Marie Ciaburri DeVilliers
Maureen Dormin DiCola
Eve Myers Doherty
Susan Pitz Duffey
Ashley Bullock Duffy

Helen Baumhauer DuMars
Eats of Eden
Karen Strom Edmondson
Christa Eslava Eiland
Elizabeth Wright Eldred
Liz Roberts English
Leigh Smith Faircloth
Ann Blackburn Faulkner
Kim Dyess Fesenmeier
Vikki Turner Finch
Meg Walsh Finkbohner
Beverly Ryan Finkbohner
Mary Demeranville Fowlkes
Valerie Laxson Fraser
Pat Balch Frazer
Irene Williams Frazer
Joanie Sapp Friedlander
Anne Hollinger Frost
Amante Toulmin Gaillard
Fanny Morrissette Gaillard
Lucy Stringfield Gallé
Annie Hunter Stabler Galloway
Joy Ogburn Gardner
Ashley Hieronymus Garstecki
Arvid Engwall Gaston
Kinta Stiegler Godwin
Tricia Paterson Graham
Prudence St. Pé Graham
Terri Peoples Gray
Janice Wheeler Greer
Guido's Restaurant
Lynn Turner Guthans
Barbara Ann Taylor Guthans
Susan Zundel Ham
Frances Thomas Hannon
Patricia Jackson Harden
Nancy Veitch Harless
Nancy Godwin Harris
Karen Nikolakis Harris
Malvereen Cromwell Harris
Elizabeth Long Harrison
Lisa Gray Hartley
Helene Holleman Hassell
Jennifer Williams Havard
Appie O'Neill Head
Louise Chamberlain Hearin
Martha Haas Hill
Mary Lucy McKnight Hirs

Allison Barbara Hodges
Millie Cowan Hollinger
Katharine Bledsoe Holmes
Susan Buford House
Brenda Respess Huddle
Nancy Kline Hughes
Susan Pharr Hume
Lori Hunter
Mary Lou Donaghey Hyland
Helen Weed Inge
Genie Radcliff Inge
Robbie Lynn Dunn Irvine
Sallye English Irvine
Jamie Norman Ison
Cammie Dunson Israel
Julianne Griffin Jackson
Liz Brocato Jackson
Sally Bragan Jackson
Greta Marie Jahnke
Deborah Booth Jardine
Carolyn Stephenson Jeffers
Treesie Greer Jeffries
Leslie Lauten Johnson
Missy Meyers Jones
Kathleen Fagan Jordan
Justine's
Carmen Elizabeth Kearley
Joan Marie Stewart Keebler
Anita Howard Keidel
Paula Burge Keith
Helen Davis Kennedy
Neil Morgan Kennedy
Mary Anne Ogletree Killion
Mary Elizabeth Kimbrough
Jo Ann Graffeo King
Paula Ingram Kiszla
Kim Crabtree Klyce
Lise Mostellar Knott
Ginger Naman Koppersmith
Marie Carwie Koury
Stacey Devine Ladas
Beth Travis Lapeyrouse
Caren Lillich Leon
Paula Miller Levi
Carol Carr Little
Lynn Meighan Little
Betsy Florey Long
Loretta's Restaurant

Austill Samford Lott
Anna McCown Luce
Dibber Bodden Lutz
Lyn Fillingim Lyle
Emilee Oswalt Lyons
Paige Gwinn Maddox
Margaret Matthews Mangham
Ruth Amundson Manley
Martha Belew Mareno
Christina Jones Marques
Tina Brauchle Martenstein
Maria Nicaud Masterson
Kathleen Stone Mayer
Margi Silva McCall
Andrew DeVaney McDonald
Ceil Smith McGehee
Boone Arendall McGinley
Cathy Waller McGowin
Corky Estabrook McGowin
Mary Pharr McGowin
Kim Judkins McKinney
Allie Rogers McLeod
Lucy Cobb McVay
Kathy Turner Meador
Laura Meador Meeker
Michael's Midtown Cafe
Christie Holmes Midkiff
Marjorie Shaddock Millette
Nancy Collier Minus
Julie Stevens Moore
Amanda Hess Morrissette
Beth Anderson Morrissette
Margaret Hunter Murray
Becky Cochran Neese
Gilaine Nettles-Williams
Cyndi Wilson Newell
Michele Fundinger Nolen-Schmidt
Bonnie Moss Norton
Sally Lott O'Neill
Kimi Stinson Oaks
Hattie Chandler Ogburn
Diana Balch Parker
Evie Roy Pearson
Karen Whiddon Peterson
Monica Schultz Peterson
Marian MacKay Pfeiffer
Amy Ferguson Pipes
Amelie Courtney Pitman

Recipe Contributors

(continued)

Deneen Territo-Evans Plessala
Sherry Spyke Pofahl
Amy Haynes Polansky
Starke Patterson Pollard
Gale Castle Pond
Nancy Brown Quittmeyer
Julie Mostellar Radcliff
Jean Faulk Radcliff
Darby Gaskins Radcliff
Janet Gardner Rawls
Sarah Pratt Rayford
Dot Ann Campbell Rayford
Doro Phister Rebarchak
Rosalind Richard
Mary Semple Riis
Erling Riis, III
Harriet Ladas Rivers
Kimberly Gilbert Roberts
Linda Meyers Robinson
Candy Bianco Robinson
Eliska Pickett Roe
Elizabeth Beck Roney
Kelsey Shiverick Russell
Martha Rutledge Catering
Elizabeth Stevens Sanders
Beth Finkbohner Sayler
Mary Lynne Farnell Schatzman
Elizabeth Bledsoe Schmahl
Leigh Wentworth Schottgen
Martelle Owens Scott
Appie Murray Sharp
Carolyn Doyle Shedd
Vivian Blackwell Sheldon
Barkley Byrd Shreve
Tracy Martin Shreve
Tara Overton Slater
Julia Touart Smith
Teresa McLean Smith
Jo Ann Smith
Jane Frances Houser Smith
Lane Ogletree Snider
Doris Carwie Solomon
Karen Long St. Clair
Cassie Champlin Steele
Laura Perdomo Stevenson
Sarah Hicks Stewart
Leslie DePauw Suffich
Nancy Newsome Tanner

Gail Schapker Tart
Marianne Sneed Taul
Susan Burke Taul
Julie Lapeyrouse Taylor
Rhonda McDuffie Taylor
Joy Warley Taylor
Virginia Hybart Taylor
Kim Armbruster Tew
The Pillars
Susan Hunnicutt Thompson
Kathy Moody Thurber
Cynthia Sconyers Tindell
Marie Goodloe Tonsmeire
Betty Reed Torbert
Martha Torres
Nancy Buerger Trawick
Donna Elliott Trenier
Elizabeth Hood Turner
Fifi Sneed Twitty
Marietta Murray Urquhart
Patricia Donaghey Valleé
Anne Mostellar Vella
Kim Mixon Verneuille
Malinda Feaster Vollmer
Trudy Carrington Vollmer
Erin Louise Vulevich
Rebecca Feaster Wahl
Jane Griffith Waite
Shannon Senn Wallace
Marijane Pachl Walmsley
Ann Brevard Ward
Carolyn Eskridge Warren
Margaret Lee Watson
Tara Ashley Webster
Kathy Whitlow Webster
Melissa Stone Weekley
Barry Taylor Weeks
Lori Leacy Wells
Jeanie Guthans Wilkins
Lynn Curran Wilkins
Liz Tew Williams
Jane Williamson
Laurel Willoughby Wilson
Priscilla Goddard Wilson
Winston Case Wright
Victoria Winston Wright
Gray Thorworth Zimlich
Jill Chenoweth Zurfluh

Recipe Testers

The Junior League of Mobile would like to thank the following people and their families,
who spent countless hours and dollars testing and evaluating the recipes for Bay Tables.

Donna Smith Ames
Cindy Wallace Angelette
Anne Kaiser Apple
Suzanne Otts Ashurst
Kristin Mendenhall Babington
Cissy Klotz Bacon
Leslie Gruenewald Baggett
Robin Meijer Barnett
Colleen Becker-Casto
Ginny Moss Behlen
Wendy Biggerstaff Bigler
Liz Murray Blankenship
Sage Morrissette Bolt
April Brister Boudreaux
Lil Shedd Bowab
Ann Simmons Bowers
Angie Case Bowman
Lucy Bowman Brady
Anne Blake Murray Brooks
Sandra Diane Bryant
Mary Courtney Cane
Joy Downey Cave
Susan Hybart Childers
Kara Coley Coats
Jeanene Quimby Cockrell
BryAnne Little Collier
Lillian Crowe Courtney
Laura Miller Courtney
Cissy Corrigan Cowart
Melanie Zoghby Cummins
Anne Marie Ciaburri DeVilliers
Susan Pitz Duffey
Karen Strom Edmondson
Elizabeth Wright Eldred
Caroline Rutledge Etherton
Ann Blackburn Faulkner
Kim Dyess Fesenmeier
Wanda Bailey Filer
Sandra Miller Finkbohner
Joy Ogburn Gardner
Ashley Hieronymus Garstecki
Lisa Byrnes Goodloe

Tricia Paterson Graham
Prudence St. Pé Graham
Cathy Waters Graham
Terri Peoples Gray
Lynn Turner Guthans
Nancy Veitch Harless
Lisa Gray Hartley
Ashley Corte Harvey
Helene Holleman Hassell
Laura Derouen Hastings
Mary Lucy McKnight Hirs
Allison Barbara Hodges
Katharine Bledsoe Holmes
Susan Buford House
Mary Lou Donaghey Hyland
Sallye English Irvine
Liz Brocato Jackson
Catharine Gordon Jernigan
Leslie Lauten Johnson
Carmen Elizabeth Kearley
Paula Burge Keith
Mary Anne Ogletree Killion
Cynthia Smith Kirk
Kim Crabtree Klyce
Stacey Devine Ladas
Mary Ann LaFleur
Beth Travis Lapeyrouse
Ann Kilpatrick Leatherbury
Paula Miller Levi
Austill Samford Lott
Tara Steiner Marshall
Maria Nicaud Masterson
Lisa Eileen McCants
Ceil Smith McGehee
Cathy Waller McGowin
Debbie Baker McManus
Lucy Cobb McVay
Erin Henry McWaters
Sharon Meatyard Metcalfe
Lori Black Metzger
Marjorie Shaddock Millette
Nancy Collier Minus

Amanda Hess Morrissette
Margaret Hunter Murray
Lucy Rencher Murray
Gilaine Nettles-Williams
Michele Fundinger Nolen-Schmidt
Cari McKay Palesano
Lisa Dickinson Peacock
Katie Hogue Pierce
Leigh Lichty Pipkin
Deneen Territo-Evans Plessala
Starke Patterson Pollard
Gale Castle Pond
Janet Gardner Rawls
Doro Phister Rebarchak
Harriet Ladas Rivers
Esther Barry Rogers
Elizabeth Beck Roney
Kim Cunningham Sewell
Andrea Jones Shane
Jo Ann Smith
Dulari Jensen Smith
Karen Long St. Clair
Leslie DePauw Suffich
Gail Schapker Tart
Susan Burke Taul
Kim Armbruster Tew
Terry Shashy Towles
Karen Neely Travis
Dee Elliott Trenier
Melanie Smith Turner
Marietta Murray Urquhart
Tricia Donaghey Valleé
Jane Griffith Waite
Ann Brevard Ward
Tara Ashley Webster
Lisa McDuffie Wells
Barbara Waller Wells
Jeanie Guthans Wilkins
Winston Case Wright
Jill Chenoweth Zurfluh

Photography Underwriters

The Junior League of Mobile would like to recognize and thank all of the following people in the community who generously helped underwrite the cost of the photography in Bay Tables.

Cheese Photograph—Betty R. McGowin

Appetizers at the Grand Hotel—1998 Sustaining Class (See List)

Tomato Photograph—Supporters of the Junior League of Mobile (See List)

Soups, Salads, Sandwiches at Dauphin Island—Laura Livingston Gewin,
*   MJLP chairman, 1984-1985*

Egg Photograph—Friends of the Junior League of Mobile

Brunch on the Porch—Past Presidents (See List)

Pasta Photograph—Dusty Wharton Walton and Nancy Tanner Walton

Pasta, Pizza, Rice and Grains at Bellingrath Gardens—The Betty Bienvilles

Poultry, Meat and Game at the Hunting Camp—Board of Directors (See List)

Seafood Photograph- Cookbook Committee (See List)

Seafood on the Wharf of Mobile Bay—Alicia Ormond Anderson,
*   Diane Anderson Ireland and Karen Anderson Williams*

Vegetables at Fort Conde—Marian MacKay Pfeiffer

Strawberry Photograph—Ann Blackburn Faulkner, Chairman, One of a
*   Kind, 1977–1981*

Champagne and Desserts at Oakleigh—Kate Blanton Dempsey,
*   Lynn Mosher Fondren, Betty Hyder Stone and Cynthia Sconyers Tindell*

Board of Directors *1997-1998*	*Board of Directors* *1998-1999*
Lucy Brady	Susan Duffey
Susan Duffey	Helene Hassell
Ellen Wingard	Sallye Irvine
Julie Friedman	Karen R. McDonald
Gail Tart	April Boudreaux
Caren Leon	Kim McKinney
Julianne Jackson	Julianne Jackson
Cathy McGowin	Wanda Filer
Kim McKinney	Margaret Murray
Amy Hamilton	Celia Sapp
LeeLee Brady	Stephanie Alexander
Gina Hedberg	Lori Myles
April Boudreaux	LeeLee Brady
Mary Anne Ball	Julie Friedman
Mary Elizabeth Kimbrough	Beth Morrissette
Leigh Faircloth	Ginger Koppersmith
Sarah Damson	Ruth Austill

1998 Sustaining Class

Donna Smith Ames
Suzanne Otts Ashurst
Mary Anne Coley Ball
Cathy Watson Barbato
Kim Tonsmeire Barnett
Maggie Hennessy Bates
Lynda Garstecki Bell
Pam Copeland Bostick
Abbie Mims Bowron
Tootsie Johns Bridges
Marbury Deaton Buckhaults
Mary Hopkins Taylor Chamblin
Susan Crain Chiepalich
Eva Sumlin Creel
Jamie Kayser Davidson
Lesleigh Lane Dodd
Elizabeth Bondurant Dominick
Carolyn Delchamps Eichold
Kathy Finney Fontana
Susie Williams Foster
Janel Norden Fowler
Lillian Riddle Gilley
Tricia Paterson Graham
Amy St. John Hamilton
Peggy Person Harkness
Malvereen Cromwell Harris
Laura Derouen Hastings
Stuart Ellis Holland
Mary Page Hope
Diane Anderson Ireland
Deborah Booth Jardine
Kathy McWilliams Killion
Tori Crowe Kneip
Kathy Morrow Latta
Peggy Levensailor Lyden
Moo Greer Martindale
Beth Wilson McDonald
Cathy Waller McGowin
Claudnette Louise McGrew
Lucy Cobb McVay
Melissa Cope Morrissette
Chris Ezekiel O'Neal

Tricia Martin Pastore
Kathy Pierce Peake
Lee Baker Pipkins
Amy Haynes Polansky
Darby Gaskins Radcliff
Joan Kassel Sands
Bowden Overbey Sarrett
Deborah Roney Scott
Pam Malpass Shedd
Dulari Jensen Smith
Margie Frazier Smith
Julie Lapeyrouse Taylor
Linda Grant Thomas
Karen Neely Travis
Jean Walker Tucker
Kathy Latham Walton
Melissa Stone Weekley
Becky Duvall Weingardt
Nancy Palombo Wettermark
Mary Jane Watkins Wilson
Kathryn Reep Zicarelli
Cynthia Hoehns Zipperly

Supporters of the Junior League of Mobile

Joy Mitchell Grodnick
Judy Screven Henson
Anne Carter Irvine
Judy Wright Matthews
Ninky McAllister Vickers
Mr. and Mrs. John H. Wright

Cookbook Committee

Liz Murray Blankenship
Elizabeth Wright Eldred
Lynn Turner Guthans
Susan Zundel Ham
Helene Holleman Hassell
Katharine Bledsoe Holmes
Sallye English Irvine
Catharine Gordon Jernigan
Mary Anne Ogletree Killion

Past Presidents

Ann Greer Adams
Carolyn Radcliff Akers
Ruth Sullivan Austill
Julie Lott Bagwell
Jane Frazer Bledsoe
Lucy Bowman Brady
Louise Shearer Brock
Eulalie Draughon Brown
Martha Clark Cameron
Joan Balch Christmas
Velma Lassiter Croom
Sarah Long Damson
Blakely Haas Davis
Sarah Druhan Davis
Mary Murray DeMouy
Caroline Rutledge Etherton
Jeaneane Brightwell Fountain
Emily Staples Hearin
Susan Oswalt Helmsing
Laura Hays Holmes
Carolyn Stephenson Jeffers
Missy Meyers Jones
Ann Karpinski Jones
Austill Samford Lott
Peggy Brinkley McClelland
Sally Tonsmeire Morrissette
Vaughan Inge Morrissette
Sally Lott O'Neill
Audrey Starke Patterson
Poodle Casey Pipes
Jean Faulk Radcliff
Madge Urquhart Rody
Carolyn Bradford Stephenson
Carol Frazer Suffich
Marietta Murray Urquhart
Margaret Ann Cumbee Waldrop
Rosemary Pritchard Walsh
Dusty Wharton Walton
Mabel Bedsole Ward

Index

About Mobile

BAY TABLES
SAVOR THE ABUNDANCE

A collection of fresh and
fabulous recipes from the
Junior League of Mobile, Inc.

YOUR ORDER	QUANTITY	TOTAL
Bay Tables $24.95 per book		$
Mobile residents add $2.25 sales tax per book		$
Alabama residents add $1.00 sales tax per book		$
Shipping and handling $3.50 per book		$
TOTAL		$

Please make checks payable to the Mobile Junior League Publications.

_____

Name

_____

Street Address

_____

City   State   Zip

( )
_____

Telephone Number

To order by mail, send to:
Junior League of Mobile, Inc.
57 North Sage Avenue
Mobile, Alabama 36607-2608
334-479-5133
334-471-3348

Photocopies will be accepted.